We live in a day of superficial k[...] o
slow down and immerse oursel[...] 's
*book "The Spiritual Discipline of Meditation" provides a helpful method on
how to dig deep into Gods Word, while nourishing the believer's soul. I highly
recommend this book, as it is beneficial for both personal and family devotions.*
- Sean Banks, Pastor, Providence Church of Williston, North Dakota

*It is with great pleasure I recommend this book by Scott Doherty. He has given
us a wonderful tool that by the power of the Holy Spirit, will draw you into the
word in a beautiful way. Meditating on Christ and His Word is a great gift of
God and He has provided, through Scott, a most useful resource. As you begin,
let me encourage you to pray II Corinthians 12:9a and ask Christ to crush your
own sinful efforts and lead you to rest in Him. Plead His mercies, die to self and
He will grow you in grace through the Word and prayer.*
- Larry Chandler, Elder, Mount Vernon Baptist Church, Atlanta Georgia

*This is not just a devotional book to add to your quiet time. It models and
teaches the spiritual discipline of biblical meditation. It will encourage and
challenge you daily. In addition it will guide you to apply historically tested
methods of learning God's Word and growing in a deeper relationship with
Him.*
- Scott Dollar, Preaching Pastor, The Way, Clarksville, Tennessee

*The Bible clearly teaches that what every believer needs is to have more faith.
But it also promises that the fountain where he can find it is the Bible itself. It is
through the constant reading, memorization, and meditation of the Scriptures
that God promises to give us the faith we need for our daily sanctification. This
is why this book is so important. It will help every christian understand, desire
and know how to grow in the spiritual discipline of meditation of the Scriptures.
He provides his reader with what has become his personal practice and
discipline and shares it with the goal of helping them grow in holiness by
meditating daily on the Scriptures. I highly recommend this book to you.*
**- Eduardo Flores, Pastor, Iglesia Bautista Reformada (Reformed Baptist
Church) Los Lagos, Costa Rica.**

*Scott's new devotional book is a wonderful addition to my personal devotional
library and will be introduced to my church as well. It is rich, deep and thought
provoking and is a wonderful tool to use in training Christians of any age in the
spiritual discipline of meditating on God's word.*
- Paul Lackey, Pastor, Living Faith Baptist Church

Many years ago, I wrote to a friend in Caracas asking him for prayer because I felt I was not overcoming sin in my life. My friend's reply was: How is your devotional life? I have read books about spiritual disciplines being aware of their importance in our spiritual growth. I even recommended those books, but I still was fighting to apply what I knew was the right thing to do. By the grace of God I eventually learned to find delight in the presence of God through prayer and meditation of the Word. A devotional book like this would have been a great help in those days of struggling because it lets you practice what you are learning. It is my desire and prayer that our Lord use this excellent devotional to show people how to find the treasures hidden in the holy meditation of the Bible.

- Alexander León, Pastor, Iglesia Bautista Reformada (Reformed Baptist Church) Los Lagos, Costa Rica.

In a world of artificial urgency and marketed chaos The Spiritual Discipline of Meditation: A Daily Devotional in the Scriptures is a potent antidote to the roaring pace of life and "bogus spirituality." Scott graphically warns that many times "without meditation, the Christian finishes (devotions) in the same condition in which he started." Working through this devotional guide shatters the possibility of this happening.

- Joel McCutcheon, Campus Chaplain, The Spanish Language Institute, San Jose, Costa Rica

The Spiritual Discipline of Meditation is a foundational resource that will benefit every believer's walk with the Lord. I recommend it for all those who seek to walk faithfully and see His power to transform their lives through His Word.

- M. David Sills, D.Miss., Ph.D.

Scott Doherty has written a masterpiece on Christian meditation! Knowing and communing with God should be the greatest goal of every human being. This book gives the reader the necessary tools and encouragements to achieve that lofty goal. The pages you are about to read are deeply rooted in the scriptures, they are centered on Christ and are historical in their approach to cultivating an intimate relationship with the Living God.

- Micah Tuttle, Missionary, Peru

The Puritans were experts at doing what some of them called, "The art of holy meditation". By this, they referred not to the anti-biblical mysticism of Eastern Religion in which one empties his mind of all thoughts, but to the biblically-

mandated practice of saturating one's mind and thoughts with the truth of Scripture so as to think God's thoughts after Him. In the midst of the hustle and bustle of life and a million and one things that distract our minds from what is truly important, Scott Doherty reminds us that "one thing is necessary" (Luke 10:42). He does this by calling us to return to the old paths, to the discipline of flooding our minds with the light of God's Word so that our hearts and lives will be impacted by the power of truth as we draw near to God in intimate communion with His Word. Your soul will be refreshed if you take heed to the burden of this book.

- Josef Urban, Missionary, Mexico

In a day where emotionally driven and mystical devotional books abound, this book drives us back to the Scripture where we belong. As the prophet Jeremiah proclaimed: "Your words were found, and I ate them, and your words became to me a joy and the delight of my heart". In like manner, this book calls us to slow down, take small bites, and chew well. I thank the Lord for the ministry of this dear brother and pray this book draws you closer to our Lord and Savior Jesus Christ.

- John Wallace

The Spiritual Discipline of Meditation

A Daily Devotion in the Scriptures

Scott Doherty

ISBN-13: 978-1501019913
ISBN-10: 1501019910

Preface

I wrote *The Spiritual Discipline of Meditation: A Daily Devotional in the Scriptures* with two purposes in mind. First, I want to teach people how to meditate on the Scriptures in a meaningful way, after the pattern of the Puritans. Second, I purposefully use a daily devotional format so readers will begin to discipline themselves in meditating on one passage of Scripture each day. Rather than just write about the Puritan form of meditation, I provide practice through meaningful daily devotions. By the end of the book, after meditating for an entire year, the reader will be trained in one of the most important spiritual disciplines.

I first learned about meditating on the Scriptures from a book called *On Being a Pastor* by Derek Prime and Alistair Begg. Prime suggested writing down one verse a day from your daily readings and then meditating on it throughout the day. I did this for years, and it was a great blessing. After a while though, by my own fault, I found myself thinking very little about the verse and application throughout the day. The testimony of the Puritans drove me to the method I use now and is the discipline found in this book. I discovered that reading, emphasizing, memorizing, and writing the verse in my own words and writing out the application revolutionized the way I meditated on the Scriptures. I believe that spending much of the time writing out your meditation makes you focus more deeply on the text and also forces you to spend time in meditation.

I was so spiritually blessed when I began to do this that I started sharing with others this method, which is not my method but one modeled after the Puritans. I received great feedback, and now I desire to share this discipline with others. The introduction of the book explains the method of meditation. Then, for the first six days, there is a meditation upon which the reader is to focus. Every seventh day the reader begins his own meditation, which he will write out in the book. In addition to personal daily meditations, this book is great for family devotions. The entire family can be involved in focusing deeply on the verse and its application. Every seventh day the family does their own meditation together. Through the daily discipline of meditating on the Scripture, I am convinced any person will gain a deeper understanding of God and His works, as well as grow closer in communion with Him.

Acknowledgments

*To God,
who awoke me from the dead when I was 28,
breathed life into me and radically changed
my heart, thoughts,
desires, and motivations
through the atoning work
of His Son Jesus Christ.*

The more you read the Bible,
and the more you meditate on it,
the more you will be astonished with it.

Charles Spurgeon

Introduction

Purpose of the Book

Today, when we hear the word meditation we immediately associate the term with a New Age practice. Sadly, the spiritual discipline of meditating on the Scriptures has become uncommon among Christians while in contrast the blending of eastern mysticism with mainstream Christian thought has risen to prominence. True, biblical meditation on the Scriptures has been replaced with a self-centered and mystic spirituality. I have known very few people in my life who have meditated on the Scriptures in a meaningful way while maintaining a disciplined time of study. There are still Christians who do so, but overall this spiritual practice has faded with the Puritans. I have found such meditation, understood in a biblical and meaningful way, brings blessing, joy, and spiritual growth. Many Christians read the Bible each day but don't meditate on it. A lack of meditation often results in lack of profit gained from devotions. Many times during devotions, without meditation, the Christian finishes in the same condition in which he started. The purpose of this book is to recover the lost spiritual discipline of meditation. In doing so, I hope to encourage Christians to grow in grace and truth and to savor the spiritual blessings of God's Word.

The Need for Meditation

God commands us to meditate on His words and obey His commands, which we see His people obeying throughout the Scriptures. (Deuteronomy 6:6-7, Psalm 19:14, 77:12, 104:34, 119:15, 27, 48, 148, 145:5). God commanded Joshua to meditate on His word. Joshua 1:8 says, "This Book of the Law shall not depart from your mouth, but you shall meditate on it day and night, so that you may be careful to do according to all that is written in it. For then you will make your way prosperous, and then you will have good success."

The word "meditate" means to think deeply on or engage in contemplation or reflection. Donald Whitney, in his book titled *Spiritual Disciplines for the Christian Life*, defines biblical meditation as: "deep thinking on truths and spiritual realities revealed in Scripture for the purposes of understanding, application, and prayer."[1] Thomas Watson defines meditation as "a holy exercise of the mind whereby we bring the truths of God to remembrance, and do seriously ponder upon them and apply them to ourselves."[2] To meditate is to absorb the Word of God. Meditation without application is not useful. We meditate in order to understand and apply God's truths. With such application we must then resolve to change.

The Puritans had purpose in meditation. In their book, *A Puritan Theology: Doctrine for Life*, Joel Beeke and Mark Jones describe the Puritan practice and purpose of meditation. They state, "The Puritans never tired of saying that biblical meditation involves thinking upon the triune God and His Word. By anchoring meditation in the living Word, Jesus Christ, and God's written Word, the Bible, the Puritans distanced themselves from the kind of bogus spirituality or mysticism that stresses contemplation at the expense of action and flights of the imagination at the expense of biblical content."[3]

George Mylne, a nineteenth century pastor, teaches on the art of meditation. He says we must, "make it a time of prayer - of communing with God. This helps the matter greatly. Take the words of Scripture-- and ask Jesus what they mean. In doing this, the mind is exercised. A glow of thought attends the effort. You honor Jesus; and He will honor you, by pouring out a largeness of capacity--a quicker mind. The interchange of thought between you and Jesus goes on apace, and you are surprised to find how long the exercise has lasted. Thus meditation grows, the more it is exercised. It feeds the soul, expands the mind, increases thought, and, best of all, it brings you into fellowship with Jesus. This is the very life and soul of meditation."[4] As Mylne describes, when we meditate on the Word of God, we commune with God. The longer we meditate, the more we understand, and the closer we draw near to God in communion.

Meditation gives us joy and delight in God. Psalm 1:2 says, "But his delight is in the Law of the LORD, and on His Law he meditates day and

---

1   D.S. Whitney, *Spiritual Disciplines for the Christian life*. (Colorado Springs: Navpress, 1991), 48.
2   Thomas Watson, *Heaven Taken by Storm* (Morgan, Pa: Soli Deo Gloria, 2000), 23.
3   Joel R. Beeke and Mark Jones, *A Puritan Theology: Doctrine for Life* (Grand Rapids: Reformation Heritage, 2012), 890.
4   George W. Mylne, *Ecclesiastes: Or, Lessons for the Christian's Daily Walk* (London: n.p., 1859).

night." The more we meditate on the Word, the more we love the Word. Psalm 119:97 says, "Oh, how I love your law! I meditate on it all day long." Meditation on the Word of God holds up a mirror to our souls and causes us to thoroughly examine and compare ourselves with Scripture, to discover our want in sanctification, to grow in the fruits of the Spirit and in our zeal for God. When we draw near to God in communion we are given a greater desire to know and love God, to grow in the grace and knowledge of God, and to become more like Christ. When we do not meditate on the Scriptures, we neglect one of the most important spiritual disciplines and hinder our spiritual growth.

Meditation Method

Each day has a devotion you will read and upon which to meditate. Every seventh day, you will do your own meditation on the selected verse. Fill in your own work every seventh day.

Read: You will be assigned a passage of Scripture so that you can understand the context of the selected verse. This enables you to understand the meaning and helps you form the application.

Emphasis: You will write out the verse in this section and then underline or highlight the key words or phrases. In the "Emphasis" section you will also pray through the verse. Read the verse with your first key word in mind. Meditate and think deeply on the key phrase. Read the verse again with your second key word emphasized and think deeply about this key word or phrase. Keep repeating the verse until you have meditated on each key word. Before you read the verse each time, pray for understanding and pray through the verse.

Rewrite: Write the verse in your own words to help you better understand. You can expand the verse for clarity.

Application: This is the section where you will spend most of your time. Think deeply, pray and discover the application of this verse to your life as a Christian in the new covenant. Write down hymns, songs, quotes, illustrations, experiences or anything else that comes to your mind. Some people are more creative than others, but everyone can be creative in some sense. Some people sketch out the application to ingrain the truth deep into their memory. Others sing the verse until they memorize it.

Writing the application can be dangerous if the verse is removed from its context or used in an erroneous hermeneutic. Don't read the verse with the goal of determining what the verse means to you. The verse means one thing, and it is your job to find out that meaning. The verse cannot mean one thing to you and another thing to someone else. Don't read the verse looking for a really deep, obscure meaning and then miss the plain meaning. The main things are the plain things. Don't read the Bible immediately assuming everything immediately applies to you directly. There are many valuable principles that you can learn and apply to your life in the Old Testament, but most of it is not speaking to you, a new covenant believer and follower of Jesus Christ.

For example, an often misquoted verse is Jeremiah 29:11 which says: "For I know the plans I have for you, declares the LORD, plans for welfare and not for evil,to give you a future and a hope." People always use this to say that God promises this to me, but by reading the first verse in chapter 29 you will read, "These are the words of the letter that Jeremiah the prophet sent from Jerusalem to the surviving elders of the exiles, and to the priests, the prophets, and all the people, whom Nebuchadnezzar had taken into exile from Jerusalem to Babylon." So unless you are a survivor of the Babylonian exile, this has nothing to do with you. God may have plans for you, but don't use this verse.

Another often misquoted verse is Matthew 18:20 which says, "For where two or three are gathered in my name, there am I among them." I have witnessed countless times someone stand up before the service at church or pray before a Bible study in a home and quote this verse. They say that because at least two or three Christians are in the same place, Jesus is with them. This, of course, brings up questions. What if there is only one person? Is Jesus not with one person? Does there have to be at least two people present for Jesus to be present? Does Jesus somehow lose His attribute of being omnipresent when there is only one person? Is Jesus not really omnipresent at all times, which would mean that He is not omnipresent? The problem with this interpretation is that the text has absolutely nothing to do with Christians gathering as a church, in a Bible study, or in fellowship. If we read the whole context of the passage we will see that this passage specifically refers to church discipline. It is a promise for guidance for the two or three who confront, and a promise for the church to claim wisdom and restoration for the erring brother.

To understand the meaning of a verse, we must first discover how the original readers or hearers of the verse understood it. It is very useful to understand the culture and customs, language and literary aspects of the book. There are many helpful resources you can use to do this like commentaries, manners and customs books, Bible dictionaries, history books and many more. Once you understand how they understood the verses, you must discover how the verse relates to you as a new covenant believer on the other side of the cross of Christ, filled with the Holy Spirit and living in this century. Once you know how it relates to you then you can figure out what you must do in your life to respond to the verse.

Some questions that you can ask of the text are: What does the text say? Who was it written by and to whom? What is the author's reason for writing? What is life like? What are the circumstances? What is the culture? What is the commercial trade or industry? From where and to where is he writing? When did he write it? What is his or their situation? What are the differences between the biblical audience and us? What is the setting? What is the time period? Old or new covenant? What is the theological principle of the text? Does the New Testament change our understanding of an Old Testament text?

After observing and understanding the text you can learn the application of the verse to your life. Once the application is clear you must be resolved to conform to the teaching of Scripture. Knowing what the verse means and how it applies to you will not change you or spiritually benefit you. You must be determined to live the verse and conform to it with regular periods of examination to see if you are still conforming to the Scriptures.

May my meditation be pleasing to him, for I rejoice in the Lord.
Psalm 104:34

Day 1

On the glorious splendor of your majesty, and on your wondrous works, I will meditate.

Psalm 145:5

Emphasis: On the glorious splendor of your **majesty** and on your wondrous **works**, I will **meditate**.

Rewrite: I will meditate on your glorious majesty and on the wondrous things you have done.

Application: As our knowledge about God increases, our praise of Him also augments. As we meditate on the majesty and wondrous works of God, we can only burst forth in praise. Before we can meditate on God, however, we must first know something of God's majesty and His wondrous works. The attributes of God are demonstrated through His works. As we see the works of God, we will see His glorious majesty. We see the wondrous works of God in the intricacy of His creation. God's majesty is displayed when we look at a breathtaking sunset or stand on the top of an enormous mountain peak. We see God's majesty in the smallest details and processes of nature. God displays His majesty in His works in so many ways, but ultimately His greatest work and majesty is displayed in Jesus Christ. The glorious rescue of the enemies of God from the condemnation and penalty of sin through the work and the person of Christ demonstrates the perfection of the majesty of God. When we fall before a blood stained cross and contemplate the cost of our salvation, we can only humbly praise God for His glorious majesty. Meditating on the work that God has done in your life will bring great encouragement through hard trials. To remind the Israelites of God's faithfulness and to encourage them that they can trust in Him, God reminds them that for "[t]hese forty years the Lord your God has been with you. You have lacked nothing" (Deuteronomy 2:7). Whenever we have doubts about our future, we must look back at the wondrous works of God in our life and renew our trust in our faithful God. Meditating on the glorious splendor of God's majesty and on His wondrous works should be the delight of Christians. Today we should look back at God's work in creation, our Savior Jesus Christ, and our salvation through Him.

Day 2

These things I have spoken to you, that my joy may be in you, and that your joy may be full.

John 15:11

Emphasis: These things I have spoken to you, that **my joy** may be in you, and that **your joy may be full**.

Rewrite: I have told these things to you so that you will have my joy in you and that you will have fullness of joy.

Application: Everyone on this earth pursues their own joy. Many search for joy in the wrong places. The greatest and only true joy can be found in Christ. If we seek joy in anything that can be lost, our joy will be lost. Life will be a series of hills and valleys. Jesus had pure joy in the midst of suffering and trials. Hebrews 12:2 states: "...who for the joy that was set before him endured the cross..." Jesus puts the joy that He has into us. When we have the joy of Christ, our joy is the fullest. When we derive our joy from Jesus, we have a constant flow of joy from the fountain of joy. How do we get this joy? Jesus spoke these things so we could have His joy. What did He speak? He said, "Abide in me, and I in you" (v. 4). "Whoever abides in me and I in him, he it is that bears much fruit" (v. 5). "If you abide in me, and my words abide in you, ask whatever you wish, and it will be done for you" (v. 7). "Abide in my love" (v. 9). "If you keep my commandments, you will abide in my love" (v. 10). How do we get this true joy? We get joy by abiding in Christ. When we abide in Jesus we will bear much fruit, which conforms us to Christ. When we abide in Jesus we have sweet communion with Him and He answers our prayers. When we abide in Jesus we abide in love, that is we know true love and can truly love. We abide in Jesus by keeping His commandments. His commandment is that we love one another as He has loved us. (v. 12) By loving one another we keep Christ's commandment, which leads to abiding in Christ, which leads to our prayers being answered and communion with God, which leads to bearing much fruit, which leads to becoming more like Christ, which finally leads to experiencing the fullness of joy. We cannot produce fruit, love, or joy in ourselves, but Jesus can when we abide in Him.

Day 3

Whoever humbles himself like this child is the greatest in the kingdom of heaven.

Matthew 18:4

Emphasis: Whoever **humbles** himself **like this child** is the greatest in the **kingdom of Heaven.**

Rewrite: Anyone who will live a life of childlike dependence and trust in God is the greatest in the kingdom of Heaven.

Application: To be humble like a child means to have a childlike trust and dependence on one's father. Children are vulnerable and lack the ability to fulfill their own desires without the help and guidance of their father. The child is dependent on the father for food, clothing, shelter, transportation, guidance, and instruction. In the same way, a Christian must surrender his will and live a life of faith, trust, and dependence on God alone. He must depend on God for His very existence and sustenance. He must not do his own will but the will of the Father. He must not advance his own cause or ideas but God's cause and ideas. If anyone would be first, he must be last of all and servant of all (Mark 9:35). The kingdom of Heaven is the goal. Being made great in the eyes of God is far greater than being great in the eyes of men, being popular on earth, or always being right. We must live a life of humility and childlike trust in our God, who upholds the universe by the word of His power (Hebrews 1:13). It is a great danger to grow in knowledge and ability. As we grow, we are tempted to rely on ourselves and our own ability and lose the simple, childlike trust in God. Losing our simple trust and dependence on God is the first step before the fall. If we want to be great, we must be a servant to all. Being great in the kingdom of Heaven may mean being unknown and insignificant in the world. Some of the greatest, Christlike servants who have ever existed or will exist are completely unknown in the world but their name is great in Heaven. Some of these servants have lived and died pouring their lives out in isolated places of the world. We may never be great in the eyes of man or preach to a thousand people but we can humbly serve God where we are at and be great in Heaven.

Day 4

The secret things belong to the LORD our God, but the things that are revealed belong to us and to our children forever, that we may do all the words of this law.

Deuteronomy 29:29

Emphasis: The **secret things** belong **to the LORD** our God, but the **things that are revealed** belong **to us** and to **our children forever**, that we may **do** all the words of this law.

Rewrite: The things that are true about God which have not been written in the Bible are hidden from us for God's purposes. Everything that is revealed to us through the Bible is all that we need to know about God, ourselves, and the world, and they are for us and our children.

Application: Not everything that is true of God has been revealed to us at this time on earth. There are things about God and His ways that we don't need to know, at this time and we probably could not grasp them if God did reveal them. There will be a time in Heaven when we learn much more about God and His ways, and we will continually learn about Him for all eternity. Jonathan Edwards, referring to the saints in Heaven, said, "Their knowledge will increase to eternity; and if their knowledge, their holiness; for as they increase in the knowledge of God, and of the works of God, the more they will see of his excellency, and the more they see of his excellency...the more will they love him, and the more they love God, the more delight and happiness will they have in him."[5] We will never be omniscient like God, therefore, we will always be learning. Because there are secret things now, we are called to trust God and His word and to humble ourselves before him, acknowledging that we don't understand everything. It should bring us joy to know God did not reveal everything to us because it proves that there are things we can still learn about God. We only know a fraction of what there is to know about God. We do know that God is love and demonstrated His love by sending His Son to die for us. Because of His love, we can now spend all eternity learning about God.

---

5 Jonathan Edwards, The Complete Works of Jonathan Edwards, vol. 2 (Great Britain: Hendrickson Publishing Marketing, LLC, 1834 reprint, 2011), 618.

Day 5

Therefore, if anyone cleanses himself from what is dishonorable, he will be a vessel for honorable use, set apart as holy, useful to the master of the house, ready for every good work.

2 Timothy 2:21

Emphasis: Therefore, if anyone **cleanses** himself from what is **dishonorable**, he will be a vessel for **honorable use**, set apart as **holy, useful** to the master of the house, ready for every good work.

Rewrite: If you mortify the sin in your life, you will be holy, useful to God, a person who God will use for honor and you will be ready for every good work.

Application: Robert Murray McCheyne said: "It is not great talents God blesses so much as great likeness to Jesus. A holy minister is an awful weapon in the hand of God." If we want to be used by God, we must first seek a holy life, set apart from sin. We must first clean ourselves from anything that is dishonorable in our lives so that we will be a vessel for honorable use. We will never be perfect, but we must never be content with our spiritual lives. We must continue to die to ourselves and live to righteousness each day. Verse 19b says, "Let everyone who names the name of the Lord depart from iniquity." Often times people live worldly, unholy lifestyles and then wonder why God is not using them in a powerful way. If we look back into history at the servants whom God most mightily used, we will see there is a common thread that runs through them all. Holiness. The carnal "Christian" watches things on television or listens to music that God absolutely hates and then he goes to church and takes the Lord's Supper. He prays for revival after he looks at pornography. He spends four hours a day on the internet but doesn't spend four minutes in his Bible. He talks more about himself than Christ. He spends more time talking to strangers about sports than about the gospel. He does all this and then asks God to use him. If we want to be used by God, we must know, seek, and do the will of God. God calls us to live our lives set apart from sin and the world, totally dedicated to Him and His perfect will which is revealed in the Scriptures. If we want to be used, we must read the Bible and obey it.

Day 6

Do you see a man who is hasty in his words? There is more hope for a fool than for him.

Proverbs 29:20

Emphasis: Do you see a man who is **hasty** in his **words**? There is **more hope for a fool** than for him.

Rewrite: Do you see a man who is hasty in his words? There is more hope for a fool than for him.

Application: Because we still have a sinful nature, we must examine all our thoughts, motivations, and desires to see if they are in accord with the Word of God. Words spoken quickly, before taking the time to think about how you should speak, often cause irreversible damage. When we respond or react in our emotions without filtering what should be said, we fall into a great snare of the devil. A quick word spoken in anger cuts a deep wound. James says "...the tongue is a fire, a world of unrighteousness" (James 3:6). We must always guard our tongues. Evil thoughts produce evil words and evil actions. "A fool gives full vent to his spirit, but a wise man quietly holds it back" (Proverbs 29:11). We must not vent every emotion and feeling we have without prudence. The more we speak in haste, the more potential we have to sin. "When words are many, transgression is not lacking, but whoever restrains his lips is prudent" (Proverbs 10:19). We must learn to bridle our tongues and not be quick to speak. How have you responded to slander, gossip, conflict, and rumors about you? Have you become angry and spoken things that you now regret? The tongue causes more hurt and damage than anything. We can't be a Christian and have an unrestrained tongue. "If anyone thinks he is religious and does not bridle his tongue but deceives his heart, this person's religion is worthless" (James 1:26). It is far better to remain silent and entrust yourself to God than to foolishly react in the first sinful emotions that come to mind. Jesus is the perfect example for us to follow. "When he was reviled, he did not revile in return; when he suffered, he did not threaten, but continued entrusting himself to him who judges justly" (1 Peter 2:23). If you continue to ignore this sin, there is more hope for a fool than you.

Day 7 – Your Meditation

Enter by the narrow gate. For the gate is wide and the way is easy that leads to destruction, and those who enter by it are many. For the gate is narrow and the way is hard that leads to life, and those who find it are few.

Matthew 7:13-14

Note: For instructions on how to fill in this page, read the introduction.
Read: Matthew chapter 7

Emphasis:_____

_____

_____

Rewrite:_____

_____

_____

_____

Application:_____

_____

_____

_____

_____

_____

_____

_____

_____

_____

_____

_____

_____

_____

_____

_____

Day 8

Jonathan said to the young man who carried his armor, "Come, let us go over to the garrison of these uncircumcised. It may be that the LORD will work for us, for nothing can hinder the LORD from saving by many or by few."

1 Samuel 14:6

Emphasis: It may be that the LORD will work for us, for **nothing can hinder the LORD** from **saving by many or by few**.

Rewrite: It may be the will of the Lord that He will work for us, for there is nothing that can hinder the Lord from accomplishing His will, and He can save by many or few or any means that He desires.

Application: Saul was concerned with numbers, but Jonathan was concerned with God's glory. Saul was quick to put himself in the protection of a cave surrounded by 600 men, but Jonathan was quick to put his life in the hand of God. God is not limited by power nor does he need anyone to help him do anything. God chooses means that will glorify him the most. We often see this in the Scriptures. In Judges chapters 6 through 8, we see that God made Gideon reduce his army to 300 men to bring deliverance from the Midianites. In the ultimate display of God's deliverance, God sent one man, His Son, born in a manger, under the law, to save a myriad of His people from every tribe and language and nation. By only one man, the Father saved a multitude in every generation. Now if God can save all His people in all the ages by only one man, how much more can he deliver us out of our desperate situation. Jonathan knew that nothing could restrain God from saving with many or few. At times, we all are faced with our inadequacies compared to what God calls us to do, but we should be comforted by this verse and reminded what God can do with many or few. No matter what the circumstance or how impossible deliverance seems, we must not look at what is seen but what is unseen. If our deliverance is dependent on our ability, we would never be delivered. When we fully and gladly surrender to God, like Jonathan, we can be confident that God will get glory out of our situation, and it will be for our good.

Day 9

I urge you, then, be imitators of me.

1 Corinthians 4:16

Emphasis: I urge you, then, be imitators of me.

Rewrite: I exhort you, imitate me.

Application: In the preceding verses, Paul explains what a life of serving Christ has been like for him. He says, "...we have become a spectacle to the world, to angels, and to men. We are fools for Christ's sake, but you are wise in Christ. We are weak, but you are strong. You are held in honor, but we in disrepute. To the present hour we hunger and thirst, we are poorly dressed and buffeted and homeless, and we labor, working with our own hands. When reviled, we bless; when persecuted, we endure; when slandered, we entreat. We have become, and are still, like the scum of the world, the refuse of all things" (1 Corinthians 4:9b-13). Interestingly, Paul then urges the Corinthians to imitate him and his ways in Christ. Paul establishes this principle of "imitating him as he imitates Christ" in various letters. In this same letter Paul says, "Be imitators of me, as I am of Christ" (1 Corinthians 11:1). In Philippians 3:17, he urges the brothers to "join in imitating me, and keep your eyes on those who walk according to the example you have in us." In Philippians 4:9 and 2 Timothy 3:10-11, Paul also exhorts Christians to imitate those who are mature in Christ and practice what they practice. Our ultimate example in the Scriptures is Christ, and we are to follow in His steps. God has also given us spiritual parents, leaders, and mentors who are an example of how a Christian practically imitates Christ in day to day life. When we read the biographies of these men and women of the faith, whom God used so powerfully, we are rightly encouraged to imitate them as they imitated Christ. When we have the privilege to be mentored by a spiritually mature believer, we find ourselves striving to imitate them as they imitate Christ. We don't imitate them in their personality, but in all that is Christ-like in them. We imitate their perseverance, boldness, love, kindness, faith, diligence, and other Christ-like attributes. Today, we must think of our own mentors who we imitate and the example we hope to set for others as we imitate Christ.

Day 10

...and that all this assembly may know that the LORD saves not with sword and spear. For the battle is the LORD's, and he will give you into our hand.

1 Samuel 17:47

Emphasis: ...and that all this assembly may know that the **LORD saves** not with sword and spear. For the **battle is the Lord's**, and He will give you into our hand.

Rewrite: So that all who see will know that the Lord does not need the sword or spear to save. The battle is not yours but the Lord's.

Application: In this well known story of David and Goliath we are reminded that God ordains by His providence the events in time so that he can glorify himself through deliverance. The cowering Israelite army was at a standstill on the battle front with the Philistines because of their fear of the giant Goliath. The lad David arose to the occasion, fueled by his desire for the glory of God, and kills the giant by himself while the cowering Israelites watch. This deliverance through David prefigures salvation through Christ, who defends us. We are not and never could be a David. We are the cowering Israelites who can do nothing. Christ is the real David, who went out before us and brought salvation and deliverance to us as we did nothing. If we are in Christ, the battle is not ours but His. Christ rules and defends us and restrains and conquers all of His and our enemies. God does not need the sword or spear to save. He does not need a great army or political power. He does not need gifted men and women to win the battle. In fact, he uses the weak things in this world to shame the wise so that all the credit and glory go to Him. The Lord, not strength in armies, determines the outcome of all battles. Every battle in our life is ordained by God for a reason, and we have an opportunity to glorify him in it. Sadly, by our nature, we try to fight these battles on our own. We take things into our own hands and try to fight our battles with money, politics, numbers and our own abilities, but the battle will not be determined by these. Go to God, who needs nothing from men, in prayer and ask Him to save you and win the battle for you.

Day 11

For you are not setting your mind on the things of God, but on the things of man.

Mark 8:33

Emphasis: For you are not setting your **mind** on the **things of God**, but on the **things of man**.

Rewrite: Your thoughts are not being consumed by heavenly things that will last in eternity, but you are thinking of worldly, temporal things that will not matter in eternity.

Application: There is an old saying that one is so heavenly minded that he or she is no earthly good. This saying could not be more wrong. Most of our day is usually spent on the daily worries of this world and not on eternal things. Most of us are so earthly minded that we are no good at eternal things. Peter was so focused on Jesus' bodily health that he was oblivious to the eternal purpose of the death of Christ, which is why Jesus rebuked him. We often do the same thing when we put all our thoughts, words, deeds and effort into this short life, which is like a grain of sand in the desert compared with eternity. At times we are so consumed by our circumstances that we are oblivious to our future in eternity. The world can only focus on the things of man, but a Christian must live for eternity. In a sermon titled *When a Preacher is Downcast* Charles Spurgeon said, "It is our duty and our privilege to exhaust our lives for Jesus. We are not to be living specimens of men in fine preservation, but living sacrifices, whose lot is to be consumed." A practical way to set our minds on the things of God is by renewing our minds in the Scripture each morning. When we start our day with our minds set on the things of God, we can live for that which is eternal. If we begin to stray, we can stop throughout the day to read the Word and pray to refocus our minds upon Christ. We must be heavenly minded and look at every circumstance, trial, relationship, and every event that occurs in our day as a God-ordained appointment with eternal bearing.

Day 12

And David said to Abishai and to all his servants, "Behold, my own son seeks my life; how much more now may this Benjaminite! Leave him alone, and let him curse, for the LORD has told him to."

2 Samuel 16:11

Emphasis: **Leave him alone**, and let him curse, **for the LORD has told him to**.

Rewrite: Leave him alone, let him do what he wills, the Lord has ordained all things, and we will trust in Him.

Application: Instead of taking action and avenging himself, David takes the curse upon himself and trusts in God to make things right. He says in the next verse, "It may be that the LORD will look on the wrong done to me, and that the LORD will repay me with good for his cursing today" (2 Samuel 16:12). When something unjust befalls us, it is often our natural inclination to seek out vengeance. How contrary to the Bible is this? We see David model the opposite here, and we saw Jesus do the same when wicked people gave false testimony against Him and when the high priest questioned Him. Scripture states Jesus remained silent (Matthew 26:63). Jesus trusted God to take vengeance and set things right. We are told in Romans 12:19, "Beloved, never avenge yourselves, but leave it to the wrath of God, for it is written, 'Vengeance is mine, I will repay, says the Lord.'" Today as we meditate on this verse, we must remember what the Bible teaches about trusting in God to make things right and not taking things in our own hands. There may be a time today or in the future when someone will wrong you, slander you, curse you, or treat you unfairly. Understand even this is the providence of God. He is giving you the opportunity to trust in Him, instead of your own efforts, to set things right. God is teaching you to depend on Him. After all, Jesus bore all your guilt and shame. He was treated unfairly and cursed in your place. Be like Christ, take a curse or slander; be silent and rest in God.

Day 13

And seeing in the distance a fig tree in leaf, he went to see if he could find anything on it. When he came to it, he found nothing but leaves, for it was not the season for figs. And he said to it, "May no one ever eat fruit from you again." And his disciples heard it.

Mark 11:13-14

Emphasis: When He came to it, **He found nothing** but leaves, for it was not the season for figs. And He said to it, "**May no one ever eat fruit from you again**." And His disciples heard it.

Rewrite: After finding no fruit on the fig tree, Jesus cursed the already barren tree so that it would never bear fruit again.

Application: Jesus didn't curse the fig tree because he had a craving for figs but couldn't eat them. There was a message behind this event. The cursing of the fig tree symbolized what was happening to the Jewish nation. Jesus came to the Jews looking for fruit but found none. They had turned away from God to a vain religion and tradition of men. Jesus tells us in Matthew 21:43: "Therefore I tell you, the kingdom of God will be taken away from you and given to a people producing its fruits." The Kingdom of God will be taken away from the leaders of national Israel and given to a people producing fruits. The church will be a new people of true believers, Jews and Gentiles, producing fruit. They will be brought from all nations and become a new nation. This should make us look at the fruit in our own lives. The fruit of the Spirit in Galatians 5 is the fruit of becoming more like Jesus in your character, doctrine, and practice. There is a strict warning against hypocrisy for all who have the outward appearance of bearing fruit but inwardly have not been changed by the Spirit of God. It is important to always examine ourselves to see if we are in the faith. Have I just learned the proper things to say, or do I really believe? Have I just learned how to behave, or do I do all things with a pure motivation to please and glorify God? Am I really changing to be more like Christ, or am I just putting on a show for men? Am I trying to please men or Christ? Do I really have biblical fruit?

Day 14 – Your Meditation

Fight the good fight of the faith. Take hold of the eternal life to which you were called and about which you made the good confession in the presence of many witnesses.

1 Timothy 6:12

Note: For instructions on how to fill in this page, read the introduction.
Read: 1 Timothy 6

Emphasis:_____

_____

_____

Rewrite:_____

_____

_____

_____

Application:_____

_____

_____

_____

_____

_____

_____

_____

_____

_____

_____

_____

_____

_____

_____

_____

_____

_____

_____

Day 15

In his hand is the life of every living thing and the breath of all mankind.

Job 12:10

Emphasis: In **His hand** is the **life** of **every living thing** and the breath of all mankind.

Rewrite: God upholds and sustains all that is living.

Application: Every person and living thing owe their lives and existence to God. Every living thing is sustained by God. In God, and by His grace, we live and move and have our being. Each breath is a gift from God. Every living thing is utterly dependent on God to remain alive. God keeps the universe running smoothly. The reason the planets remain in orbit is because God upholds them. God sustains the life of the smallest bacteria to the greatest beast. Amazingly, God upholds the life of the most wicked people on earth. God upheld the life of Hitler when Hitler murdered millions. God upheld our lives when we were His enemy and we lived in hate and rebellion against Him. Hebrews 1:3 declares Jesus upholds the universe by the word of His power. The most unfathomable fact is that even when Jesus was brutally beaten and then crucified on the cross, He upheld the very lives of those who were killing Him. He gave them their very being and strength which enabled them to torture and kill Him. This is an amazing thought. In a greater way than sustaining the lives of the wicked, Jesus promises to sustain the life of the Christian until the end. 1 Corinthians 1:7–8 says, "so that you are not lacking in any gift, as you wait for the revealing of our Lord Jesus Christ, who will sustain you to the end, guiltless in the day of our Lord Jesus Christ." We will never perish because the God who gives us life and saved us will also sustain us. The promise in John 10:28-29 applies to all true believers: "I give them eternal life, and they will never perish, and no one will snatch them out of my hand. My Father, who has given them to me, is greater than all, and no one is able to snatch them out of the Father's hand." As we meditate, we must rejoice that God sustains all things by the word of His power.

Day 16

So Solomon did what was evil in the sight of the LORD and did not wholly follow the LORD, as David his father had done.

1 Kings 11:6

Emphasis: So Solomon did what was evil in the sight of the LORD and **did not wholly follow the LORD,** as David his father had done.

Rewrite: Even though Solomon did good things in the name of the Lord, and he did follow Him in some way, he failed to follow the Lord fully and did evil in the sight of the Lord.

Application: Let this not be said about me! "He followed the Lord but not wholly. He did evil in the sight of the Lord." What a dreadful thing to be said about a person. Our good does not outweigh our bad. It is said that you can do everything right and no one notices, but if you do one thing wrong it can destroy you (Ezekiel 33:13). How many pastors have preached boldly, served God faithfully, had successful ministries, and then one day they commit adultery and all is lost. Their preaching is counted as hypocrisy, and their ministry is destroyed overnight. Solomon started well but finished badly. Matthew Henry tells us, " He left his first love, lost his zeal for God, and did not persevere to the end as he had begun; therefore it is said he was not perfect, because he was not constant; and he followed not God fully, because he turned from following him, and did not continue to the end."[6] It is so dangerous to put your guard down, to become complacent in your walk, to stop examining yourself, and to fall into a life of ease. We must be given fully to God and His work constantly, day after day, until we die. We must pour out our lives for the sake of Jesus Christ and the advancement of His kingdom. We must not dwell on or look for the comforts of this world or a life of ease. We must use our short lives for the work of God while we still have strength and finish the race. We must stay awake! Stay awake!

---

6 Henry, *Matthew Henry's Commentary on the Whole Bible*, 1 Kings 11:1–8.

Day 17

And he arose and came to his father. But while he was still a long way off, his father saw him and felt compassion, and ran and embraced him and kissed him.

Luke 15:20

Emphasis: And he arose and came to his father. But while he was still a long way off, his **father saw** him and **felt compassion**, and **ran** and embraced him and kissed him.

Rewrite: Filled with love and compassion at the sight of his lost son, the father ran and embraced him and kissed him.

Application: Everyone is familiar with the parable of the prodigal son, but the biblical application is often lost. Many believe the point of the parable is to show how a rebellious son can return to God. Many parents have told their child that he was saved when he said a prayer at the age of 10. The child never demonstrated any evidence of salvation and rebelled against his parents and God all through high school and beyond. The assumption that the child is actually saved is a big one. The parents cling to the story of the prodigal son in the hope that their son will come home to them and to God.   There is nothing wrong with longing for a rebellious son to come home, but that is not the point of the parable. If we read the whole context we see that Jesus is telling the parable in the presence of tax collectors and sinners in one group and the Pharisees in the other group. The parable is not about one lost child who rebelled and one who stayed home but of two lost, spiritually dead children. The younger son represents the tax collectors and sinners while the older son who stayed home represents the Pharisees. The whole point of the parable is not lost or saved children, judgmental Pharisees, or wicked, rebellious sinners. The point is to show the love of the father. The father's love was so great that he saw his disgraceful son, and he ran to him with a compassionate embrace. His love was unconditional. He longed for his child to come home to him. He saw the brokenness and repentance in his son and rejoiced. Like the angels in Heaven (Luke 15:7), the father rejoices over a sinner who repents. We must be reminded of our sad condition when God saved us and of His amazing love for us.

Day 18

This is a light thing in the sight of the LORD.

2 Kings 3:18

Emphasis: This is a **light thing** in the **sight of the LORD**.

Rewrite: This thing that is impossible for men is nothing for the Lord.

Application: When we think in a worldly sense, we see that things are impossible at times, but when we think from God's perspective, we realize nothing is impossible for God; all things are easy in the eyes of God. When Israel and Judah united forces to fight against the rebellion of the Moabites, Israel and Judah ran out of water after a seven day march and thought they would perish. They sought the Lord through Elisha the prophet, and the Lord turned a dry stream bed into flowing water and pools. The water kept coming until the whole country was filled with water. In the morning when the sun shone on the water, it looked like blood to the Moabites. The Moabites thought that Israel and Judah fought against each other, so the Moabites ran to the spoil and instead were killed by the Israelites. In this way God brought victory. This miracle was nothing for God. God created all things, sustains all things, and controls all things. He does impossible things to show His power and glory. Everything is impossible without God, but nothing is impossible with God. God makes the impossible, possible for wicked men when He sent His own Son, born of a woman, to live a perfect life and die a perfect death in our place. If God saved us, which was absolutely impossible for us to achieve in ourselves, then God can do anything. "He who did not spare his own Son but gave him up for us all, how will he not also with him graciously give us all things?" (Romans 8:32) We must remember today, as we meditate on this verse, that our hard circumstances are but a light thing to God. He has ordained our circumstances for His purposes and glory which will be for our good. We will see more of God through hard times.

Day 19

For our sake he made him to be sin who knew no sin, so that in him we might become the righteousness of God.

2 Corinthians 5:21

Emphasis: For **our sake** He made **Him** to be **sin** who **knew no sin**, so that **in Him** we might become the **righteousness of God**.

Rewrite: Because of God's love for us, the Father made Jesus, who was perfect in every way, without sin, to be sin, that is to take all of our sin and bear the penalty for it, so that in Jesus we have His righteousness imputed to us and we become the righteousness of God.

Application: This verse is arguably the most important verse in all of Scripture for understanding the meaning of the atonement and justification. God made Jesus to be sin. God initiated it, not us. Christ was regarded and treated as if He was like us, a sinner, even though He never sinned. Jesus, for our sake, bore our sins in His own body on the tree (1 Peter 2:24). Christ was our substitute on the cross, and He bore the wrath of God in our place to satisfy the divine justice of God. This is called substitutionary atonement. Because Christ bore our sin and paid our penalty, we are justified. Justification was an act of God's grace, that He initiated, where He pardoned all our sins, and accounted us as righteous in His sight. This was only possible because of the righteousness of Jesus Christ imputed to us, which we received by faith alone. Christ has provided the atoning sacrifice as our substitute, for the sins of all who believe (Romans 3:23-25). Isaiah 53:4-12 is this prophecy that Christ fulfilled. Christ bore our griefs and carried our sorrows. He was wounded for our transgressions and crushed for our iniquities. His chastisement brought us peace, and we were healed by His stripes. The Father laid on Jesus the iniquities of us all. His imputed righteousness makes many to be accounted righteous. We imputed our sin to Jesus, which He bears the punishment for the sin, and in return, the righteousness of Christ is imputed to us. Now God regards or treats us as having the legal status of righteousness. What more motivation do we need to serve and obey the living God? We must be more motivated to serve Him with all our lives, just as He gave His life.

Day 20

For I will defend this city to save it, for my own sake and for the sake of my servant David.

2 Kings 19:34

Emphasis: For I will defend this city to save it, **for my own sake** and for the **sake of my servant David.**

Rewrite: I will accomplish all things for my own sake and the sake of my people.

Application: Verse 31 reveals the motivations of God for defending the city. It says that the zeal of the Lord will do this. God is a jealous God (Exodus 20:5). God has zeal and jealousy for His own honor and name, and when He makes a promise, He keeps it for the sake of the fame of His name. The second reason for defending the city was for the sake of the promise God made to David. Matthew Henry comments on this point, "I will do it for my servant David's sake; not for the sake of his merit, but the promise made to him and the covenant made with him, those sure mercies of David. Thus all the deliverances of the church are wrought for the sake of Christ, the Son of David."[7] This verse brings great comfort to us because we learn of God's zeal and jealousy for His own name and for His promises. We can be confident in and trust in the promises that God reveals in Scripture. This is confirmed in one of the most comforting verses in the Bible, Romans 8:28, which says, "And we know that for those who love God all things work together for good, for those who are called according to his purpose." When we begin to understand the character of God and His sovereignty over all creation, we can take great comfort in trusting Him for all things and casting all our anxiety and cares on Him. Knowing God loves us beyond anything we can imagine and that He is working out all things for His glory and our good, makes it a great joy to step back, view things from an eternal perspective, and fully trust in God in all things.

---

7   Henry, *Matthew Henry's Commentary on the Whole Bible*, 2 Kings 19:20–34.

Day 21 – Your Meditation

For God has not called us for impurity, but in holiness.

1 Thessalonians 4:7

Note: For instructions on how to fill in this page, read the introduction.
Read: 1 Thessalonians 4:1-12

Emphasis:_____
_____
_____

Rewrite:_____
_____
_____

Application:_____
_____
_____
_____
_____
_____
_____
_____
_____
_____
_____
_____
_____
_____
_____
_____
_____
_____
_____
_____
_____
_____

Day 22

In this is love, not that we have loved God but that he loved us and sent his Son to be the propitiation for our sins.

1 John 4:10

Emphasis: In this is **love, not that we** have loved God but that **He loved us** and sent His **Son** to be the **propitiation** for our sins.

Rewrite: This is true love, not that God returns His love when we love Him, but that He loved us first, unconditionally.

Application: He loved us.   All of eternity will be spent striving to understand why God loved us.   There was nothing in us that was lovable. Why would God crush His own perfect Son in our place?   The doctrine of the love of God is often taken to two extremes.   One extreme is to believe that God is always wrathful against the world and only loves His people.   This view always focuses on God as hard, severe, fierce, and wrathful, and the people who hold this view, like a fearful child unwilling to come to a wrathful father, stay far from communion with God.   The other extreme of the doctrine of the love of God teaches that God is love and nothing else.   God loves all people unconditionally and equally.   God does not care about sin because He is love.   People who hold this view are not worried about their sin, they don't pursue holiness, and they live worldly and unchanged lives.   This is a grievous error.   God does hate sin, and He is wrathful against all workers of iniquity.   God will punish sinners because He is just and loving.   Because He is loving, He must be just, and therefore He must punish lawbreakers.   If God let wicked, God-hating sinners go free without satisfying justice then God would be wicked and corrupt Himself.   The only way God can bring sinners into communion with Him is to satisfy His justice by punishing someone in the sinner's place. That is why the second half of the verse says, "and sent his Son to be the propitiation for our sins." God satisfied His justice by crushing His own Son in our place so that we could be reconciled to Himself.   We must set our thoughts on the eternal love of the Father, and we will find true joy.

Day 23

Seek the Lord and his strength; seek his presence continually!

1 Chronicles 16:11

Emphasis: Seek the LORD and **His strength**; seek His **presence continually**!

Rewrite: Search for the Lord and His strength and His presence without ceasing.

Application: After going through so many trials, David is established and the ark is brought back to Jerusalem and placed in the tent that David had pitched for it. David sings a song of thanksgiving. His primary concern has been seeking God, and now it has paid off, which is why verse 10 says, "...let the hearts of those who seek the Lord rejoice!" How we fail at this so much. How we fail at seeking communion with God, seeking His strength and presence. James 4:8 tells us, "Draw near to God, and he will draw near to you." What a great promise upon which we can depend! God will draw near to us as we communion with Him. Often we get in a spiritual rut, and we feel distant from God. We feel dead spiritually. The solution is to seek God, seek communion with Him. Our strength and weakness is directly related to the amount of time we spend in communion with God through the Word and prayer. The result of neglected communion with God is weakness and spiritual deadness. Our fellowship or communion with God is essential but most often neglected.   That is why Puritan authors like John Owen wrote volumes on communion with God.   Meditating on this verse today reminds us to reflect on our relationship and communion with God. Has it been neglected?   We must strive to get a glimpse of God and His goodness. We must violently pursue Him with all that we are. We must fight against everything in our lives that seeks to steal away our time of communion with God. We must vow to make communion with God a top priority every day. The consequences of neglecting communion are disastrous, and the benefits of seeking Him are immeasurable. We have the promise in the book of James: "Draw near to God, and he will draw near to you."

Day 24

And you, Solomon my son, know the God of your father and serve him with a whole heart and with a willing mind, for the LORD searches all hearts and understands every plan and thought.

1 Chronicles 28:9a

Emphasis: And you, Solomon my son, **know** the God of your father and **serve** Him with a **whole heart** and with a **willing mind**, for the **LORD searches** all hearts and **understands every plan and thought**.

Rewrite: And Solomon, my son, you must seek to know the God of your father and to serve Him with all of your being, for the Lord searches and understands every plan and thought that is in your heart.

Application: Once we know the true and living God, our only response can be to serve and obey Him with our whole heart and a willing mind. If we have no desire to serve and obey Him it is because we do not really know Him. If we know Him but don't serve Him then we worship Him in vain. The second part of the verse reveals the omniscience of God. He searches all hearts and understands every plan and thought of man. This means that we can't fool God or get away with anything. He knows everything (1 John 3:19-24). We may be able to have secrets before men, but we cannot hide anything from God. Matthew Henry comments on this verse, "We must therefore be sincere, because, if we deal deceitfully, God sees it, and cannot be imposed upon; we must therefore employ our thoughts, and engage them in God's service, because he fully understands all the imaginations of them, both good and bad."[8] Knowing that God is seeing our every thought should make us not only serve Him with all our souls but also to war against the sin in our minds. If we fight and conquer sin in our mind then it won't manifest itself outside of our mind. Knowing that God is sitting beside us and that He knows our thoughts should bring great fear to us when we are doing something we know is wrong. Every lustful look, every bad television show, and every sinful motivation is seen by God.

---

8   Henry, *Matthew Henry's Commentary on the Whole Bible*, 1 Chronicles 28:1-10.

Day 25

He will swallow up death forever; and the Lord GOD will wipe away tears from all faces

Isaiah 25:8a

Emphasis: He will swallow up death forever; and the Lord GOD will wipe away tears from all faces.

Rewrite: The Lord will destroy death forever and wipe away all our tears.

Application: We live in a fallen world of suffering, death, and tears. No one looks forward to the pains of death. No one longs to suffer, mourn, or cry, but the reality of life in this sin-filled world is that we must go through the pains, sin, and misery of this life, and then die. Before the death and resurrection of Christ, the great enemy of death stung and conquered its foes. Death had a stronghold on everyone. The only way to remove the fear of death was to destroy death forever. Isaiah prophesied about the day this would happen. There was only one way that death could be swallowed up; it was through the death of Christ on the cross. Christ abolished death and brought life and immortality to light through the gospel (2 Timothy 1:10). Now death is destroyed and no longer has a stronghold on the Christian. We hold tightly to the promise of God in Revelation 21:4, which says, "He will wipe away every tear from their eyes, and death shall be no more, neither shall there be mourning, nor crying, nor pain anymore, for the former things have passed away." We long for the day of no more suffering, pain, and tears. Because Christ swallowed up death forever, countless martyrs were able to embrace their deaths while singing hymns. Someone once said that the most dangerous person in the world was the one who had no fear of dying. When the Spirit of God dwells in the Christian, He removes all fear of death from him. Paul tells us that at our resurrection, through Christ, we will receive this promise. When the perishable puts on the imperishable, and the mortal puts on immortality, then shall come to pass the saying that is written: "'Death is swallowed up in victory.' 'O death, where is your victory? O death, where is your sting?'" (1 Corinthians 15:53–55). We no longer have a spirit of fear, but power.

Day 26

Why do you call me 'Lord, Lord,' and not do what I tell you?

Luke 6:46

Emphasis: **Why** do you call me **'Lord, Lord,'** and **not do** what I tell you?

Rewrite: Why do you say that I'm your master and then disobey me.

Application: This should bring great conviction to the hypocrite. Countless people profess that Jesus is their Lord and that they are a follower of Christ, but they live as though God never gave them a law to obey. They live in disobedience to God at the same time they tell everyone that they belong to Him. Before we were saved, we were slaves to sin, and now that we are saved by Christ, we are slaves to our Master, Jesus Christ. He is not the hard task master of sin but a loving Master who not only saves us, protects us, and provides for us, He adopts us into His family, and we receive all of the rights and privileges as sons and daughters of God. The question is, why do we call Jesus our master, the one who has all authority and power and to whom respect, to whom allegiance and obedience is due, and then rebel against Him in our sin? A true Christian is not only a hearer of the Word but a doer of the Word as well. We have what some have called acceptable sins. Sins we know that we do but in our minds they are little, and, therefore, we don't fight too hard against them to kill them. We justify them instead. We compare our sin with bigger sins of others, and we just accept our own sins. Why do we say we are followers of Christ and then don't follow Him? As we meditate on this verse today, we should examine ourselves and seek out the answers to these questions. Maybe it is because we are not really a true follower of Christ. Maybe we are still engulfed in the world and love the world more than Christ; we love our sin more than Christ. Later in Luke 9:23, Jesus says, "If anyone would come after me, let him deny himself and take up his cross daily and follow me." We must daily fight sin and obey God. Let us fight the good fight and obey our loving, gracious, kind, and glorious God today.

Day 27

But when he was strong, he grew proud, to his destruction.

2 Chronicles 26:16a

Emphasis: But when he was **strong**, he grew **proud**, to his **destruction.**

Rewrite: With his growing strength came growing pride, which destroyed him.

Application: Uzziah became king of Judah when he was 16 years old. He replaced his father Amaziah, who was murdered after he turned away from the Lord. Uzziah started out by doing what was right and seeking God. As long as he sought God, God made him prosper. However, after a life of prosperity, ease and strength, he became proud and was destroyed. God struck him with leprosy in the forehead; he was isolated to a separate house until he died years later. We should be familiar with Proverbs 16:18 that says, "Pride goes before destruction, and a haughty spirit before a fall." Uzziah experienced this verse. Often we have been humbled when we were sure of ourselves and fell, maybe not as hard as Uzziah, but we fell and were humbled. We see this so often in men who are in prominent positions. The majority of the kings who we see in the Bible are marked with pride which led to adultery, murder, oppression, persecution, and especially idolatry. 1 Timothy 3:6 declares that one of the requirements for a prospective elder in a church is he, "...must not be a recent convert, or he may become puffed up with conceit and fall into the condemnation of the devil." Pride is the root of all our sins. It has destroyed the lives of many of its victims. When we are humble, it is much easier to seek and depend on God instead of ourselves. When we have strength and success, by our sinful nature, we are tempted to seek to do things in our own selves and depend on ourselves instead of God. Pride is a character trait of the devil, the world, and false teachers. It often manifests itself in self-righteousness, positions of authority, inexperience, power, and wealth. Today we must examine our strength, pride, and dependence on God. We must continually fight against pride our whole lives, and we must try to mortify it in our lives before it mortifies us.

Day 28 – Your Meditation

But now in Christ Jesus you who once were far off have been brought near by the blood of Christ.

Ephesians 2:13

Read: Ephesians chapter 2

Emphasis:_____

_____

_____

Rewrite:_____

_____

_____

Application:_____

_____

_____

_____

_____

_____

_____

_____

_____

_____

_____

_____

_____

_____

_____

_____

_____

_____

_____

_____

Day 29

So even to old age and gray hairs, O God, do not forsake me, until I proclaim your might to another generation, your power to all those to come.

Psalm 71: 18

Emphasis: So even to **old age** and gray hairs, O **God, do not forsake me**, until I **proclaim** your might to another generation, **your power to all** those to come.

Rewrite: So now that I am old, O God, do not leave me, until I proclaim your might and power to one more generation.

Application: David, the author of this Psalm, had been taught by God and had proclaimed His wondrous works from a young age (v. 17). David's longing now is just a little more time in his old age to proclaim the excellencies and works of God to the next generation. David wanted to finish well. Notice the contrast between David and the nominal Christian. David sought more years to proclaim the goodness of God just as David had done for most of his life. The nominal Christian seeks retirement in his old age. David sought to pour out the last years of his life for God. The nominal Christian seeks a life of ease, recreation, and naps in the last years of his life. David desired to finish strong. The nominal Christian seeks to finish easy. David sought to die proclaiming. The nominal Christian seeks to die in his sleep. After a life of serving God, David only desired to serve Him more. The nominal Christian thinks he has earned his right to rest. David trusted in the might and power of God. The nominal Christian trusts in the stock market and his 401k. We must not retire from God. We must keep seeking, serving, and proclaiming so that when it is time to die, we can just simply die. We will not have regrets. No one on their death bed has ever said that they wish they had not given so much of their life to God. We must make the best use of our time and take heed to the exhortation that Paul gives in Ephesians 5:15-16, which says, "Look carefully then how you walk, not as unwise but as wise, making the best use of the time, because the days are evil."

Day 30

And do not be grieved, for the joy of the LORD is your strength.

Nehemiah 8:10b

Emphasis: And do not be **grieved,** for the **joy of the Lord** is your **strength.**

Rewrite: Do not be distressed, you have the joy of the Lord, which is your strength.

Application: The word translated into English as "strength" doesn't refer to physical strength which makes you physically strong. The word "strength" here means a place of refuge, fortress, means of safety or protection. It is the same word in Psalm 91:2 which is translated as "fortress". The joy of the Lord is our fortress, refuge, and stronghold. This is not a carnal joy that we get from eating a good meal; it is a holy joy that is drawn from God. We have joy in the love and goodness of God. We have joy in the person and works of God. We have joy in our salvation through Jesus Christ. This joy, drawn from God, is the fuel that gives us great motivation and desire to serve and obey Him. We must never seek joy from anything we can lose. If we hope to get joy out of any material thing or person, we will lose our joy when we lose the object of our joy. Because the Christian can never lose God, he will always have joy, even in trials. We must seek this joy from God so that it will strengthen us for good works, which God prepared beforehand, that we should walk in them. If Jesus Christ is our Lord and refuge in times of hard trials then these promises are for us. When we realize that God is our refuge, fortress, and the Almighty, Sovereign of the world, we can draw great joy from this. This promise does not apply to us if we are not in close fellowship with God. So the question is, do we live in close fellowship with God? Is God our rock, fortress, and deliverer in whom we trust? If not, we have no joy. As we meditate on this verse, we must be urged by it to make God our refuge in all the problems in our lives. When we meditate on the goodness and love of God and on His Son Jesus who bore our penalty and gave us His righteousness, then we will have great joy and will gain strength to live in the assurance that this great God is our refuge in all the issues we face today.

Day 31

For if you keep silent at this time, relief and deliverance will rise for the Jews from another place, but you and your father's house will perish. And who knows whether you have not come to the kingdom for such a time as this?

Esther 4:14

Emphasis: For if you **keep silent** at this time, relief and deliverance will rise for the Jews from **another place**, but you and your father's house will **perish**.

Rewrite: If you don't intercede now, God will use someone else to bring deliverance, but you will suffer loss.

Application: Mordecai, in his strong faith, boldly proclaims that if Esther does not step up and intercede, God will bring deliverance from somewhere else. Even though Mordecai had no idea where deliverance would come from in this impossible and desperate situation, he completely trusted God for it. He encouraged Esther that this may have been the plan from God all along, that she would be made queen to intercede and to save the Jews. Esther had fear; Mordecai had courage. Esther was looking at the circumstance while Mordecai was looking to his great, sovereign God in Whom all things are possible. We are often faced with similar challenges when we have a chance to speak up in a situation that could ruin us in the sight of the world. Other times it is a chance to help someone financially. God will take care of this person no matter what, but He gives us the opportunity to do it for His glory and our good. Sometimes we have a chance to volunteer for something or help someone do something. It will take a lot of our time and the work may not be fun. God will accomplish this work and help the person no matter what, but He gives us the opportunity for our good and His glory. It comes down to the matter of selfishness. If we are worldly minded, we are selfish. If we are heavenly minded then we are selfish to do good works. We understand that our reward is in Heaven and that we get the greatest true joy from serving and obeying God. We must look for these opportunities to stand up, do good, and serve.

Day 32

And he said, "Naked I came from my mother's womb, and naked shall I return. The LORD gave, and the LORD has taken away; blessed be the name of the LORD."

Job 1:21

Emphasis: Naked I came from my mother's womb, and naked shall **I return.** The **LORD gave**, and the **LORD has taken** away; **blessed be** the name of the LORD.

Rewrite: I came into this world with nothing, and I will leave with nothing. The Lord gives, and He takes away. Blessed be His name.

Application: After losing just about everything earthly in his life, Job humbled himself before God, mourned, and accepted the providence of God in his life. He proved to show himself content, like the apostle Paul, in times of abundance and times when he had nothing. From Genesis 3:19 we know that we were taken from the dust and will return to it when we die. This is a reality we don't think of much but should think of much more, especially when we lose focus and begin to spend our time and money on living for the things this world has to offer. When we begin to think getting that new house or other desired object will bring happiness, we have already lost our contentment. When we focus on accumulating material things or seeking a more comfortable life, we have lost our contentment. We can easily fall into this trap just like the rich man with the rich land. He accumulated so much stuff that he kept building bigger barns to store it all. He spent all his time building his kingdom on earth. He thought that if he stored up enough stuff in his younger years, then in his later years, he could relax, eat, drink and be merry (Luke 12:16-21). But it didn't work out good for him. God called him a fool, took his life, and gave his goods to another. We must learn contentment and take the exhortation from Paul to Timothy seriously. He says, "But godliness with contentment is great gain, for we brought nothing into the world, and we cannot take anything out of the world. But if we have food and clothing, with these we will be content. But those who desire to be rich fall into temptation, into a snare, into many senseless and harmful desires that plunge people into ruin and destruction (1 Timothy 6:6-9).

Day 33

Nathan said to David, "You are the man!

2 Samuel 12:7

Emphasis: Nathan said to David, "**You** are the man!

Rewrite: You are thinking of another, but you are the man!

Application: It was a nice spring day for a normal spring battle. This time though was different because David the king did not go to battle, but he instead sent Joab and all Israel to fight the Ammonites. David stayed home in leisure, which was a decision he would later regret. So David was on his roof, and from his roof he sees a beautiful woman bathing; he lusted and invited the woman to his house. David found that she was married, but this didn't stop him from having his way with her. The woman, known as Bathsheba, was now pregnant with the king's child. David panics and comes up with a devious plan to hide his sin. He writes a letter to Joab instructing him to put Uriah, Bathsheba's husband, in the heat of the battle and to then abandon him so that Uriah would die in the battle. Joab carried out his orders, and Uriah dies in battle. The scandal was a success, the adultery and murder are hidden from everyone, that is except God. More than nine months go by, the baby is born, and the scandal is still hidden, but as the Scripture says, "...be sure your sin will find you out" (Numbers 32:23b). During this time when David hides his sin, he becomes weak and sick physically; he loses his joy; he loses his witness; he loses his power. God gives David plenty of time to make things right, but David persists in hiding his sins. In walks Nathan, a respected prophet of God with a message for David. He tells a story of injustice; David becomes angry and demands justice to come on this wicked man in the story. Nathan turns to David with a bold, authoritative voice and says, "You are the man!" It is so easy to see sin in other people, yet it is even easier to be blind to our own sin. How often do we hide or justify our sins but accuse others of the same sin. We sweep our sins under the rug. We forget that hiding our sin has consequences. Those things that no one knows about that come up every once and awhile, as your conscience bears witness against you, will eat you up inside and begin to harden your heart until you confess them.

Day 34

And immediately all the crowd, when they saw him, were greatly amazed and ran up to him and greeted him.

Mark 9:15

Emphasis: And immediately all the crowd, when they **saw** Him, were **greatly amazed** and **ran** up to Him and greeted Him.

Rewrite: Immediately everyone in the crowd saw Jesus and were so amazed that they could do nothing else but run to Him.

Application: After Peter, James and John descended the mountain with Jesus after Jesus was transfigured, they came to the other disciples who were arguing with the scribes. When they saw Jesus, the crowd became silent. They were amazed and ran to Him. The disciples and crowds had seen Jesus many times, but this time the text says that they were *greatly amazed*. Why were they so amazed this time? Was the face of Jesus different after He had been transfigured? Was His face similar to the face of Moses when he came off the mountain? It is hard to say, but we do know that when the crowd caught a glimpse of Jesus, they were greatly amazed, and they ran to Him. Are we not to be amazed at Jesus as well? The thought of Jesus in His person and work on the cross for us should cause us to drop everything and run to Him. We should sit in amazement at His love and sacrifice for us. Jesus is worthy of all our love, adoration, worship, and praise. He is our highest priority. When we get a glimpse of the beauty of Christ, all we can do is be amazed and worship Him. A right understanding of the worth of Christ will motivate us to face any hardship and trial. This understanding will humble us and refocus our lives. Just as the crowd stopped all their arguing and ran to Christ when they saw Him, we will forget about all our pride and vanity of this world at the first glimpse of Him. Today we should meditate with great amazement on the person of Christ, and as we do, all the worries of this world will slowly fade away for a moment.

Day 35 – Your Meditation

Consider him who endured from sinners such hostility against himself, so that you may not grow weary or fainthearted.

Hebrews 12:3

Read: Hebrews chapter 12

Emphasis:_____
_____
_____

Rewrite:_____
_____
_____

Application:_____
_____
_____
_____
_____
_____
_____
_____
_____
_____
_____
_____
_____
_____
_____
_____
_____
_____
_____
_____

Day 36

But you are doing away with the fear of God and hindering meditation before God.

Job 15:4

Emphasis: But you are doing away with the **fear of God** and **hindering meditation** before God.

Rewrite: Your lack of fear of God is hindering your meditation of Him.

Application: The ESV translates the word *meditation,* but the KJV uses the word *prayer.* Eliphaz assumes that Job has no fear of God and that his prayer or meditation is hindered. Although Eliphaz wrongly accused Job, his principle is true. If a man has no fear of God, he will have no desire to pray or meditate on the Scripture. If you are not in a regular habit of communing with God through meditation and prayer, then you show that you do not fear God or desire to be in communion with Him. When we don't fear God then our prayers and meditations will be without fruit. We will leave our prayer time unaffected and without comfort. To not fear God is sin, and sin will hinder our prayers and meditation. Isaiah 59:2 says, "...but your iniquities have made a separation between you and your God, and your sins have hidden his face from you so that he does not hear. Before coming in communion with God in prayer and meditation, we must examine ourselves for sin that will hinder our prayers and meditation. Scripture states if we have sin that we have not confessed in our life, our prayers will be hindered (Psalm 66:18, Isaiah 59:1-2, Jeremiah 11:10-11). Other things that hinder our prayer and meditation are: rebellion (Proverbs 28:9), broken relationships, such as you are fighting with your spouse (1 Peter 3:7), unbelief (James 1:6-7), selfishness (James 4:3), and pride (James 4:6). We must continue to be on guard and examine ourselves daily and then fight, mortify, and kill any sin we discover. Charles Spurgeon encourages us in our battle with sin, he says of sin, "Christ has crucified it, "nailing it to his cross." Go now and mortify it, and the Lord help you to live to His praise, for sin with all its guilt, shame, and fear, is gone. [9]

---

[9]   Charles H. Spurgeon, *Morning and evening: Daily readings* (Complete and unabridged; New modern edition.). Peabody, MA: Hendrickson Publishers, 2006).

Day 37

...he commanded our fathers to teach to their children, that the next generation might know them, the children yet unborn, and arise and tell them to their children, so that they should set their hope in God.

Psalm 78:5b-7a

Emphasis: ...He **commanded** our **fathers** to **teach** to their **children**....so that they should set their **hope in God.**

Rewrite: God gave us His word to teach our children so they would put their hope in God.

Application: This is an instructional and historical Psalm which teaches us that we must learn from the past. It recounts the history of Israel and their mistakes. The Psalm urges fathers to teach their children about the past and learn from it. They should learn from the mistakes of their forefathers, and they should learn about the greatness of God through His character and works. History is always very valuable for learning. God preserved the knowledge of His wonderful works through all the feasts and by all the songs focusing on them. We do the same thing today with all the great hymns which sing of the works of God and glory of Christ. Also, specific days like Christmas and Easter, which focus on the birth of Christ and His resurrection, respectively, remind us of the truth of God and hope in Him. Romans 15:4 says, " For whatever was written in former days was written for our instruction, that through endurance and through the encouragement of the Scriptures we might have hope." Hope is the result of teaching our children about who God is, what He did in the past, and what He is doing today. Proverbs 22:6 says, "Train up a child in the way he should go; even when he is old he will not depart from it." The principle of this verse in Proverbs is the same as this verse in Psalm 78. We teach our children about God and explain the way they should go so that they will set their hope in God. This verse is wisdom, not a promise. This verse does not promise that if you raise your child in the ways of the Lord then he will be saved. Only God can save the child, no matter how good you raise him. Our children have hope as we teach them the works of God.

Day 38

For in a single hour all this wealth has been laid waste.

Revelation 18:17

Emphasis: For in a **single hour** all this **wealth** has been **laid waste.**

Rewrite: In a single hour, all was lost.

Application: This verse is speaking of the great city of Babylon and of all that was in it being destroyed in one hour. This is a shocking reality of how fast things can change in your life. On October 29, 1929, Black Tuesday, the stock market crashed and the Great Depression went global. Many rushed to sell their stocks but could not, and they went bankrupt almost overnight. Banks closed overnight and life-savings were lost. All the wealth of men was laid waste in a single hour. How do we see the riches of this world? How do we react when we see wealthy people accumulate more things while we scrape by? How would we feel if all the wealth of the world was destroyed in one night? How would we feel if all of our material possessions were destroyed in a fire? Matthew 6:19-21 is a warning to us; it says, "Do not lay up for yourselves treasures on earth, where moth and rust destroy and where thieves break in and steal, but lay up for yourselves treasures in heaven, where neither moth nor rust destroys and where thieves do not break in and steal. For where your treasure is, there your heart will be also." Can we obtain wealth without it penetrating our hearts? When we lay up our treasures in Heaven and focus on eternity, we gain a promise. Jesus tells us in Mark 10:29-30, "Truly, I say to you, there is no one who has left house or brothers or sisters or mother or father or children or lands, for my sake and for the gospel, who will not receive a hundredfold now in this time, houses and brothers and sisters and mothers and children and lands, with persecutions, and in the age to come eternal life." We must live for eternity, not retirement. It's not only our money that can be destroyed in a single day, but our own lives as well. Death is a reality we don't want to think about much, but we must. In his famous resolutions, Jonathan Edwards wrote, "Resolved, to think much on all occasions of my own dying, and of the common circumstances which attend death." When we think of our death and the brevity of life, we can only focus on eternity.

Day 39

Just so, I tell you, there will be more joy in heaven over one sinner who repents than over ninety-nine righteous persons who need no repentance.

Luke 15:7

Emphasis: Just so, I tell you, there will be more **joy in Heaven** over **one sinner** who **repents** than over ninety-nine righteous persons who need no repentance.

Rewrite: There is more rejoicing in Heaven over one lost sinner who repents than over ninety-nine righteous persons who have never strayed.

Application: This is an amazing reality that we should think deeply on. From this verse we get a glimpse of what is happening in the heavenly realms. When one lost sinner is enlightened to the knowledge of Christ by the work of the Spirit, and he turns from his sins to God, all of Heaven stands up and takes notice. Myriads of myriads of angels break out in rejoicing when just one sinner repents (Luke 15:10, Revelation 5:11-12). What a sight this must be in Heaven! Meditating on this scene should bring us great joy throughout the day. The second half of the verse is directed towards the Pharisees and scribes (v. 2), who proclaimed that they were like the righteous person who needed no repentance. Jesus is saying that all of Heaven is not really impressed with their "righteousness" that they proclaim before men, but all Heaven rejoices over repentant sinners. The Pharisees and scribes were unrepentant, self-righteous sinners, and, therefore, there is no rejoicing in Heaven over them. This should encourage us in many ways. God loves us, and all of Heaven is concerned for us and our repentance. When God saved us, it was a day of rejoicing in Heaven. The poor, broken, insignificant man in the deepest jungle who is not known by many people in the world and despised by the ones that know him, probably does not grasp his worth in Heaven. If he could only get a glimpse of Heaven at the moment of his conversion, he would have enough joy and love for Christ to carry him for the rest of his life. We should also be encouraged to repent. God requires that we repent from all of our sins, and the angels rejoice over repentance. No one in Heaven or on earth likes an unrepentant sinner. We must live a life of repentance.

Day 40

Bear with me a little, and I will show you,
for I have yet something to say on God's behalf.

Job 36:2

Emphasis: Bear with me a little, and I will show you, for **I** have yet something to say **on God's behalf.**

Rewrite: Listen to me because I have something to say to you from God.

Application: We have all heard people say, "God told me to tell you...." Most of the time it turned out that what they had to tell you was not from God at all but from their own sinful imagination. It was the same with Elihu here. Elihu was the youngest of Job's "miserable comforters," and he was very proud. Verse 4 says that Elihu claimed he had perfect knowledge. How dangerous and foolish is this? If God is going to correct or discipline someone, most likely He will do it through the Scriptures, preaching, or another person, but in the case of His use of another person, the other person usually has no idea that he is correcting you on God's behalf. Someone will say something unwittingly that will speak of your secret sin and cut you to the heart. We must have extreme caution when someone comes to us with a "word" from God, and we must have equal caution when we think God is "telling" us to speak to someone on His behalf. Someone once came to Charles Spurgeon after Spurgeon finished preaching and said God told him that he must preach at Spurgeon's church the following night. Spurgeon looked at him with a smile and said it was funny because God never told him that. Sometimes we think that we hear from God when it is really our own emotions. There is an old saying that says, "When emotions run high, discernment runs low." Discernment is a practice that we must learn. The more we understand of the Bible, the more we will be able to discern. We must practice discernment when people come to us with a "word" from God, and we must practice the same discernment when we think that God is giving us a word to tell someone. The majority of the time that we think we have a word from God for someone, it is pride, and we must not fall into the same trap as Elihu.

Day 41

If your enemy is hungry, give him bread to eat, and if he is thirsty, give him water to drink, for you will heap burning coals on his head, and the Lord will reward you.

Proverbs 25:21-22

Emphasis: If your **enemy** is hungry, **give** him bread to eat, and if he is thirsty, **give** him water to drink, for you will heap **burning coals** on his head, and the Lord will **reward** you.

Rewrite: If your enemy is hungry or thirsty, meet his need, by doing this, your graciousness will cause him to be ashamed of his wickedness toward you, and the Lord will reward you.

Application: Jesus tells us that we must love our enemies and bless those who persecute us (Matthew 5:44). Paul quotes this Proverb in Romans 12:20 when he is teaching that Christians should not avenge themselves but leave vengeance to God. Paul later goes on to say that we should not be overcome by evil but overcome evil by doing good. This teaching differs greatly from the old covenant teaching of an eye for an eye. The principle of this old covenant teaching is that the punishment should fit the crime. However, in the new covenant, we are supposed to give grace to those who do not deserve it. In the same way that Jesus Christ gave His life for undeserving sinners who deserve Hell, we are to demonstrate grace to our enemies. We can demonstrate our grace and love towards our enemies in practical ways like showing undeserved kindness to them. This is quite a contrast to how the world of non-Christians handle their enemies. The world says that you should smite your enemy, that revenge is acceptable, and that pay back is inevitable. How much different should we be than the world? When everyone around us is always avenging themselves, how much brighter will the love of Christ shine when we love our enemies. When we show unmerited kindness and love towards people who want to crush us, we demonstrate something the world is not capable of. By helping, showing kindness, and demonstrating our love in practical ways, our enemies feel guilt for their behavior and often times will be won over by our love. As burning coals melt wax, so is the heart of the enemy melted.

Day 42 – Your Meditation

So therefore, any one of you who does not renounce all that he has cannot be my disciple.

Luke 14:33

Read: Luke 14:25-33

Emphasis:_____
_____
_____

Rewrite:_____
_____
_____

Application:_____
_____
_____
_____
_____
_____
_____
_____
_____
_____
_____
_____
_____
_____
_____
_____
_____
_____
_____
_____
_____

Day 43

And Abraham lifted up his eyes and looked, and behold, behind him was a ram, caught in a thicket by his horns. And Abraham went and took the ram and offered it up as a burnt offering instead of his son.

Genesis 22:13

Emphasis: And Abraham went and took the ram and **offered it** up as a burnt offering **instead of his son**

Rewrite: Abraham offered the ram as a burnt offering instead of his son.

Application: In this well known event, Abraham, in obedience to God, was told to kill his son for a burnt offering, but God stopped him and provided a substitute. This is a picture of the gospel. Abraham looks and sees a sacrifice whose head was surrounded by thorns. This sacrifice would bring salvation to Isaac by becoming Isaac's substitute. The sacrifice would be killed and burned instead of Isaac. This is the principle of substitutionary atonement. At this moment a substitution was made which God provided; a son was saved, a promise was kept, salvation was accomplished, the gospel was foreshadowed, another attribute of God was revealed, the covenant with Abraham was confirmed, and God's name was again glorified. God demonstrates this attribute of provision in salvation. In the same way that Abraham trusted in God to provide a way out of a desperate situation, those who trust in God will receive provision from God in the way of His only Son as a substitute and sacrifice for their sin. God will always see to it that all things will be provided for His people, for their good and His glory. God will see to it because He has ordained all that comes to pass. When His people are in distress, He will never leave them or forsake them. At the most critical time, the Lord will intervene. God, in the greatest difficulties, when all human assistance is vain, will make a suitable provision for the deliverance of those who trust Him. God shows us through trials that we can depend on Him and that we can trust in Him no matter how impossible the circumstances seem to be. God will provide a way out for His glory and our good. Unlike the world, we must trust in Him in every trial and every aspect of our lives. He will never disappoint.

Day 44

Your boasting is not good. Do you not know that a little leaven leavens the whole lump?

1 Corinthians 5:6

Emphasis: Your boasting is not good. Do you not know that a **little** leaven **leavens the whole lump**?

Rewrite: You should not boast about this. Do you not know that a little sin spreads like yeast through a whole batch of dough.

Application: Here Paul was dealing with sin within the church that was left unchecked and not dealt with. We know from verse one that the heinous sin was reported to Paul, and that the sin in the church was well known throughout the region. It was bringing dishonor to the name of Christ because it was being tolerated. Sin must be dealt with in our own lives immediately. We must do all we can to mortify our sin. Every eye is on the Christian to find hypocrisy so that unbelievers can point at him and dishonor Christ. When we let sin fester in us and do not deal with it violently, it begins to pollute our whole being in the same way that a little leaven leavens the whole lump of dough. We become a hypocrite. Spurgeon once said that if any man's life at home is unworthy, he should go several miles away before he stands up to preach. When he stands up, he should say nothing. Sin destroys everything. In a garden there are always weeds. Sometimes the weeds are hidden under you plants and flowers and can't be seen. The garden looks beautiful from the surface. The problem is that the weeds are small and hidden at first. If you don't search for them under the plants and flowers and uproot and kill them, then they will continue to grow, take over the garden and kill all of your plants and flowers. The little weed of sin that we hide from the world to look good on the surface will eventually sprout up, come into the open and destroy us. Sin always finds us out. All sin is eventually destroyed. We must search out every weed of sin in our lives and destroy it before it destroys us.

Day 45

For while we were still weak, at the right time Christ died for the ungodly.

Romans 5:6

Emphasis: For while we were still **weak**, at the right time **Christ died** for the **ungodly**.

Rewrite: While we were unable to do anything, at the perfect time Christ died for the wicked.

Application: We have often heard one of the world's ignorant maxims that says, "God helps those who help themselves." This couldn't be farther from the truth. As we see in this verse, God helps those who can't help themselves. This is the whole point of the gospel. No one in the world will be saved until they stop trying to save themselves. We couldn't be right with God nor atone for our sins, so God sent a Savior and Substitute who made us right with God and atoned for our sin. When we were weak, without strength, in deplorable condition, dead in our sin, and unable to awake ourselves from the dead, Christ died for us. What a truth and what a great and merciful God! It is so comforting to know we were not saved by first helping ourselves. We were not only helpless, we were ungodly, guilty, and wicked. We were condemned people with no hope in ourselves or the world. I tried to help myself by keeping God's commandments and being good, but all I found was sin and misery. The law condemned me. The law showed me that I could not help myself and that I needed someone who could help me. The grace of God then pointed to a Savior who was without sin and who desired to pay the penalty of sin for the ungodly, helpless dead man. A few verses later, Romans 5:8 says, "but God shows his love for us in that while we were still sinners, Christ died for us." Christ sought us and bought us with His blood. We know this at the point of our conversion, but it seems that at times we forget it. After we have been saved for a while, we start trying to help ourselves instead of going to the throne of grace to be helped. We try to do things in our own strength without God. We depend on our knowledge or experience instead of God. Without God we can do nothing. We must meditate on this fact and humbly go to Him.

Day 46

Open your mouth wide, and I will fill it.

Psalm 81:10b

Emphasis: **Open** your mouth wide, and **I will fill it.**

Rewrite: Open your mouth wide, and I will satisfy you.

Application: In Bristol, England in the year 1836, George Mueller opened his first orphan house and took in 26 children. This verse, *Open your mouth wide, and I will fill it*, rang in the head of Mueller over and over. Mueller never directly or indirectly asked anyone for money; he simply prayed and trusted God to meet all of his needs. He stepped out on faith, opened his mouth wide, and God filled it. When he died at the age of 93, God had provided over one million dollars (today's currency) for the care of the over 10,000 orphans he ministered to in his lifetime. At the age of 70, he stepped out in faith again and became a missionary for the next 17 years. He preached in over 42 countries. George Mueller opened his mouth wide, and God filled it. We learn from verse 16 that filling a mouth means to satisfy; it says, "But I would feed you with the finest wheat. I would satisfy you with wild honey from the rock." God promises to satisfy Israel if they will flee from idolatry. Verses 9 and 10 say, "You must never have a foreign god; you must not bow down before a false god. For it was I, the LORD your God, who rescued you from the land of Egypt. Open your mouth wide, and I will fill it with good things." What God is saying to Israel is to stop longing to be satisfied from foreign gods. He reminds them that He is the all-powerful, true God who rescued them from Egypt. He calls them to simply open wide their mouth, trust in Him implicitly, and He will satisfy their desires. Mueller took this literally and proved this verse to be true. We must think about our own lives and how often we look to the things of the world to satisfy us. If we only had a better job, a nicer house, a better boss, the perfect wife, more money or better behaved children, then we would be satisfied. We spend all our time seeking satisfaction from these things but never obtain anything lasting. As we seek to be filled by these "false gods," God calls us to flee from idolatry and put our trust in Him to satisfy us. We must open our mouths wide to God, and He will fill it.

Day 47

One who sows discord among brothers

Proverbs 6:19

Emphasis: One who sows **discord** among **brothers**

Rewrite: God hates the person who divides brothers.

Application: In verse 16 we get the context. There are six things that the Lord hates, seven that are an abomination to Him. One who sows discord among brothers is one of the things God hates. God hates all sin, and He hates all sin completely. He does hate certain sins, however, in a special way. The seven sins listed here hurt our neighbor. Whenever there is a controversy among Christians, it seems that our sinful nature comes out, and we find ourselves gossiping, slandering, taking sides, or playing on both sides of the fence. The sinful part of us enjoys discord among brothers because it makes us look good and others look bad. This is what we did when we were without Christ and in the world, but this is a grievous sin against God, and He hates it. It is pride. It is sin for which you will be disciplined. We must keep a unity of spirit with all brothers and sisters in Christ, and we must be peacemakers, not sowers of discord. We must walk in all humility and gentleness, with patience, bearing with one another in love, eager to maintain the unity of the Spirit in the bond of peace (Ephesians 4:2–3). God is glorified in peace, not discord. The world is always in discord, but Christians should live in and model peace. How good and pleasant it is when brothers dwell in unity (Psalm 133:1)! Paul exhorts Timothy to: "Have nothing to do with foolish, ignorant controversies; you know that they breed quarrels. And the Lord's servant must not be quarrelsome but kind to everyone, able to teach, patiently enduring evil, correcting his opponents with gentleness. God may perhaps grant them repentance leading to a knowledge of the truth, and they may come to their senses and escape from the snare of the devil, after being captured by him to do his will" (2 Timothy 2:23–26). There will always be contention and quarrels among brothers as long as we live on this earth and have our sinful nature. The question is how we will respond to contention. Will we be the peacemaker, or will we sow discord and cause division? We must be like Christ in all things.

Day 48

So you also, when you have done all that you were commanded, say, 'We are unworthy servants; we have only done what was our duty.'

Luke 17:10

Emphasis: So you also, when you have **done all** that you were **commanded**, say, 'We are **unworthy servants**; we have only done what was **our duty**.'

Rewrite: So you also, when you have done all that was required of you, say, "We are unworthy servants who have done only our duty."

Application: God does not owe us anything. We owe God more than we could ever pay. We owe God everything. Sometimes when we simply obey God and do what is required of us, we expect a reward from God. We think God is more pleased with us because we did what He asked, but in reality, God will never be more pleased with us than He is now because our status before God is not based on our works but on Christ's righteousness. We receive the righteousness of Christ, and God is pleased with us based on His righteousness, not our own. When we do good or model Christ-like behavior, we are just doing our duty. We are unworthy servants that have been ransomed by the blood of Christ. We were slaves to sin, and now we are slaves to a loving Master. It is said that when we do good, it goes unnoticed, but when we do something bad, everyone notices, and we are disciplined. We can spend years doing the right thing in the eyes of the world, but when we make a mistake it could destroy years of good behavior. This, for the most part, is true. When we do good, it is only our duty. We are supposed to do good. We are not supposed to do what is evil, and when we do, we pay the consequences for our actions. Whatever we do in service for God is only our duty. The most greatly used servants of God have always considered themselves unworthy servants. Charles Spurgeon said not to make too much of preachers; for when they have done all, they are unprofitable servants. He is saying that the results from our obedience are determined by God alone. We are just unworthy servants who are obeying God and doing our duty. The results are God's. This thought should humble us.

Day 49 – Your Meditation

I have not departed from the commandment of his lips;
I have treasured the words of his mouth more than my portion of food.

Job 23:12

Read: Read Job chapter 23

Emphasis:_____

_____

_____

Rewrite:_____

_____

_____

Application:_____

_____

_____

_____

_____

_____

_____

_____

_____

_____

_____

_____

_____

_____

_____

_____

_____

_____

_____

Day 50

The mouth of the righteous is a fountain of life

Proverbs 10:11

Emphasis: The **mouth** of the righteous is a **fountain of life**

Rewrite: The words of a righteous person pour out life.

Application: The Puritan John Flavel preached a series of 42 sermons titled, *The Fountain of Life: A Display of Christ in His Essential and Mediatorial Glories.* The sermon series was focused on the excellencies of Christ as the fountain of life. Flavel was spot on in showing that Jesus Christ is the fountain of all life. Christ is the heir, creator, and sustainer of all things (Hebrews 1:2-3). Everything exists by Christ and for Christ (Hebrews 2:10), and all glory, honor, and power is due to Him. Christ is the fountain of life from which all life springs. This proverb also says that the mouth of the righteous is a fountain of life. We also see in Proverbs that the teaching of the wise (Proverbs 13:14), the fear of the Lord (Proverbs 14:27), and good sense (Proverbs 16:22) are a fountain of life. When we are being sanctified, or conformed to Christ, we begin to have the mind of Christ. We begin to think like Christ. Our mouth is the outlet of our minds. The things that we want to let out of the mind come out of our mouth. Our mouths are a fountain of life with the potential to speak the pure and clean words of God. Our speech can be deceitful or truthful; it can be rash or hurtful, and it can bring healing. Our speech can be wise or perverse, and it can speak joy or bitterness. James describes it as "a restless evil, full of deadly poison. With it we bless our Lord and Father, and with it we curse people who are made in the likeness of God. From the same mouth come blessing and cursing" (James 3:8–10a). We have so much potential to do good or to do evil with our mouth, but the mouth of the righteous should be a fountain of life, not death. If we now belong to Christ, the fountain of life, we are fed from His pure and living words. As we conform to the image of Christ, our words should as well. The more we know the words of Christ, the more we will speak them. We must process all the thoughts in our minds and then speak the words of Christ. The Christian's speech should be a fountain of life to all those around him, saved or lost.

Day 51

to an inheritance that is imperishable, undefiled, and unfading, kept in heaven for you

1 Peter 1:4

Emphasis: to an **inheritance** that is imperishable, undefiled, and unfading, kept in **Heaven** for you

Rewrite: We have an inheritance in Heaven that is eternal, perfect, and will never pass away.

Application: The Puritans meditated on the subject of Heaven more than any other subject. They longed for their inheritance and most of all to be with Jesus. Peter uses the word *inheritance* because an inheritance that is kept in Heaven means that we have not received it yet. This is important because the majority of Christians live a hard life of struggles. This earth is not our reward. We are strangers and exiles on this earth (Hebrews 11:13). We suffer on this earth and long for a time when there will be no more sin, pain, and tears. Before God saved us, this world was all we had. We were strangers and aliens to Heaven. Now we are no longer strangers and aliens, but we are fellow citizens with the saints and members of the household of God in Heaven (Ephesians 2:19). Meditating on the glories of Heaven and our inheritance that awaits us will get us through hard times of trials. Sadly, the only time most Christians think about Heaven is when they are unhappy on earth. When they are living it up in the world and enjoying the pleasures of the world, Heaven is a distant thought. It should not be so. Because of Jesus Christ we are now children of God through adoption, "and if children, then heirs—heirs of God and fellow heirs with Christ" (Romans 8:17). Heaven is imperishable; it can never pass away or be destroyed. Heaven is undefiled which means there is no more sin and misery. The fallen world, our sinful flesh, and the devil make life on earth miserable when we are controlled by them, but Heaven is pure, holy, and perfect. Heaven is unfading. It never gets old, wears out, or loses its beauty. It's like a beautiful fall day when the leaves are in the glory of all their colors. On earth they fade, die, and fall, but in Heaven everything is always in its prime. This inheritance is waiting for the children of God.

Day 52

The king's heart is a stream of water in the hand of the Lord;
he turns it wherever he will.

Proverbs 21:1

Emphasis: The **king's heart** is a stream of water in the hand of the Lord; **He turns it wherever He will.**

Rewrite: The king's heart is like a river directed by God; He turns it where He wants.

Application: There is nothing out of the control of God. He is sovereign. He works all things together for our good and His glory (Romans 8:28). He kills and brings to life; The LORD makes poor and makes rich; He brings low, and He exalts (1 Samuel 2:6-7). He rules over all nations. None is able to withstand Him (2 Chronicles 20:6). He preserves all that exists (Nehemiah 9:6). In His hand is the life of every living thing (Job 12:10). He makes nations great, and He destroys them (Job 12:23). What He desires, He does, and no one can change Him (Job 23:13). He reigns and rules the nations (Psalm 22:28). His counsel stands forever, and the plans of His heart to all generations (Psalm 33:11). He is the great King, He subdues people, He chose our heritage and reigns over the nations (Psalm 47:2-8). The world and its fullness belongs to Him (Psalm 50:10-12). His kingdom rules over all (Psalm 103:19). He made everything, He needs nothing, He sustains everything, and determines where each man will dwell and how long He will live (Acts 17:24-26). God changes the minds of men and turns them where He wants. The sovereignty of God is a tremendous comfort to us because there is not a situation in our lives or in the world that is outside of the control of God. God has all in His control. Whenever disaster seems inevitable or a situation impossible, God can change it in one second. We fight with politics and campaigns, but when God changes the hearts of those involved, everything changes instantly. When we truly understand this, we will spend much more time in prayer to our sovereign God who turns hearts.

Day 53

"Shall we receive good from God, and shall we not receive evil?"

Job 2:10

Emphasis: Shall we **receive good from God**, and shall we not **receive evil**?

Rewrite: Shall we rejoice and accept good things from God but be angry when evil comes upon us from God?

Application: Sometimes Christians think that only good comes from God and we are to only expect good things from God. However, God uses the hard trials in our lives to conform us to Christ far more than He uses the times of ease and prosperity. When it is always sunny, the land turns into a desert and nothing grows. For something to grow and be healthy you need both sun and storms. Paul tells us in Romans 5:3-4, "Not only that, but we rejoice in our sufferings, knowing that suffering produces endurance, and endurance produces character, and character produces hope." Hard times, trials, and suffering teaches us to endure through these times, which begins to build Christ-like character, which gives us more hope. Jesus suffered more than anyone on this earth, and in 1 Peter 2:21 we see that we must follow the path of Christ in suffering. He says, "For to this you have been called, because Christ also suffered for you, leaving you an example, so that you might follow in his steps." We must not let times of trouble and trials quench our zeal for God nor make us forget about all of His mercies. Throughout the hardest trials we must remember the greatest mercies of God, above all, Jesus Christ, who gave us everything we did not deserve and took every evil thing upon Himself that He did not deserve for our sake. Again Paul encourages us in Romans 8:18, "For I consider that the sufferings of this present time are not worth comparing with the glory that is to be revealed to us" We must accept the evil in our lives as an opportunity to glorify God and become more like Jesus.

Day 54

For lack of wood the fire goes out, and where there is no whisperer, quarreling ceases.

Proverbs 26:20

Emphasis: For lack of wood the fire goes out, and where there is **no whisperer, quarreling ceases.**

Rewrite: The fire dies out without fuel, and a quarrel will stop when gossip stops.

Application: Gossip is the fuel of all quarrels, and it is always damaging to the person who spreads the gossip, the hearer of the gossip, and the people involved in the gossip. Ultimately gossip is damaging to the church and the glorious name of Jesus Christ. Is it not strange that we are so tempted to justify gossip? In verse 22 of this Proverb it says, "The words of a whisperer are like delicious morsels; they go down into the inner parts of the body." To hear something slanderous about another person exalts our pride because we think we are better than the person being gossiped about. In our sinful nature, we especially love to hear gossip about someone who is actually a better person than us. Pride, jealousy, and gossip are all connected. Scripture not only forbids us to gossip but also to not listen to gossip. We often justify gossip by saying the gossip is true. Whether it is true or false, it is still gossip, and it is a sin. Gossip always has bad intentions and is destructive. To determine whether something is gossip we must ask ourselves what is the purpose of the information, are we part of the solution, and would we talk about this person the same way if he was standing next to us. If we talk about a person in a way that we would not talk face to face with that person, we are gossiping. When we kill gossip, the quarrel will stop. When someone comes to us with gossip, he must be rebuked. We are to speak evil of no man (Titus 3:2). Ephesians 4:29 gives us a model to follow; it says, "Let no corrupting talk come out of your mouths, but only such as is good for building up, as fits the occasion, that it may give grace to those who hear." Gossip is something everyone struggles with; that means we must spend more time and effort mortifying this sin.

Day 55

a living dog is better than a dead lion.

Ecclesiastes 9:4

Emphasis: a **living dog** is better than a **dead lion.**

Rewrite: There is more hope for a living wretch than a dead prince.

Application: While there is life, there is hope. There is no hope to change for the dead. There is no second chance after death. In the place where the tree falls, there it will lie (Ecclesiastes 11:3). There is more hope for the most wicked person that is alive on this earth today than for the most popular and powerful dead man. As long as there is breath in the body, there is hope for the soul. We often look at our wayward child and all the mistakes he makes and wonder if he can ever change. We look at our best friend who is more hardened to the gospel than he ever was and wonder if there is hope. Another year has gone by in the life of our parents, and they are still not saved; so we begin to wonder if there is hope after all. We should take comfort because there is hope for a living dog. God can change everything in the blink of an eye. In fact, changing people while they are still alive is the chief business of God concerning His people. "For the Son of Man came to seek and to save the lost" (Luke 19:10). While there is life, there is opportunity to prepare for death. God calls all men to repent and believe, and He gives countless chances for man to do this while he lives. Angels did not have a second chance. "...God did not spare angels when they sinned, but cast them into Hell and committed them to chains of gloomy darkness to be kept until the judgment" (2 Peter 2:4). A dead lion is as useless as a dead man. The dead have no more opportunity. "For the living know that they will die, but the dead know nothing, and they have no more reward, for the memory of them is forgotten" (Ecclesiastes 9:5). Napoleon came to understand this. He said, "I marvel that where the ambitious dreams of myself and of Alexander and of Caesar should have vanished into thin air, a Judaean peasant Jesus should be able to stretch his hands across the centuries, and control the destinies of men and nations." All of Napoleon's power and fame died with him. He is a dead lion, but all who breathe have hope.

Day 56 – Your Meditation

Whoever conceals his transgressions will not prosper, but he who confesses and forsakes them will obtain mercy.

Proverbs 28:13

Read: Read Proverbs 28:13

Emphasis:_____

_____

_____

Rewrite:_____

_____

_____

Application:_____

_____
_____
_____
_____
_____
_____
_____
_____
_____
_____
_____
_____
_____
_____
_____
_____
_____
_____
_____
_____
_____
_____
_____

Day 57

Vanity of vanities, says the Preacher, vanity of vanities! All is vanity.

Ecclesiastes 1:2

Emphasis: Vanity of vanities, says the Preacher, **vanity** of vanities! All is vanity.

Rewrite: Everything is beyond meaningless. There is no meaning in anything.

Application: Sometimes this life on earth seems so vain, only consisting of endless cycles of repetition, the same endless struggles, the same endless longings that never give lasting satisfaction. This is the fallen world in which we live. The rancher gets up early, works until dark. It is time to calve again; he works the long night shifts just to get the cows out and pregnant again. Branding, preparing the fields, hoping for a break in the weather to plant. Hoping for rain and sun so the grass will grow. Time to fix fences and then the first cutting of hay. Hoping for no rain. He works hard in the heat all day and now longs for cooler weather. Time for the second cutting. All the hay is put up, fall is here, and it is time to move the cows down from the high country, winter moves in, feeding in blizzards, breaking ice, fixing fence, time to calve again, and the cycle repeats year after year, day after day. The endless repetition of natural seasons and cycles never produces anything new and so appears to be without purpose. At times we may ask what we are living for. The world continually searches for lasting purpose in life through gaining wisdom, in pleasure, in career, and in wealth. The preacher in the book of Ecclesiastes sought purpose in all of these things as well, but his search ended in death and judgment. He found that sin leads to death, sin brings judgment, and everyone must die. At the end of his search, he concluded that the whole duty of man was to fear God and keep His commandments (Ecclesiastes 12:13). The whole duty of man includes true faith in the living God as well as works, which are the inevitable result of genuine faith. Even though we go through trials and toils on earth, we are comforted in that all our trials and toil are not vanity at all but are working together for good, for those who love God and are called according to His purpose.

Day 58

I am a rose of Sharon, a lily of the valleys.

Song of Solomon 2:1

Emphasis: **I am a rose** of Sharon, a **lily** of the valleys.

Rewrite: I'm a like one of the beautiful roses or lilies that grows on the plain of Sharon.

Application: The Song of Solomon has the broadest range of interpretation than any other book in the Bible. The early Jews interpreted the book as an allegory of God's love for Israel, and then until the nineteenth century it was interpreted as an allegory of Christ's love for His bride, or the church. John Owen, the greatest English theologian of the seventeenth century, said, "This whole book called 'The Song of Solomon' describes the communion between the Lord Christ and his saints."[10] Since the nineteenth century it has been interpreted as a love poem about the love of a man and woman. Even if it is about the love between a man and woman, what does marriage represent but the model of Christ and the church. All of Scripture has a purpose, and every book points to the beloved Christ and the redemption of God's people through Him. When we read this verse what must we think of besides the beauty of the beloved Christ? John Owen comments on this verse, "The Lord Christ is compared to all that is most glorious and beautiful in his creation. He is, in the heavens, as glorious as the sun, and as the bright morning star. Among the beasts he is like the lion, the lion of the tribe of Judah. Among the flowers, Christ is as beautiful and as glorious as the rose and the lily."[11] To gaze upon the beauty and perfection of our Lord Jesus will satisfy us deep in our souls. When we meditate on the beauty of Christ, we long for the day when we will be in His presence. David did as well in Psalm 27 when he said, "One thing have I asked of the LORD, that will I seek after: that I may dwell in the house of the LORD all the days of my life, to gaze upon the beauty of the LORD."

---

10 John Owen, *Communion with God.* (Carlisle, Pa: The Banner of Truth Trust , 1991), 45.

11 Owen, *Communion with God,* 39.

Day 59

And being in agony he prayed more earnestly; and his sweat became like great drops of blood falling down to the ground.

Luke 22:44

Emphasis: And being in **agony** He **prayed more earnestly**; and His sweat became like great drops of blood falling down to the ground.

Rewrite: Because of His great agony, He prayed more fervently; and His sweat become like blood falling to the ground.

Application: Our attempts to understand the suffering and agony of Jesus in the Garden that night will always fail. This mystery is so profound that our finite minds can't understand it fully. Why was Jesus in agony? Was He scared of the pain of crucifixion that awaited Him? There have been countless Christians slaughtered for the sake of the gospel over the past centuries. Countless have suffered for truth and have gone to their painful, torturous deaths with great joy imitating our Savior Jesus Christ. Was Jesus sweating blood because He feared the physical pain of death? No. If this were the case then these countless martyrs were much more courageous than Jesus. They would have made Jesus look like a coward if He was afraid of the pain. Jesus was not scared of the pain of death; He faced something far different. The day before Jesus would be crucified, after eating the Passover meal in the upper room, He separated Himself from His disciples to be with His Father in prayer. He prays in verse 42, "Father, if you are willing, remove this cup from me." What is the cup Jesus wants removed? Psalm 75:8 tells us about this cup, "For in the hand of the LORD there is a cup with foaming wine, well mixed, and he pours out from it, and all the wicked of the earth shall drain it down to the dregs." The cup is the judgment and wrath God being poured out on the wicked, and all the wicked of the earth must drink it down to the dregs. This cup that Jesus is praying about is the full cup of God's wrath, the dregs included, about to be poured out on Him as He substitutes Himself in our place. Jesus was in agony because He was about to swallow the full fury of the wrath of God and be ground to powder. He did this all because of His redeeming love for us. The love of God should compel us to die to sin and to love God.

Day 60

What to me is the multitude of your sacrifices? says the LORD; I have had enough of burnt offerings of rams and the fat of well-fed beasts; I do not delight in the blood of bulls, or of lambs, or of goats.

Isaiah 1:11

Emphasis: What to me is the multitude of **your sacrifices**? says the LORD; I have **had enough** of burnt offerings of rams and the fat of well-fed beasts; **I do not delight** in the blood of bulls, or of lambs, or of goats.

Rewrite: Do I care about all your sacrifices? I have had enough of your vain offerings which cannot please me.

Application: God is rebuking Judah through the prophet Isaiah because of their hypocrisy. The people of Judah were diligent in keeping the required sacrifices, but they turned it into legalism; their hearts were far from God. God set up the ordinances to turn their hearts to true worship, but they turned the worship of God into a legalistic system to earn God's favor. Isaiah says later (Isaiah 29:13) that the people of Judah worshiped God in vain, honoring Him with their lips, but their hearts were far from Him. Jesus quotes this verse in Matthew 15:7-9 and applies it to the Pharisees and scribes of His day. The Pharisees continued the hypocritical traditions of the people of Judah in turning the worship of God into a legalistic system of vain worship. They turned the worship of God into a show designed to attract attention to themselves. Even their prayers were in vain as they stood on street corners and in the synagogues making long, elaborate prayers so that they could receive praise from men (Matthew 6:5). When they fasted they disfigured their faces to make sure everyone knew they were fasting because they sought the praise of men over the praise of God. They desired to please men with their religious piety, but their hard hearts were an eternity from God. God is still the same way today. He is not impressed with our religious activities, the amount of time we pray or read the Bible, or all the things we do for the church if these things conceal our sinful hearts. God hates hypocrisy. If we outwardly do what God requires but with a sinful heart, grudgingly, or to impress men, our service is in vain and we are proved to be hypocrites. God desires a clean heart, not sacrifice.

Day 61

Behold, God is my salvation;
I will trust, and will not be afraid;

Isaiah 12:2

Emphasis: Behold, **God** is **my salvation**; I will **trust**, and will not be **afraid**.

Rewrite: Stop and think, God is the one who can save me; I will trust in Him and will not be scared.

Application: Isaiah writes this praise song about a future time of deliverance for the people of God after the fall of Assyria when God's kingdom would arise, led by the Righteous Branch, the Messiah (Isaiah 11:1-12:6). This would be a time of rejoicing and thanks to God, who is mighty to save. The readers are called to behold. To behold is to stop, focus your attention, and gaze upon something. The fact that God is our salvation should cause us to sit in wonder. The author of creation is also the author of salvation. No one could have rescued us from Hell but God Himself. He who saved us from the penalty of sin, through Christ's substitutionary atonement, is the same One who will continue to uphold, sustain, and deliver us. Just as we trust Him for our eternal salvation, we must trust Him for our temporal difficulties on this earth. We must not be afraid of anything since the mighty God who saved us, will keep us (John 10:28-30). In order to encourage the believer to put his confidence and trust in God, the author of Hebrews quotes Joshua 1:5, which says, "I will never leave you nor forsake you." He applies this promise to New Testament believers and then goes on to say that because God will never leave you nor forsake you, you can confidently say, "The Lord is my helper; I will not fear; what can man do to me?" (Hebrews 13:6) Now that we are Christians, we no longer have a spirit of fear, for God gave us a spirit not of fear but of power and love and self-control (2 Timothy 1:7). When we grasp that God is our salvation, we will find it easy to trust in the founder and perfecter of our faith (Hebrews 12:2). The center verse in the Bible gives us the same message, it says, "It is better to take refuge in the LORD than to trust in man" (Psalm 118:8).

Day 62

But he would withdraw to desolate places and pray.

Luke 5:16

Emphasis: But He would **withdraw** to desolate places and **pray.**

Rewrite: He would get alone in order to pray and commune with God.

Application: How often do we need to get away to a desolate place just to pray, meditate, examine ourselves, and commune with God, but we fail to do it? Getting alone with God to have real communion with Him in prayer is essential every day, but we often neglect this great privilege. We actually can come before the living, sovereign God of the universe. The creator and sustainer of all things enables us to come before Him through Christ, and He calls us to come to Him. We have the privilege of offering up our desires to God. How can we neglect such a great joy and privilege? Logically we should not, but because we still have a sinful nature and our flesh is weak, we struggle with prayer and communion with God, perhaps more than any other discipline. David Brainerd, missionary to the Native Americans in the eighteenth century, followed the example of Jesus; he said, "When you cease from labour, fill up your time in reading, meditation, and prayer: and while your hands are labouring, let your heart be employed, as much as possible, in divine thoughts." Jesus spent a great amount of time in prayer. Prayer was constant in the life of Jesus. He was continually in communion with the Father. When we compare our prayer life with the prayer life of Jesus, we are probably ashamed. Getting alone with God in prayer, meditation, and communion is as essential to our spiritual life as air is for our physical lives. We must set some time apart every day to be with God and never break the appointment. It would be very good to lock ourselves away somewhere on a regular basis to cry out to God. We should set aside one day a month to spend all day alone with God, whether it is a day spent praying in the woods or a locked room at the church. We must not put this off any longer. We must be alone with God today.

Day 63 – Your Meditation

But to all who did receive him, who believed in his name, he gave the right to become children of God, who were born, not of blood nor of the will of the flesh nor of the will of man, but of God.

John 1:12-13

Read: John 1:1-13

Emphasis:_____
_____
_____

Rewrite:_____
_____
_____

Application:_____
_____
_____
_____
_____
_____
_____
_____
_____
_____
_____
_____
_____
_____
_____
_____
_____
_____
_____

Day 64

For the LORD is a God of justice

Isaiah 30:18b

Emphasis: For the LORD is a God of **justice**.

Rewrite: God is just.

Application: In this passage from the book of Isaiah we learn about a very important attribute of God: His justice. The whole reason for Christ's death on the cross hinges on the justice of God. God is just so He must uphold His law and punish all lawbreakers. A man was caught killing five people, and he stood before the judge. All the evidence was against him. The judge found him guilty, and the man declared himself to be guilty as well. Before the judge sent him to prison, however, the murderer pleaded with the judge. He said, "Judge, please let me go free because I am a good person. I have done much more good than bad in my life. I have helped elderly women, and I have given money to the poor." The judge responded, "It doesn't matter if you have done more good than bad; you broke the law so the penalty must be paid." God is the same as this just judge. If God really is love then He must punish lawbreakers. God must uphold the law or He would be unjust. Because God is loving, He must be just as well. God must punish sinners because He is loving. The good news for the Christian is that God, out of His love, sent His Son to die in our place. There was no other way to satisfy justice, forgive sin, and reconcile people to God. Jesus had to be made sin in our place to satisfy the divine justice of God. We should be so grateful that God is just for the same justice that demands all lawbreakers to pay the penalty for sin and be destroyed, now demands salvation for believers; Jesus satisfied the divine justice of God when He paid, in full, the penalty for our sin. It would be very unjust and wicked for God to send a believer to Hell because the sinner's fine has already been paid. Because of Christ paying for the penalty of our sin and then giving us His perfect righteousness, we are accounted as righteous, and therefore, according to divine justice, God must grant us salvation and bring us to Heaven. God is always fair, just, and loving, which we rejoice in. As we think of God's justice, we should rejoice in Christ's satisfaction of it.

Day 65

for my people have committed two evils: they have forsaken me, the
fountain of living waters, and hewed out cisterns for themselves, broken
cisterns that can hold no water.

Jeremiah 2:13

Emphasis: for my people have committed two evils: they have
forsaken me, **the fountain of living waters**, and hewed out cisterns for
themselves, broken cisterns that can hold no water.

Rewrite: My people have done two evil things: they have abandoned
me, the fountain of living waters, for their own broken cisterns.

Application: In verse 12, all of Heaven is called to be shocked and
appalled at the stupidity of Israel. The people had abandoned and
forsaken God, the fountain of living waters, for their own worthless idols
that could do no good for them. They traded the living God for
worthlessness, and they became worthless (Jeremiah 2:5). A cistern was
dug into the ground and sealed so that it could collect rain and runoff or
the people would fill the cisterns up with buckets of water. The cistern
was the worst place to get water because it was stagnant and dirty. When
the cistern broke, the water leaked out and all that was left was mud,
sediment, and sludge. The best water was clean, pure, running water.
This is the picture we see here. Israel traded God, who was Himself the
fountain of pure living water; they traded life itself, for a stagnant
cesspool of disease and death. They traded the best water for the worst
water. Living water is found in Christ. Jesus said He was the source of
living water. In John 4:13-14, He said, "Everyone who drinks of this
water will be thirsty again, but whoever drinks of the water that I will
give him will never be thirsty again. The water that I will give him will
become in him a spring of water welling up to eternal life." Jesus calls
all who thirst to come to Him, and out of His heart will flow rivers of
living water (John 7:38). Trusting in anything besides Christ will leave
us without help in difficult times. It is amazing that we have access to
the source of life, but we often go to the world for help in times of
trouble. We must not be like Israel and trade the living God for the
world.

Day 66

and the Lord has laid on him the iniquity of us all.

Isaiah 53:6b

Emphasis: and the LORD has **laid on Him** the **iniquity of us** all.

Rewrite: The Father put all of our sins on Jesus.

Application: In no other place in the Old Testament are the prophesies and descriptions of Christ's atoning work on the cross made so clear as in Isaiah 53. The Father placed all of our sins on His sinless Son and then crushed Him (v. 10) in our place to pay the penalty for our sins. Jesus bore our griefs and carried our sorrows (v. 4). He was pierced for our rebellion and crushed for our sins (v. 5). He took our beating, and by His wounds we are healed (v. 6). He was delivered up for our trespasses and raised for our justification (Romans 4:25). The Father made the perfect, sinless Son to be sin so that we may become the righteousness of God (2 Corinthians 5:21). "He himself bore our sins in his body on the tree, that we might die to sin and live to righteousness" (1 Peter 2:24a). John Piper explains that, "The way Christ defeated death and disease was by taking them on himself and carrying them with him to the grave. The horrible blows to the back of Jesus bought a world without disease."[12] Isaiah made these prophesies about 700 years before Christ came into this world. We now have the benefit of looking back at these prophesies and seeing so clearly how Jesus fulfilled them. The people of Isaiah's day looked forward to the time of the Messiah, but we can look back to the prediction of the Messiah, His coming, and the fulfillment of the predictions. We don't have to hope for a future Messiah that is supposed to come; we can look to Christ who did come and die for us. It was planned before the foundation of the world. The Father put our sin on Christ; He suffered, paid our fine, died, was buried, and three days later He rose, conquering death and bringing redemption to His people. We are the most privileged generation that has ever existed, and we bear a great responsibility for what we do with this knowledge. What a great sin it is to reject Jesus.

---

12 John Piper, *Fifty Reasons Why Jesus Came to Die*. (Wheaton, IL: Crossway, 2006), 55.

Day 67

No one ever spoke like this man!

John 7:46

Emphasis: No one ever **spoke** like **this man!**

Rewrite: No one ever spoke the way that Jesus spoke.

Application: No one had ever spoken like Jesus. Ever since He was a child the people were amazed by Him. They were amazed at His ability to heal (Matthew12:23, Mark 2:12). They were amazed at His silence to defend Himself (Matthew 27:14). They were amazed at His power (Mark 1:27, Luke 4:36). They were amazed at His teaching (Mark 10:24). They were amazed at His understanding and answers (Luke 2:47). They were amazed at His resurrection (Luke 24:22). They were amazed at His death (Matthew 27:54), and they were amazed by the words that He spoke. In Luke 4:22 we read that after Jesus finished speaking, all the people spoke well of Him and marveled at the gracious words that were coming from His mouth. The temple guards were even amazed with the words of Jesus because they sought to arrest Him for His teachings, but they could not even find any thing against Him. They had to return to the Pharisees and give an account of why they didn't arrest Jesus. They responded that, "No one ever spoke like this man!" Philip Schaff, Christian Historian of the 19th century, spoke of the uniqueness of Jesus when he said, "Jesus of Nazareth, without money and arms, conquered more millions than Alexander the Great, Caesar, Mohammed, and Napoleon; without science and learning, he shed more light on things human and divine than all philosophers and scholars combined; without the eloquence of school, he spoke such words of life as were never spoken before or since, and produced effects which lie beyond the reach of orator or poet; without writing a single line, he set more pens in motion, and furnished themes for more sermons, orations, discussions, learned volumes, works of art, and songs of praise than the whole army of great men of ancient and modern times." No one has ever spoken like Jesus nor done anything like Jesus. This is our amazing Savior, and we should be left in awe of Him each time we meditate on His person and work. Jesus Christ is the most amazing subject upon which we can think.

Day 68

I am the first and I am the last; besides me there is no god.

Isaiah 44:6b

Emphasis: I am the first and I am the last; besides me there is no god.

Rewrite: I am the first and the last; no other god exists outside of me.

Application: In this passage in Isaiah, Israel can rejoice in the God whom they trust because He is the first and the last, and there is no other god besides Him. All the gods of the nations are idols. The Lord God is Israel's King and Redeemer, and He is the commander of the armies of Heaven. He is the first and the last. God the Father calls Himself by this title again in Isaiah 48:12, but the amazing thing is that Jesus Christ boasts of this same title in Revelation 1:17 when He says, "Don't be afraid! I am the First and the Last. I am the living one. I died, but look—I am alive forever and ever! And I hold the keys of death and the grave." Again in Revelation 2:8 and 22:13, Jesus claims this title for Himself. The amazing thing is that this proves the divinity of Jesus. If Jesus is not God, then this is a huge contradiction in the Scripture. There would be two people claiming they are the first and the last and that there is no other besides them. The only way this can be reconciled is if Jesus is God. Both the Father, Son, and Holy Spirit are the first and the last, and there is no other besides them; all three are one God. There is no god besides the one true God. In the book of Isaiah this truth is emphasized repeatedly. We read it in Isaiah 43:10-11, 45:5-6, 14, 18, 21, 22, and 46:9. There is only one God and Savior. Acts 4:12 says, "And there is salvation in no one else, for there is no other name under heaven given among men by which we must be saved." There is only one God who has always existed, and there is only one hope, one substitute, one savior, one redeemer, one salvation, and one sovereign Lord over all. Christians have great hope in this fact because we know we serve the one, true and living God. We have it right. All the nations are following after false gods, but our God made the Heavens. We can rejoice today because the true and living God found us. He sought us and bought us with His redeeming blood. We are adopted sons of the only God who exists. What a day of rejoicing this should be!

Day 69

Do not work for the food that perishes, but for the food that endures to eternal life...

John 6:27a

Emphasis: Do not work for the **food that perishes**, but for the **food that endures to eternal life**

Rewrite: Do not work for the food that keeps you alive temporarily, but for the food that will give you eternal life.

Application: Jesus just finished feeding five thousand people then withdrew to a mountain by Himself. The crowd was searching for Jesus and found Him on the other side of the sea. They were not seeking Jesus because they saw His miracles and were entertained nor because they sought eternal life. They were seeking Him because they liked the free meal they got and wanted to fill their stomachs (v. 26). Jesus tells them to stop laboring for the food that perishes and start laboring for the food that endures to eternal life.   The food that perishes is all the things of this world like wealth, pleasure, prestige, status, and material possessions. These are the things that never bring lasting satisfaction. These are the temporal things that leave you hungry after you have had them for a short time. Jesus said this same thing in a different way in the book of Matthew. He said, "Do not lay up for yourselves treasures on earth, where moth and rust destroy and where thieves break in and steal, but lay up for yourselves treasures in heaven, where neither moth nor rust destroys and where thieves do not break in and steal. For where your treasure is, there your heart will be also" (Matthew 6:19–21). We are to labor for the things that will benefit our soul for all eternity. In verse 28, the people ask Jesus the next logical question, "What must we do, to be doing the works of God?" Jesus answered them, "This is the work of God, that you believe in him whom he has sent." The food that doesn't perish is believing and trusting in the person and work of Jesus. Believing in Christ benefits us not only on this earth as we receive the benefits of salvation and knowing God, but also for all eternity. We must daily trust in Christ for all things and labor to be conformed to His image.

Day 70 – Your Meditation

Whoever believes in the Son has eternal life; whoever does not obey the Son shall not see life, but the wrath of God remains on him.

John 3:36

Read: John chapter 3

Emphasis:_____

_____

_____

Rewrite:_____

_____

_____

Application:_____

_____

_____

_____

_____

_____

_____

_____

_____

_____

_____

_____

_____

_____

_____

_____

_____

_____

_____

Day 71

And the LORD said to me: "The prophets are prophesying lies in my name. I did not send them, nor did I command them or speak to them. They are prophesying to you a lying vision, worthless divination, and the deceit of their own minds.

Jeremiah 14:14

Emphasis: The **prophets** are prophesying **lies in my name**. I did not send them, nor did I command them or speak to them.

Rewrite: The prophets are deceiving people to think that I send them and told them to speak these things, but they are not from me. They lie and deceive.

Application: Often we hear people and church leaders saying things that are not biblical, but they claim they are speaking on the behalf of God. Sadly, we have seen this throughout history; we still see it today, and we will see it in the future. Jesus tells us that false prophets will lead many people astray (Matthew 24:11). Peter spoke of false prophets in the time of the Old Testament, and he warned that they would sneak into the church in his day as well. He says in 2 Peter 2:1-2, "But false prophets also arose among the people, just as there will be false teachers among you, who will secretly bring in destructive heresies, even denying the Master who bought them, bringing upon themselves swift destruction. And many will follow their sensuality, and because of them the way of truth will be blasphemed." There always has been and always will be false teachers until Christ returns and sets all things right. The goal of false teachers is to twist and blaspheme the truth. People still listen to false prophets today. Why do people listen to false teachers? They listen because the false prophets always tell the people what they want to hear instead of what they need to hear. Timothy warns that because people hate sound teaching they will accumulate for themselves teachers to suit their own passions (2 Timothy 4:3). In 1 John 4:1, John teaches us how to respond to false teaching. He says to not believe every spirit, but test the spirits to see whether they are from God, because many false prophets have gone out into the world. We must be like the Bereans and test everything we hear by the Bible and then stand on the truth.

Day 72

There is therefore now no condemnation for those who are in Christ Jesus.

Romans 8:1

Emphasis: There is therefore now **no condemnation** for those who are **in Christ Jesus.**

Rewrite: Now we are not condemned because we are in Christ Jesus.

Application: When Adam sinned, he brought condemnation to all men (Romans 5:18). The world is now condemned (1 Corinthians 11:32). When we were separated from Christ, we had no hope, and we were without God in the world (Ephesians 2:12). We condemned ourselves because of our sin and because we rejected the only hope of pardon. Whoever does not believe is condemned already, because he has not believed in the name of the only Son of God (John 3:18). Now that we are in Christ, everything has changed. We are no longer condemned but pardoned. "Who is to condemn? Christ Jesus is the one who died—more than that, who was raised—who is at the right hand of God, who indeed is interceding for us" (Romans 8:34). We are not condemned because Christ was condemned for us. When Christ bore our sins and paid our penalty, we were freed from our condemnation in the same way that a man on death row is free to walk out of prison as a free man when his fine has been paid. John Piper says, "There is no double jeopardy in God's court. We will not be condemned twice for the same offenses. Christ has died once for our sins. We will not be condemned for them. Condemnation is gone not because there isn't any, but because it has already happened."[13] When the Father made Jesus, who knew no sin, to be sin in our place, we became the righteousness of God (2 Corinthians 5:21). This one act of righteousness led to justification and life for all men (Romans 5:18). Because Christ took our condemnation upon Himself and paid our fine, we are free and can never be condemned again. What a great relief to know that He who began a good work in us will bring it to completion at the day of Jesus Christ (Philippians 1:6).

---

13 Piper, *Fifty Reasons Why Jesus Came to Die*, 43.

Day 73

And to this people you shall say: 'Thus says the LORD: Behold, I set before you the way of life and the way of death'.

Jeremiah 21:8

Emphasis: And to this people you shall say: 'Thus says the LORD: Behold, **I set before you** the way of **life** and the way of **death.'**

Rewrite: The Lord says: choose life or death.

Application: Jeremiah had already warned that Jerusalem would be destroyed, but the leaders ignored, denied, mocked and persecuted him for his prophesies. Now he tells them that God is giving them a choice. They can stay in the city and be killed by sword, famine and pestilence or surrender to the Chaldeans and live (v. 9). It is amazing that even in the middle of the greatest disaster, when there seems to be no hope, God gives us a way out. In His mercy, He always gives a way out of the messes in which we find ourselves. As Christians we have a promise that God is faithful, and He will not let us be tempted beyond our ability, but with the temptation He will also provide the way of escape, that we may be able to endure it (1 Corinthians 10:13). In every situation, no matter how impossible it may seem, God has ordained it and has provided a way out. In fact, we have the opportunity to glorify God in every trial in our lives. We must always ask how we can glorify God in our particular trial. Ultimately, God in His mercy, gives us a way of escape from sin, death, and destruction through Jesus Christ. God says: trust Christ and live or reject Him and die. Christ is our only option, our only hope, and our only way to escape the penalty of our sins. Jesus says, "I am the resurrection and the life. Whoever believes in me, though he die, yet shall he live, and everyone who lives and believes in me shall never die" (John 11:25–26). The Bible is full of dichotomies. There is no sitting on the fence. You are either following Christ or running away from Him; you are loving God or hating Him; you are trusting Christ or rejecting Him; you hate what is evil or you love it; you accept sin or kill it. In every situation we have the choice to do good or evil, to trust or deny, to stand or run, or to love or hate. We always have an option, a way of escape and a choice.

Day 74

I am the light of the world. Whoever follows me will not walk in darkness, but will have the light of life.

John 8:12

Emphasis: I am the **light** of the world. Whoever **follows me** will not walk in **darkness**, but will have the light of life.

Rewrite: I am the light of the world. If you follow me you will not have to walk in the darkness because I am the light of life.

Application: This is the second of seven of the "I am" statements in the book of John. Jesus says that He is the bread of life (6:35), the door of the sheep (10:7), the good shepherd (10:11), the resurrection and the life (11:25), the way, and the truth, and the life (14:6), and the true vine (15:1). Jesus makes the ultimate "I am" statement in John 8:58 when He says, "Truly, truly, I say to you, before Abraham was, I am." In this bold statement, Jesus declares Himself to be Yahweh, God Himself, which is why the people immediately tried to stone Him (v. 59). Jesus is everything, and all things were created through Him and for Him (Colossians 1:16). Here we see that Jesus is the light of the world or the light of life. The pillar of fire in the Old Testament was a guiding light for the people of Israel. It was their guidance and protection and symbolized the presence of God. Jesus is the pillar of fire that guides, protects, and brings us into the presence of the Father. Jesus, the author and sustainer of life, gives light and life to His people. The light of Christ removes the darkness in our lives. Jesus said, "I have come into the world as light, so that whoever believes in me may not remain in darkness" (John 12:46). The light of Christ exposes our sins and shows us who we really are and reveals our need for a Savior. Christ is our light, and we must put away the deeds of darkness and follow the light of Christ. We must live our lives in a way that shows Christ is our guide, our protector, our joy, our blessing, and our life in contrast to darkness and death. We must always ask ourselves how the light of Christ shining into our lives has changed us and be sure that it is continually changing and conforming us. We must reflect the light of Christ in the world and live as a light to those in darkness.

Day 75

*"For thus says the L*ORD*: David shall never lack a man to sit on the throne of the house of Israel, and the Levitical priests shall never lack a man in my presence to offer burnt offerings, to burn grain offerings, and to make sacrifices forever."*

Jeremiah 33:17-18

Emphasis: "For thus says the LORD: David shall never **lack a man** to sit on the **throne** of the house of Israel, and the Levitical **priests** shall never **lack a man** in **my presence** to offer burnt offerings, to burn grain offerings, and to make sacrifices **forever**."

Rewrite: The Lord says: David will have a descendant as king forever, and there will always be a priest to intercede forever.

Application: This is a very important prophecy about Christ. In verses 14 through 16 God promises to fulfill the covenant with Israel and Judah by raising up a righteous Branch from the line of David that will reign and execute justice and righteousness. Jesus, in His first coming, set up His reign, and in His second coming, He will execute justice and righteousness. In these verses (17-18), we see God's promise to have a descendant from the line of David as king forever and a priest continually interceding for the people of God. Jesus fulfills the roles of the eternal priest and king from the line of David. Luke 1:32-33 explains the eternal kingship of Jesus; it says, "The Lord God will give to him the throne of his father David, and he will reign over the house of Jacob forever, and of his kingdom there will be no end." As long as Jesus sits on the right hand of the throne of God and rules the world, the covenant with David is fulfilled. There is no more need for a human king to reign nor an earthly priest to intercede for the people of God anymore. An earthly priest must offer sacrifices daily, which can never take away sins, but when Christ offered for all time a single sacrifice for sins, He sat down at the right hand of God. For by a single offering He has perfected for all time those who are being sanctified (Hebrews 10:11-14). How glorious to have as our Redeemer an eternal priest who has reconciled us to God and continually intercedes for us and an eternal king who rules and defends us and conquers all His and our enemies! Our Lord reigns!

Day 76

Jesus answered, "It was not that this man sinned, or his parents, but that the works of God might be displayed in him.

John 9:3

Emphasis: Jesus answered, "It was not that this man **sinned**, or his parents, but that the **works of God** might be **displayed in him.**"

Rewrite: It was not because of the sin of him or his parents, but it is so the power and glory of God could be shown in him.

Application: In this account we see Jesus heal a man who was blind from birth. The common Jewish belief of the day was that any physical illness, disease, disability or any suffering was caused by the sin of that particular person or, as in this case, the sin of the parents. Clearly the child did not sin in the womb which caused him to be born blind so the people added that the disability could be from the sin of the parents. Even though sin does have consequences and will result in suffering, not all suffering is a result of specific sins of the person. Paul was given a thorn in the flesh to keep him from becoming conceited (2 Corinthians 12:7). Again in Galatians 4:13 we read that God ordained a bodily ailment in Paul so that he would preach the gospel to the Galatians. We all know the story of Job and his suffering, which was not the result of a particular sin of his. Of course, Jesus is the greatest example. He had no sin and suffered more than any person who has lived. In this situation, Jesus clearly says that the man's blindness from birth was not because of his sin or his parents sin but so that the mighty works of God could be displayed in him. This man was born blind so that Jesus could heal him, which showed His power and sovereignty as well as proved that Jesus was who he said he was. Many times we find ourselves in the middle of some tragedy, not because of our sin, but so that God can display His power to us and so we will be conformed to the image of Christ. We were once like this blind man. We were born spiritually blind until Jesus sought us and made us see spiritually for the first time. We were once blind and now we see. Jesus continues to make us see clearly through trials. When we suffer, we have an opportunity to see Him display His power, which in turn, glorifies Him.

Day 77 – Your Meditation

For whoever is ashamed of me and of my words in this adulterous and sinful generation, of him will the Son of Man also be ashamed when he comes in the glory of his Father with the holy angels.

Mark 8:38

Read: Mark 8:31-38

Emphasis:_____

_____

_____

Rewrite:_____

_____

_____

Application:_____

_____

_____

_____

_____

_____

_____

_____

_____

_____

_____

_____

_____

_____

_____

_____

_____

_____

_____

Day 78

I give them eternal life, and they will never perish, and no one will snatch them out of my hand.

John 10:28

Emphasis: I give them **eternal life**, and they will **never perish**, and no one will **snatch them** out of **my hand**.

Rewrite: I give them eternal life, they will never lose it, and no one can take them away from me.

Application: It grieves the Holy Spirit when we doubt the promises of God. Jesus clearly promises here that when He gives us eternal life, we can't lose it. We never earned our salvation, and we can't lose it. The whole understanding of the gospel rests here. If we had any ability to gain or keep our salvation, then Jesus did not need to come and die for us. Jesus lived a life that we were unable to live, and He died a death that we deserved. Jesus helped us when we could not help ourselves. To say that a Christian can lose the salvation that he was given by God is to deny and reject the promise of God that we read here. To do this is sin. Charles Spurgeon comments on this verse, "How can we ever grieve him by doubting his upholding grace? Christian! It is contrary to every promise of God's precious Word that thou shouldst ever be forgotten or left to perish." [14] We must understand that our salvation was bought by the precious blood of Christ and that we are kept by the same. We will never perish, and no one, including ourselves, can remove us from the Father's hand. Jesus says in the next verse (v. 29), "My Father, who has given them to me, is greater than all, and no one is able to snatch them out of the Father's hand." We must repent of and fight against the sin of unbelief and hold fast to the promise of God that when he gives the gift of eternal life, we cannot perish or lose the gift. John 6:40 proclaims the will of God concerning how to receive this gift; it says, "For this is the will of my Father, that everyone who looks on the Son and believes in him should have eternal life, and I will raise him up on the last day." Believe in Him and you will never perish!

---

14 C.H. Spurgeon, *Morning and evening: Daily readings* (Complete and unabridged; New modern edition.). (Peabody, MA: Hendrickson Publishers, 2006), June 26.

Day 79

Arise, cry out in the night, at the beginning of the night watches! Pour out your heart like water before the presence of the Lord!

Lamentations 2:19a

Emphasis: Arise, **cry out** in the night, at the beginning of the night watches! **Pour out** your heart like water before the **presence of the Lord!**

Rewrite: Wake up, cry out to the Lord! Pour out your heart to the Lord in His presence.

Application: At the end of the book of Jeremiah, we read about the destruction of Jerusalem by the Chaldean army and the exile of Judah, which was predicted by the prophets for many years. In this book of Lamentations we read Jeremiah's expressions of sorrow over the destruction that he had prophesied for forty years. Here we read that Jerusalem must cry out to God and turn to Him once again. The second half of the verse says that they should do this for the sake of their children. Even if God will not show mercy to the exiled generation, they should turn to God for the sake of the next generation. The Lord has done what He purposed (v. 17), and now everything has been destroyed. The only option left is to pray in desperation. Pouring out your heart like water before the presence of the Lord means to go to the Lord in fervent and desperate prayer. Many times we fall into the same trap as Judah. We ignore many red-flags and warnings until everything catches up to us and we find ourselves in a bad situation. It is only then do we pour out our hearts in the presence of God. He gives us warnings, but we ignore Him. We ignore Him when times are easy and then we find ourselves in desperation. We read of this same desperate plea in Psalm 119:147, which says, "I rise before dawn and cry for help; I hope in your words." We must be crying out to God in fervent, zealous prayer when times are easy or difficult. When we find ourselves in times of ease and our devotion to God and our prayer life begin to become complacent, we must fight harder and not let our guard down. If we really understood that we have an opportunity, in Christ, to go into the presence of God in prayer, we would pray much more and do far less.

Day 80

Love one another with brotherly affection. Outdo one another in showing honor.

Romans 12:10

Emphasis: **Love one another** with brotherly affection. **Outdo one another** in showing honor.

Rewrite: Be genuine in our love for one another. Purposely honor one another.

Application: Paul exhorts the Romans to "love one another with brotherly affection." When we first believed, we were brought into the Body of Christ and became, not only an adopted son of God, but part of the family of God. Even though we may have nothing in common with a member of the Church, if we have Christ, we have in common the only thing that matters. We are called to love our fellow Christians unconditionally, not based on their personalities. When we love one another and function the way the Body of Christ was designed to function, we bear the fruit of truly being born of God (1 John 4:7). We see many exhortations concerning how we should treat one another in the New Testament. We are called to "live in harmony with one another" (Romans 12:16); to "welcome one another" (Romans 15:7); to "comfort one another, agree with one another, live in peace" (2 Corinthians 13:11); to "serve one another" (Galatians 5:13); to "bear one another's burdens" (Galatians 6:2); to "be kind to one another, tenderhearted, forgiving one another" (Ephesians 4:32); to "encourage one another and build one another up" (1 Thessalonians 5:11); to "exhort one another every day" (Hebrews 3:13); to confess our sins to one another and pray for one another (James 5:16); to "show hospitality to one another without grumbling" (1 Peter 4:9). We are exhorted to not provoke or envy one another (Galatians 5:26). We must not lie to one another (Colossians 3:9) or speak evil against one another (James 4:11). Finally, we must not grumble against one another (James 5:9). These are amazing exhortations that we fail to fulfill perfectly. We must read through and meditate on these exhortations to see where we are failing and then purposely put these into practice each day.

Day 81

The steadfast love of the Lord never ceases; his mercies never come to an end; they are new every morning; great is your faithfulness.

Lamentations 3:22-23

Emphasis: The **steadfast love** of the LORD never **ceases**; **His mercies** never come to an end; they are **new every morning**; great is **your faithfulness.**

Rewrite: The loving-kindness of the Lord will never end; His mercies will never fail; they are renewed each morning; great is your faithfulness.

Application: After bearing much suffering and affliction (vv. 1-21), the speaker remembers that there is hope (v. 21). His hope is the steadfast love of the Lord which never ceases. He trusts in the mercy of God, which will never end. He depends on the mercy of God to awaken him each morning, and each day he is amazed by the great faithfulness of God that is sustaining him. If we had no hope then we would live a life of constant misery and despair. Even in the worst situations, if we have hope, we can look forward to renewal which encourages us to press on through hard times. When we understand the unending mercies of God, we will understand that no matter how bad a situation is, it could be much worse. God continually restrains evil and controls all situations. It is by the mercy of God that we wake up each morning, and it is His great faithfulness, not ours, that strengthens us to get through each day. As long as we breathe, there is hope and there always will be. No person nor situation is hopeless when we have a sovereign, unchangeable, merciful God who governs the world. The Christian can endure any trial and even death itself when he relies on the mercy of God that is new every morning. We can say with Paul in 2 Corinthians 4:8-9, "We are afflicted in every way, but not crushed; perplexed, but not driven to despair; persecuted, but not forsaken; struck down, but not destroyed." Every morning as we awake, we have the opportunity to see the mercy of God and to reflect the glory and the faithfulness of God. If we never went through trials, suffering, and affliction, we would never see the greatness of God's faithfulness and mercy. Today we can demonstrate God's mercy in the way we handle our daily problems.

Day 82

And I will give them one heart, and a new spirit I will put within them. I will remove the heart of stone from their flesh and give them a heart of flesh

Ezekiel 11:19

Emphasis: And I will give them **one heart**, and a **new spirit** I will put within them. I will **remove the heart of stone** from their flesh and give them a **heart of flesh**

Rewrite: I will unite them with one heart, and I will put a new spirit in them. I will remove their hard, stubborn heart and give them a tender and loving heart towards me.

Application: Ezekiel lived and prophesied among the exiles of Judah in Babylon. Ezekiel was speaking to a group of very broken and discouraged people who had seen their city and homes destroyed and now were slaves in a foreign land. Even though God punished Israel for their gross idolatry and breaking the covenant, God now brings hope to a captive people. God promises that He will give them one heart, and a new spirit He will put within them. He will remove their hearts of stone from their flesh and give them hearts of flesh. The promise is repeated in Ezekiel 36:26-37, but we also see God's motive for doing this in 36:22-23. It is not for the sake of the house of Israel that He is giving them this promise, but for the sake of His holy name. He will vindicate the holiness of His great name so that the nations will know He is the Lord. We see that God is giving this promise for His own name sake and so that His name will be glorified among the nations. We also see the promise to restore Ezekiel's people to their land and to bring the new covenant blessings. Jeremiah also predicted the new covenant (Jeremiah 31:31-34). It is amazing that this new covenant was instituted by Christ, the mediator (Hebrews 9:15), and all those in Christ receive this promise of a new heart and spirit. If anyone is in Christ, he is a new creation (2 Corinthians 5:17). This promise to Israel is fully realized in the church (Hebrews 8:7–13; 9:15). The only way that you can love God is because He gives the Christian a new heart and spirit through the regenerating work of the Spirit, and for that we should weep with joy.

Day 83

By this all people will know that you are my disciples, if you have love for one another.

John 13:35

Emphasis: By this **all people** will **know** that you are **my disciples**, if you have **love for one another.**

Rewrite: Your love for one another will show that you belong to me.

Application: The world can never truly understand the meaning of unconditional love. Christ modeled unconditional love for us when He suffered the wrath of God in our place. Christ, being perfect, was condemned and suffered in our place and in return gave us His righteousness. We are sinners who deserve the wrath of God, but through Christ we get the reward of Christ's righteous life. This is true love. Unbelievers will recognize us by our love more than by our doctrine. True doctrine should result in loving unconditionally. If you have sound doctrine but are unloving, then your testimony is in vain. The deeds we do in love show to the world that we are followers of Christ. Christians have been demonstrating this for a long time. The reason there are hospitals and orphanages is because of Christianity. The reason that widow burning has ceased in India and indigenous tribes in the Amazon have stopped burying children alive with their deceased fathers is because of Christianity. Jesus gives the new command, "just as I have loved you, you also are to love one another." The old command was to love your neighbor and hate your enemy (Matthew 5:43), but Jesus calls Christians to not only love their fellow Christians but to love their enemies (Matthew 5:44-45). The command to love your enemy is not found in any other religion. We must model the love and compassion of our heavenly Father, and this will prove we are children of God. John warns us that whoever hates his brother is not of the light, or is not a true believer (1 John 2:9-11). Again in 1 John 3:10 we see that love is an evidence of being a Christian. Today we must strive to love everyone as Christ loves us. The more we love the unlovable people in our lives, the more we show the glory of Christ. The more unlovable a person is, the greater opportunity we have to reflect the glory of Christ by loving them.

Day 84 – Your Meditation

See to it that no one takes you captive by philosophy and empty deceit, according to human tradition, according to the elemental spirits of the world, and not according to Christ.

Colossians 2:8

Read: Colossians chapter 2

Emphasis:_____

_____

_____

Rewrite:_____

_____

_____

Application:_____

_____

_____

_____

_____

_____

_____

_____

_____

_____

_____

_____

_____

_____

_____

_____

_____

_____

_____

_____

_____

Day 85

And they shall know that I am the LORD

Ezekiel 5:13

Emphasis: And they shall **know** that **I am the LORD.**

Rewrite: And they will know that I alone am Lord.

Application: This phrase is used in the book of Ezekiel seventy-two times in reference to judgment on idolatry and against the abominations of Israel and the nations. God will vindicate His name and judge and punish all those who sin against Him so that they will know He is the Lord. God was performing His judgments and bringing nations to their knees so they would know that there is only one God, the God of all nations, and He is holy. The enemies of God would know that God is the Lord of all. Jesus, when He walked the earth, performed countless miracles to validate His ministry and to prove He was God. His works proved who He said He was, the Christ, the Son of the living God (Matthew 16:16, Mark 14:58), the great "I am" Himself (John 8:58). When Jesus returns, He will return in all His glory for judgment, and then all will know that He is the Lord (Revelation 11:18). When the enemies of Christ realize Jesus is Lord, they will hide themselves in the caves and call the mountains and rocks to fall on them and hide them from the Lamb because of their fear of wrath and judgment (Revelation 6:15-17). God will reveal that He is Lord to all nations and people by His judgment, but He has also already revealed Himself to His people through the person and work of Jesus Christ. The Christian is blessed in knowing that God is Lord through the awakening work of the Holy Spirit in regeneration. Now the Christian is no longer under the wrath of God but the loving discipline of God. God providentially ordains things in our lives, and He allows us to face consequences for our actions to sanctify us and to remind us that He is Lord. The question for us to meditate on today is, "What is God doing in our lives now to show us that He is Lord?" All our trials, discipline, suffering, and blessings are to show us that He is Lord. How are we responding to the way that God is revealing Himself? Are we hiding with fear or rejoicing that He is Lord?

Day 86

And if I go and prepare a place for you, I will come again and will take you to myself, that where I am you may be also.

John 14:3

Emphasis: And if I go and prepare **a place for you**, I will **come** again and will **take you to myself**, that **where I am you may be** also.

Rewrite: If I leave this earth to prepare a place for you then I will return to get you and take you with me.

Application: After Jesus bore our sins and paid the penalty on the cross, He died, was buried, and three days later He rose from the dead.   He remained on earth for 40 days and then ascended to Heaven and now sits at the right hand of the Father until all His enemies are put under His feet.   The men of Galilee saw Jesus ascend into Heaven, and an angel told them that Jesus would one day return in the same way that they saw Him leave (Acts 1:11).   In Revelation 22:20, Jesus promises to return soon. The Christian longs for the day of either Christ's return or his own death because both scenarios will put him in the arms of Christ for all eternity. In verse one in this chapter, Jesus calls the disciples to trust and believe in Him for their true happiness in eternity. We are to be happy because Jesus has prepared a place for His people, and He confirms this promise in verse two when He says, "If it were not so, would I have told you that I go to prepare a place for you?" The disciples were troubled and needed assurance so Christ said this to bring them, and us, comfort. This promise will help the Christian get through any trial. On our worst day, we do well to remember Christ died for us, and we have a home in Heaven. Every Christian longs to be where Christ is because he longs to be with Christ. The greatest joy anyone will ever have is when he is in the presence of Jesus Christ. All of our greatest joys on this earth will seem almost like misery compared to the joy of being with Jesus in Heaven. Although there will be a lot to do and see in the new Heavens and the new earth, the greatest joy and satisfaction we will receive will be basking in the glory of Christ. During any hard trial, we must take time to be alone with God and meditate on this promise that we will one day be with Christ and have eternal, unspeakable joy.

Day 87

I myself will be the shepherd of my sheep, and I myself will make them lie down, declares the Lord GOD.

Ezekiel 34:15

Emphasis: **I myself** will be the **shepherd** of **my sheep**, and I myself will make them lie down, declares the Lord GOD.

Rewrite: I will be the true shepherd of my people, and I will care for them, declares the Lord God.

Application: In this passage, the worthless shepherds of Israel have failed to shepherd the flock of Israel of which they were in charge. They were using their position for dishonest gain and feeding themselves instead of the people (vv. 1-10). The shepherds of the church are the pastors, and with this position comes great responsibility. Just as in the days of Ezekiel, the pastors today must feed the sheep the pure Word of God and be an example in all things. The under-shepherds of the church, who are charged with the care of souls, will have a great deal to answer for on the day of judgment because they will be judged with greater strictness (James 3:1). Despite the failure of human shepherds we have hope because Jesus Christ is the true shepherd of the sheep and will never fail. The shepherds of Israel failed and became corrupt, so God said He would be their shepherd. The Lord is our shepherd (Psalm 23). Jesus Christ is the true good shepherd, and unlike the worthless shepherds of Israel, He laid down His life for the sheep (John 10:11,15). God tells Israel that He will not only be their shepherd but that He will make them lie down (Psalm 23:2). Matthew Henry explains that making them lie down means, "a comfortable rest after they had tired themselves with their wanderings, and a constant continuing residence; they shall not be driven out again from these green pastures, as they have been, nor shall they be disturbed, but shall lie down in a sweet repose and there shall be none to make them afraid."[15] Despite the failure of corrupt leaders in the church, our good Shepherd will always lead us to the truth of His Word, care for us, and give us rest from our failures.

---

15 Henry, *Matthew Henry's commentary on the whole Bible*, Ezekiel 34:7–16.

Day 88

Abide in me, and I in you. As the branch cannot bear fruit by itself, unless it abides in the vine, neither can you, unless you abide in me.

John 15:4

Emphasis: **Abide** in me, and I in you. As the branch cannot **bear fruit** by itself, unless it abides in the vine, neither can you, **unless you abide in me.**

Rewrite: Remain with me, and I will remain with you. A branch cannot give fruit unless it is part of the life-giving vine. You cannot give fruit either unless you are part of me.

Application: To abide in something is to remain with it, be part of it, or continue with it. Remaining with Jesus will bear fruit. Evidence that you are in Christ is that you will bear fruit. Remaining with Christ and bearing fruit is a non negotiable for a Christian. If you don't remain and bear fruit, it proves you are not a Christian. Verse six says any person who does not remain with Christ will be burned, and verse eight says bearing much fruit proves you are a Christian. Not everyone who outwardly follows Christ is really a Christian (John 6:66). In 1 John 2:19 we see again that not continuing or abiding is proof that you are not part of Christ. It says, "They went out from us, but they were not of us; for if they had been of us, they would have continued with us. But they went out, that it might become plain that they all are not of us." It is impossible to produce fruit in your life without Christ (John 15:5). Fruit is answered prayer, joy and love (vv. 11-12), and we read in Galatians 5:22-24 that fruit is love, joy, peace, patience, kindness, goodness, faithfulness, gentleness, and self-control. In 2 Peter 1:5-8 we see that fruit is virtue, knowledge, self-control, steadfastness, godliness, brotherly affection, and love. The only way to develop this Christ-like character is to be in and abide in Christ. It is very clear that if you are not growing in these qualities then you are not in Christ. No fruit, no Christ. The carnal, fruitless Christian does not exist. For the Christian, serving, abiding in, and obeying God brings great joy (v. 11). We must continually examine ourselves and our fruit to see if we are in the faith (2 Corinthians 13:5). Our joy is a great evidence of our abiding. Do you have joy?

Day 89

And the name of the city from that time on shall be, The LORD Is There.

Ezekiel 48:35

Emphasis: And the name of the **city** from that time on shall be, **The LORD Is There.**

Rewrite: The name of the city will be, The Lord is There.

Application: No longer will the city be called Zion or Jerusalem or the land called Canaan; this new city that will be in the glorious land will be called *Jehovah Shammah or* The Lord Is There. The Lord will be there forever. This is in contrast to the beginning of Ezekiel's vision where God departed from the temple, the city, and the presence of the people. In this new city, the Lord will be there, and all those who trust in Him will be in His presence as well. We get a greater glimpse of this city in Revelation 21. This new city will be where God dwells permanently. Verses 3 and 4 say, "The dwelling place of God is with man. He will dwell with them, and they will be his people, and God himself will be with them as their God. He will wipe away every tear from their eyes, and death shall be no more, neither shall there be mourning, nor crying, nor pain anymore, for the former things have passed away." The presence of the Lord brings times of refreshing for the Christian (Acts 3:20), which is in contrast to the wicked who will suffer the punishment of eternal destruction, away from the presence of the Lord and from the glory of His might (2 Thessalonians 1:9–10). This vision is about the presence of God dwelling among the people of God. Revelation 22:3-4 says, "No longer will there be anything accursed, but the throne of God and of the Lamb will be in it, and his servants will worship him. They will see his face, and his name will be on their foreheads." Even now, being in the presence of God brings joy and refreshing for the Christian. This is something we must be reminded of because the pressures and stresses of life on this cursed earth often distract us from God and communion with Him. The importance of prayer, daily Bible reading, and worshiping with a biblical church cannot be stressed enough. These are the means that God has given to keep us focused and in communion with Him.

Day 90

If this be so, our God whom we serve is able to deliver us from the burning fiery furnace, and he will deliver us out of your hand, O king. But if not, be it known to you, O king, that we will not serve your gods or worship the golden image that you have set up.

Daniel 3:17-18

Emphasis: If this be so, **our God** whom we serve is **able** to deliver us from the burning fiery furnace, and He will deliver us out of your hand, O king. **But if not**, be it known to you, O king, that **we will not serve your gods** or worship the golden image that you have set up.

Rewrite: Oh King, if you throw us in the furnace, our God whom we serve can deliver us, but if He doesn't, we will never serve or worship you or your gods.

Application: Three men stood before the most powerful man in the world and were questioned about where their loyalties fell. They had the opportunity to explain away their behavior and comply with his wishes. They could have compromised by justifying idol worship this one time. They could have said that, by law, they must obey the king. They could have accepted the new culture and bowed down or justified it by saying they were not hurting anyone. What they did instead was bold, faithful, and courageous. They first refused to answer the king or excuse their behavior because it was such a clear issue to them (v. 16). They then said they were loyal to the true God only; they spoke of His sovereign power, and finally they surrendered to the will of God. They chose to be faithful to God until death itself, which is a shadow of Christ's willingness to die in our place. God did choose to deliver them (Daniel 3:19-30) to show His power and sovereignty. At times, we find ourselves in a providential situation where we must take a stand for our faith in God. God ordains these situations for countless reasons, but one reason is to give us an opportunity to trust in Him instead of men. We must always obey God rather than men (Acts 5:29). When we suffer for righteousness, in the same way as with Shadrach, Meshach, and Abednego, Christ is with us in the fires of persecution. God uses the fiery furnace of affliction to refine our faith and to purify us.

Day 91 – Your Meditation

He who dwells in the shelter of the Most High will abide in the shadow of the Almighty.

Psalm 91:1

Read: Psalm 91

Emphasis:_____
_____
_____

Rewrite:_____
_____
_____

Application:_____
_____
_____
_____
_____
_____
_____
_____
_____
_____
_____
_____
_____
_____
_____
_____
_____
_____
_____
_____

Day 92

For we do not present our pleas before you because of our righteousness, but because of your great mercy.

Daniel 9:18

Emphasis: For we do not present our **pleas** before you because of our **righteousness**, but because of your **great mercy.**

Rewrite: We are pleading before you, not because we deserve anything from you, but because you are a merciful God.

Application: As Daniel pleads with God in prayer for mercy with fasting and repentance (v. 3), he reveals his humility and dependence on God. He doesn't have an attitude of entitlement, nor does he think that his righteousness deserves an answer to his prayer. He pleads with God because he knows that God is a God of mercy. The only basis for Daniel's plea was the mercy and grace of God. Daniel knew that both he and Israel were unworthy of the favor of God, so he pleads for God's unmerited favor. He pleaded for deliverance based on God's name sake. We saw David (1 Chronicles 21:13) and Job (Job 9:15) plead for mercy, and throughout the Psalms, the prayers are filled with cries for mercy. We must be like the tax collector and always cry out for the mercy of God in our prayers. "The tax collector, standing far off, would not even lift up his eyes to heaven, but beat his breast, saying, 'God, be merciful to me, a sinner!'" (Luke 18:13) We deserve God's punishment and wrath, but in His mercy He sent His Son to rescue us, which was the ultimate display of mercy. God sent Jesus, not because He had to save us or we deserved to be saved, but because He loves us and wants to show us mercy. We must hold on to this attribute of God and plead for it. The prophecies of Jeremiah about the 70 years of captivity encouraged Daniel to plead desperately with God for mercy. Daniel longed for the prophecy to be fulfilled so he could see God's people and city restored. Like Daniel, when we see our sins and what we deserve, it should cause us to pray more earnestly. Psalm 143:1 is a model of how we should pray: "Hear my prayer, O LORD; give ear to my pleas for mercy! In your faithfulness answer me, in your righteousness!" God is a God of mercy and will answer us because of His mercy.

Day 93

And this is eternal life, that they know you the only true God, and Jesus Christ whom you have sent.

John 17:3

Emphasis: And this is **eternal life**, that they **know you** the only true God, and Jesus Christ whom you have sent.

Rewrite: Eternal life is to know the only true God and Jesus Christ.

Application: In this high priestly prayer, Jesus intercedes for His people. Eternal life is knowing and belonging to God and to His Son Jesus Christ. 1 John 5:20 says that Jesus is the true God and eternal life. Jesus has the words of eternal life (John 6:68), is the way to eternal life, the truth of eternal life and eternal life itself (John 14:6). Eternal life is not only an unending existence; it is a life of immortality, knowing and learning about God. Knowing God is the greatest joy in eternity. When we understand this we can say with Paul, "Indeed, I count everything as loss because of the surpassing worth of knowing Christ Jesus my Lord" (Philippians 3:8). The lawyer asked Jesus what he must do to inherit eternal life. Jesus gave the answer in John 3:15-16 and countless other places in the gospels when He said whoever believes in Him will have eternal life. The way to gain eternal life is to know God through His Son Jesus. A few verses later, Jesus was getting ready to leave His disciples. They were troubled by this and that they would lose all the joy of having Jesus with them, but Jesus assures them of the opposite in His prayer. He says in verse 13, "But now I am coming to you, and these things I speak in the world, that they may have my joy fulfilled in themselves." Joy came to the disciples because Jesus brought them eternal life through His life, death, and resurrection. The fullness of joy is found in the presence of God. Psalm 16:11 says, "You make known to me the path of life; in your presence there is fullness of joy; at your right hand are pleasures forevermore." We long for the presence of God, and when we die, the fullness of this joy will be realized. After a life of serving God, He will say to us, "Well done, good and faithful servant. Enter into the joy of your master" (Matthew 25:21).

Day 94

And I will have mercy on No Mercy, and I will say to Not My People,
'You are my people'; and he shall say, 'You are my God.'

Hosea 2:23

Emphasis: And I will **have mercy** on **No Mercy**, and I will say to **Not My People**, '**You are my people**'; and he shall say, 'You are my God.'

Rewrite: I will have mercy on those who received no mercy, and I will say to those who are not my people, you are my people; and they will say, you are my God.

Application: We saw in chapter one that Hosea's wife bore three children that God used as symbols for prophecies. One daughter was named No Mercy, which symbolized God bringing judgment on Israel, no longer showing mercy to Israel because of their sin. Her other child was named Not My People, which symbolized God's rejection of Israel. In chapter two we see God's desire to show mercy on Israel again sometime in the future because of the covenant He made with them. The amazing thing is that we find this verse quoted by the apostle Paul in Romans 9:25. Hosea wrote to the 10 apostate northern tribes of Israel before the Assyrian exile, but Paul, here, in Romans 9:22-26 applies these two prophecies (Hosea 2:23 and 1:10) about the future salvation of Israel to the Gentiles. Through Jesus, both believing Jews and Gentiles, have become "sons of the living God." As He did with Israel in the past, so now God calls those who were not His people, His people, both Jews and Gentiles (v. 24). God promises to show mercy to people who have no mercy and that are not His people so that they can know mercy and become God's people. To be called God's people means to be the most ungodly harlot that deserves no mercy but only wrath, and become restored, embraced, and loved by a great merciful God. When we trust in Christ, we are shown great compassion and mercy from our loving God. Though we were enemies of God, we are now adopted sons of God, and we receive all the rights and privileges of the sons of God. We deserved Hell, but, through the love of Christ and His work on the cross we are given the gift of eternal life. We deserved no mercy but received more mercy and compassion than we can even grasp.

Day 95

O Death, where are your plagues? O Sheol, where is your sting?

Hosea 13:14

Emphasis: O **Death,** where are your **plagues**? O **Sheol**, where is your **sting**?

Rewrite: O Death, where is your terror? O Sheol, where is your sting?

Application: The book of Hosea ends with a call for Israel to return to God and seek His forgiveness (14:1–9). In this verse we see a glimpse of future hope. God gives hope in spite of the consequences of Israel's fall to Assyria and the destruction, exile, and suffering. God has plans for His people in spite of death and the grave. When we read this verse it should bring to mind the Messianic hope, which Christ fulfilled on the cross. Christ defeated death in His victory of it at His resurrection. The threat of death as a punishment for sin is no longer a threat for the Christian. Paul quotes this verse in 1 Corinthians 15:55 in context of the bodily resurrection, which is where we experience victory over death and eternal judgment through Christ. He then follows it up in the next few verses with the great victory over the sting of death; he says, "The sting of death is sin, and the power of sin is the law. But thanks be to God, who gives us the victory through our Lord Jesus Christ." For the people of God, death has no power over them. By cleansing people of sin, Jesus destroys the grip of death on them and releases them from their slavery to the fear of death. In Hebrews 2:14-15 it says, "through death he might destroy the one who has the power of death, that is, the devil, and deliver all those who through fear of death were subject to lifelong slavery." Every unbeliever has a fear of death, and when you have a fear of death then you are a slave to this fear. Josef Tson of the Romanian Missionary Society said that a man who has no fear of death is the most dangerous person in the world. Josef, who suffered much persecution, said in the face of danger that, "The world's weapon is killing but our weapon is dying." Why can a Christian martyr go to the stake while singing hymns? Because for the Christian, death has no power over him anymore. Christ has defeated death and removed its sting, which removes our fear. We must think today, "Are we afraid of death?" Why?

Day 96

But it displeased Jonah exceedingly, and he was angry.

Jonah 4:1

Emphasis: But it **displeased** Jonah exceedingly, and he was **angry.**

Rewrite: The outcome angered Jonah exceedingly.

Application: After the big fish released Jonah, he reluctantly went to Nineveh and proclaimed judgment on the great city of his enemies (3:4). Jonah was hoping God would judge them and wipe them out, but he knew that God was gracious, merciful, slow to anger, abounding in steadfast love, and relenting from disaster, which is why Jonah did not want to go to Nineveh in the first place (4:2). To Jonah's surprise, the people of Nineveh repented in sackcloth and ashes (3:5-6). God relented of the disaster (3:10), which angered Jonah. Jonah did not understand that God was Lord over all nations, not just Israel, and He would get His message of repentance to all the nations in the world. Jesus gives us more insight on the account of Nineveh. In Matthew 12:41 Jesus says, "The men of Nineveh will rise up at the judgment with this generation and condemn it, for they repented at the preaching of Jonah, and behold, something greater than Jonah is here." Jesus used the account of Nineveh to condemn the scribes and Pharisees for their unrepentant hearts and to show that true repentance is required before a holy God. We must ask ourselves if we are like Jonah at times. What would we think if a great enemy of the faith repented and trusted in Jesus? How would we feel if our greatest enemy, someone who made our lives miserable for many years, repented and gave his life to Jesus? Would we be bitter and angry at God like Jonah was? Do we want God's justice to fall on some people so that they will be crushed, yet we seek mercy for others? Do we pray for God to crush people instead of show mercy to them? This is sin. Jesus tells us to love our enemies (Matthew 5:44, Luke 6:27,35). How much more should we love our friends, relatives, and fellow Christians? Do we have a narrow view of God's love for people? Do we think that God only desires our little circle of people to know and love Him, while the vulgar, God-hating kid on the street is outside the grace of God? We must examine our heart for bitterness, which is a grievous sin.

Day 97

Multitudes, multitudes, in the valley of decision! For the day of the LORD is near in the valley of decision.

Joel 3:14

Emphasis: Multitudes, multitudes, in the **valley of decision**! For the **day of the LORD** is **near** in the valley of decision.

Rewrite: Immense multitudes are in the valley of judgment! The time for the Lord to judge the world has come.

Application: The valley of Jehoshaphat now becomes known as the valley of decision (vv. 2, 12). The message is clear; judgment is coming. Though God has tarried long, in our minds, in bringing judgment on all His enemies, one day all the people who have ever lived will stand before the judge of the universe. We see a snapshot of this great day of judgment in Revelation 20:12, which says, "And I saw the dead, great and small, standing before the throne, and books were opened." Earth and sky flee from the presence of the judge (Revelation 20:11) as He enters the scene. The judge is none other than Jesus (2 Timothy 4:1, John 5:26-27). This day will bring terror to all those who have rejected the Lord. Joel 2:11 says, "The LORD utters his voice before his army, for his camp is exceedingly great; he who executes his word is powerful. For the day of the LORD is great and very awesome; who can endure it?" This valley is called the valley of decision because the eternal destiny of all men will be revealed. Contrary to popular belief, the valley of decision is not a place where people decide to accept Christ as their Savior. The only one deciding anything in this valley is God and Him alone. This is judgment. There are no more chances to repent and believe. Every knee will bow, and every tongue shall confess to God (Romans 14:11). The enemies of God will be crushed and thrown into the lake of fire (Revelation 20:15), and the people of God will receive their inheritance that has been prepared for them (Matthew 25:34). What will this great day be like for you? Knowing this day is coming, how should we live our lives on this earth? Who do we know that will stand on the wrong side of this valley of decision? We must stay awake, examine ourselves, and pray without ceasing.

Day 98 – Your Meditation

Seek good, and not evil, that you may live

Amos 5:14

Read: Amos chapter 5

Emphasis:_____
_____
_____

Rewrite:_____
_____
_____

Application:_____
_____
_____
_____
_____
_____
_____
_____
_____
_____
_____
_____
_____
_____
_____
_____
_____
_____
_____
_____

Day 99

"Behold, the days are coming," declares the Lord GOD, "when I will send a famine on the land— not a famine of bread, nor a thirst for water, but of hearing the words of the LORD.

Amos 8:11

Emphasis: "Behold, the **days are coming**," declares the Lord GOD, "when I will send a **famine** on the land— not a famine of bread, nor a thirst for water, but of **hearing the words of the LORD.**

Rewrite: The day will come when the Lord will send a famine, not of food or water, but of hearing the word of God.

Application: God will no longer tolerate Israel and their rejection of the Word of God which was spoken through Amos. Israel must make an end of sin or God will make an end of them and send them into exile where the Word of God would no longer be found. We see this same thing happening in many parts of the world today. Many people today have hardened themselves to hearing the words of the Lord. They have not only become ignorant of the Word of God, but they have stopped tolerating it. Steven Lawson said, "This present-day 'famine' of 'hearing the words of the Lord' must be traced back to a famine of preaching the Word."[16] If preaching doesn't become more true and biblical, the people will lose respect for the Word and reject it. Like Israel, if we continually trample under foot the Word of God, judgment in the form of a famine of the Word of God will come upon us. God will send preachers to tickle our ears. If a person continually rejects the Word of God year after year, there will come a point when they will not be able to find it anymore. It may not mean that the person will not hear the Word of the Lord, but that person will not listen anymore. Their heart will become so hard and their conscience so dull that they will be numb to hearing and listening to the Word of God. They will be despondent to the command to repent and believe the gospel. God will give them up to their own lusts (Romans 1:18-31). Are we like this? How have you responded to the Word of God over time?

---

16 Steven J Lawson, *Famine in the Land: A Passionate Call for Expository Preaching.* (Chicago: Moody, 2003), 98.

Day 100

Jesus said to him, "Have you believed because you have seen me?
Blessed are those who have not seen and yet have believed.

John 20:29

Emphasis: Jesus said to him, "Have you believed because you have **seen** me? **Blessed** are those who have **not seen** and yet have **believed**.

Rewrite: You have believed because you have seen me, but blessed are those who have not seen and still believe.

Application: We have all heard people say, countless times, that if God would come down and show Himself to them, then they would believe. The sad thing is that these people would still not believe even if God did appear to them. When Jesus told the parable of the rich man and Lazarus, the rich man begged father Abraham to send him back from Hades to his father's house to warn his five brothers not to come to the place of torment. Abraham's response proved that seeing will not result in believing; he said, "But Abraham said, 'They have Moses and the Prophets; let them hear them.' And he said, 'No, father Abraham, but if someone goes to them from the dead, they will repent.' He said to him, 'If they do not hear Moses and the Prophets, neither will they be convinced if someone should rise from the dead'"(Luke 16:29–31). The Bible was written so that we may believe that Jesus is the Christ, the Son of God, and that by believing we may have life in His name (John 20:31). If a person will not believe the Bible then he will not believe or trust in God even if He does appear before him. A person is blessed with salvation when he believes without seeing. 1 Peter 1:8-9 says, "Though you have not seen him, you love him. Though you do not now see him, you believe in him and rejoice with joy that is inexpressible and filled with glory, obtaining the outcome of your faith, the salvation of your souls." 2 Corinthians 5:6–7 says, "We know that while we are at home in the body we are away from the Lord, for we walk by faith, not by sight." Until that glorious day when we fall asleep and pass over to be in the presence of Jesus for all eternity, we must believe and walk by faith. We must mortify all doubts that dwell in us and fully surrender every part of our lives to Him who is worthy of all our trust.

Day 101

And the LORD appointed a great fish to swallow up Jonah. And Jonah was in the belly of the fish three days and three nights.

Jonah 1:17

Emphasis: And the LORD **appointed** a great fish to swallow up Jonah. And Jonah was in the belly of the fish **three days and three nights.**

Rewrite: The Lord ordained that a great fish swallow Jonah. Jonah was inside the fish for three days and three nights.

Application: We see here that Jonah was not swallowed by a random, big fish by chance; God appointed the fish. God, in His sovereignty, ordained, from the foundation of the world, that the fish would swallow Jonah and keep him there for three days and three nights. Jonah was not swallowed by the fish to be punished, but to be rescued. Jonah was in the middle of the sea and needed to be rescued from drowning. God rescues Jonah by sovereignly preparing and directing a big fish to swallow him and take him to shore. God shows His sovereignty in many instances in this account of Jonah. He appointed the fish (v. 17), the plant (4:6), the worm (4:7), and the east wind (4:8). In Jonah 2:9 we see that God is sovereignly in control of salvation. Ultimately God sovereignly ordained this event to show a shadow of the death and resurrection of the Messiah. Jesus would be swallowed up by death and delivered from the grave three days later. When the scribes and Pharisees asked Jesus for a sign, He told them, "An evil and adulterous generation seeks for a sign, but no sign will be given to it except the sign of the prophet Jonah. For just as Jonah was three days and three nights in the belly of the great fish, so will the Son of Man be three days and three nights in the heart of the earth" (Matthew 12:29-40). Many people in our generation ask for a sign so that they can believe. However, they will get the same sign as the scribes and Pharisees, which is the sign of Jonah. If people will not believe the biblical account of the death and resurrection of Jesus, then they cannot be saved. Just as God sovereignly appointed the fish, plant, worm, the east wind, and salvation, God has appointed every word of the Scriptures to direct us to Christ and our need for Him. If we reject the ordained rescue plan of God then we cannot be rescued.

Day 102

Christ Jesus, whom God put forward as a propitiation by his blood, to be received by faith.

Romans 3:25a

Emphasis: Christ Jesus, whom **God put forward** as a **propitiation** by His blood, to be received by faith.

Rewrite: God publicly displayed His Son Jesus as the one who would remove sin and absorb His wrath with His own blood.

Application: Because of the love and justice of God, He had to send His Son Jesus to earth to die for our sins. Propitiation is a sacrifice that appeases, or absorbs the wrath of God against sin so that justice can be satisfied.   There are two parts of the work of the atonement, expiation and propitiation. Expiation is the removal of sin, and propitiation is the absorbing or appeasing of God's wrath against sin. God sent His own Son to bear the penalty of sin in our place. 2 Corinthians 5:21 says, "For our sake he made him to be sin who knew no sin, so that in him we might become the righteousness of God." Jesus became the object for God's hatred of sin, and He absorbed all the wrath and anger of God against sin, which turned God's wrath to favor. All of God's wrath, fury, and hatred for sin was coming at us like the explosion of a nuclear bomb. We had nowhere to run or hide. The wake of the destruction of the bomb was coming and would destroy everything in its path. Just when we were about to be consumed, God, the author of the wrath, sent forth His own perfect Son to stand in front of us. Jesus stood between us and the coming wrath, which was meant for us because of our sin. Jesus protected us and absorbed every ounce of wrath, fury, and hatred for sin upon His own head. In doing this, the wrath of God against us was appeased and we received God's favor. Christ drank the wrath of God down to the dregs so that we would not have to. We receive propitiation by putting our faith and trust in Jesus, the only One who could satisfy divine justice and appease the wrath we deserved. To say there is another way to Heaven outside of Christ is blasphemy.

Day 103

He has told you, O man, what is good; and what does the LORD require of you but to do justice, and to love kindness, and to walk humbly with your God?

Micah 6:8

Emphasis: He has told you, O man, **what is good**; and what does the LORD require of you but to do **justice**, and to love **kindness,** and to walk **humbly** with your God?

Rewrite: Uphold justice, show mercy, and walk humbly with your God; this is what is good and required by the Lord.

Application: Israel ignores the root problem of their sin and tries to pacify God with sacrifices. Sacrifices don't mean anything if you are neglecting what God has commanded that you do. Keith Brooks gives great insight to this. He says, "Sacrifices and ceremonies have their value from the reference they have to Christ, the great propitiation, but if the believer disregards their meaning, they are an abomination. Thousands of rams and rivers of oil cannot take the place of one little stream of the blood of Christ, the power of which is truly appropriated to the heart."[17] God does not want superficial offerings, vain, repetitious prayers, or His people to go through the motions while they do religious things. God wants changed lives and for people to bear good fruit like justice, mercy, love, kindness, and humility. Israel had neglected to bear any of these fruits. The rulers did not do justice (Micah 3:1), nor mercy (3:2), and they were far from humble (3:11). Do we find ourselves going through the motions in our service to God? Are we doing our duty because we feel that we must, but in reality our hearts are far from God? We must take time to examine ourselves to see if we are doing what the Lord requires, that is, growing in justice, kindness, and humility. Do we treat all people fairly at all times? If people were asked to describe us, would they use the word "kindness" as one of our qualities? Do we show mercy to those who do not deserve it? Are we walking before God in humility, or are we living in our own might and power?

---

17 Keith L. Brooks, *Summarized Bible: Complete Summary of the Old Testament* (Los Angeles, CA: Bible Institute of Los Angeles 1919), Micah 6

Day 104

Then they left the presence of the council, rejoicing that they were counted worthy to suffer dishonor for the name.

Acts 5:41

Emphasis: Then they left the presence of the council, **rejoicing** that they were counted **worthy to suffer** dishonor **for the name**.

Rewrite: They left the council and rejoiced that God counted them worthy to suffer for the name of Jesus.

Application: No one who has ever lived or will live has suffered more than Jesus. Jesus went through all the sin and misery of this world, including death itself, which He tasted for everyone (Hebrews 2:9). He learned obedience through suffering (Hebrews 5:8), and He was made perfect through suffering (Hebrews 2:10). He suffered in order to sanctify people through His own blood (Hebrews 13:12). At the cross He suffered the full fury of the wrath of God for every sin committed by His people. The disciples were witnesses to His suffering, and they heard Him say they must suffer as well. In Matthew 5:10, Jesus called those who suffer for righteousness sake, blessed. Jesus also promised that His followers would suffer. He said in John 15:20, "Remember the word that I said to you: 'A servant is not greater than his master.' If they persecuted me, they will also persecute you." We know that all who desire to live a godly life in Christ Jesus will be persecuted (2 Timothy 3:12). The apostles rejoiced because they were counted worthy to suffer for Jesus because they knew that suffering produces endurance, and endurance produces character, and character produces hope (Romans 5:3–4). If we share abundantly in Christ's sufferings, so through Christ we also share abundantly in comfort (2 Corinthians 1:5). Suffering conforms us to Christ. Peter says we have been called to suffer, because Christ also suffered for us, leaving us an example, so that we might follow in his steps (1 Peter 2:21). Suffering is not an option for a Christian. If you make a stand for Christ, the world will hate you and persecute you. We must count it all joy to suffer because God is counting us worthy; "...this light momentary affliction is preparing for us an eternal weight of glory beyond all comparison" (2 Corinthians 4:17).

Day 105 – Your Meditation

The LORD is slow to anger and great in power, and the LORD will by no means clear the guilty.

Nahum 1:3

Read: Nahum chapter 1

Emphasis:_____
_____
_____

Rewrite:_____
_____
_____

Application:_____
_____
_____
_____
_____
_____
_____
_____
_____
_____
_____
_____
_____
_____
_____
_____
_____
_____
_____
_____

Day 106

For the wicked surround the righteous;
so justice goes forth perverted.

Habakkuk 1:4b

Emphasis: For the wicked surround the righteous; so **justice** goes forth perverted.

Rewrite: There are more wicked than righteous; therefore there is no justice.

Application: This is Habakkuk's complaint. He is frustrated because it seems to him that God is not answering his prayer (v. 2). He cries out for God to bring justice because he is surrounded by evil, violence, corruption, destruction, strife and contention (v. 2-3). He assumes that since all of this sin and evil exists and has not been dealt with, then there is no justice anymore. The problem with Habakkuk's complaint is that he assumes. Habakkuk does not know anything about what God is doing behind the scenes. When God answers Habakkuk's complaint in verse five, He reveals that He is answering his prayer. He says, "Look among the nations, and see; wonder and be astounded. For I am doing a work in your days that you would not believe if told." God was already dealing with the complaints and prayers of Habakkuk but in a way Habakkuk did not think of. It is often the same with us. We want God to answer our prayers in the manner that we think is right and in our time. God was already raising up the Chaldeans to bring judgment on the wickedness. This was God's way and God's timing in bringing judgment and justice. Many people today assume that because evil still exists, God has not dealt with it. How can we know the details of God's providential plan to deal with evil? We may not know the details, but we know that God has already solved the problem of evil by sending His Son to die on the cross in the place of evil men. God's divine justice demands that sin be punished, and when Christ died on the cross, He defeated death and satisfied justice. One day there will be no more evil on earth because everything evil will be in Hell. Even though at times it seems that evil is prevailing on the earth, God said He would end evil, and He is progressively accomplishing this and will accomplish it in the end.

Day 107

*I will punish the men who are complacent, those who say in their
hearts, 'The LORD will not do good, nor will he do ill.'*

Zephaniah 1:12

Emphasis: I will punish the men who are **complacent**, those **who say in
their hearts,**'The LORD will not do good, nor will he do ill.'

Rewrite: I will punish the men who ignore their sin because they think
the Lord will not do good or bad to them.

Application: The prophet Zephaniah writes to a complacent Judah
before its fall to Babylon.   Zephaniah warned that Judah would be
punished, but Judah wallowed in their sin for so long without immediate
consequences that they thought the Lord would never punish them.
People still follow this pattern of complacency today. They say that they
have lived a long time in sin and God has not punished them yet. Some
people do not think of their death or the state of their souls before God.
They say they will live wild and free their whole lives and then get right
with God on their death bed. The Bible says that it is through the fear of
the Lord that men depart from sin (Proverbs 16:6). If they don't fear
God, they will be complacent about their eternal salvation and dwell in
their sins. These people will ignore the coming judgment while they
continue to build their houses, plant their crops, and live out their
worldly dreams, but just as in the days of Zephaniah, the great day of the
Lord is near (v. 14). Whether a sudden accident sends you to judgment
or Christ returns in judgment, clearly God will judge all sin. In the days
of Judah's rebellion, before their destruction by Babylon, God sent a
warning through the prophet Zephaniah that judgment would soon come.
God says in verses 17 and 18a, "I will bring distress on mankind, so that
they shall walk like the blind, because they have sinned against the
LORD; their blood shall be poured out like dust, and their flesh like
dung. Neither their silver nor their gold shall be able to deliver them on
the day of the wrath of the LORD."   How long will you live in
complacency, be dull to your sin, and ignore God's warning of judgment.
God already sent the solution to your sin by sending His precious Son to
die in your place and reconcile you to God. Only believe and be saved.

Day 108

But you denied the Holy and Righteous One, and asked for a murderer to be granted to you, and you killed the Author of life, whom God raised from the dead.

Acts 3:14-15

Emphasis: But you **denied** the Holy and Righteous One, and asked for a **murderer** to be granted to you, and **you killed** the **Author of life,** whom God raised from the dead.

Rewrite: You rejected the Holy and Righteous One, accepted a murderer, and killed the Author of Life, whom God raised from the dead.

Application: A crowd began to gather after the lame man was healed, so Peter took the opportunity to preach to the crowd (vv. 11-12). He begins by explaining and exalting Jesus and then tells the Jews very bluntly that they were responsible for denying and killing Jesus, the Author of life. We read in Luke 23:18-25 that after rejecting and calling for the death of Jesus, the Jews called for "Barabbas, a man who had been thrown into prison for an insurrection started in the city and for murder." The Jews chose the most vile man to be released instead of Jesus, who being the Author of life, was upholding their lives as they were calling for His death. This seems like the most incredible thing anyone could do. To give life to a wicked man while a perfectly innocent man dies is absurd. Amazingly, Barabbas is a picture of us. We are the most wicked people who deserve death, but Jesus came, lived a perfect life, and died for us, satisfying divine justice. We deserve to be hanging on that cross, but Jesus willingly put Himself there for us. We were credited with Jesus' righteousness, and He was credited with our sin in that great exchange on the cross. Jesus paid the penalty for our sin, and we were legally released from our punishment. Then, three days after Jesus gave up His last breath, the Father raised Jesus from the dead as confirmation that His sacrifice was accepted and justice was satisfied. Every time we reject the Holy and Righteous One and His sacrifice for our sins, we kill the very Author of life. Every time we love our sin more than Jesus, we reject Jesus, choose the ugliness of sin and prove our hatred for the life-giving God. You cannot serve two masters.

Day 109

*These are the things that you shall do: Speak the truth to one another;
render in your gates judgments that are true and make for peace.*

Zechariah 8:16

Emphasis: These are the things that you shall do: Speak the **truth** to
one another; render in your gates **judgments that are true** and make for
peace.

Rewrite: You should do this: tell the truth to one another and uphold
justice in your courts and strive for peace.

Application: In verse 15 God proposes bringing good to Jerusalem and
to the house of Judah, and then in these verses (16-17), God gives
instructions to His people on what they should do. They are to first
speak truth to one another because God is truth and He hates lies (v. 18).
Next, they are to uphold justice in their courts and seek peace. Paul
quotes this verse in Ephesians 4:25, stating, "Therefore, having put away
falsehood, let each one of you speak the truth with his neighbor, for we
are members one of another." God hates when justice is corrupted, when
His people devise evil in their hearts against one another, and when they
love false oaths (v. 17). If our hearts are corrupt with sin, then our
outward actions will produce lies, corruption, and fighting. Despite the
simplicity of these instructions, God's people then and now have never
been able to fulfill these duties. To be obedient to these instructions, a
new heart and new desires must be given by the work of the Holy Spirit
in regeneration. Psalm 15:1-2 says, "O LORD, who shall sojourn in your
tent? Who shall dwell on your holy hill? He who walks blamelessly and
does what is right and speaks truth in his heart." Since no one walks
blamelessly and does what is right and speaks truth, then no one is able
to dwell with God. God knew this so He sent hope to us. In Zechariah
9:9-10, God announces a message of hope. God is sending our righteous
King to us with salvation. He will come humbly, mounted on a donkey,
and He will bring good news to the nations and rule the whole earth.
God had to send His perfect Son to obey in our place because we loved
our sins more than obedience to God. How great is the love of God that
He would rescue us from our sins and obey in our place?

Day 110

And there is salvation in no one else, for there is no other name under heaven given among men by which we must be saved.

Acts 4:12

Emphasis: And there is **salvation** in **no one else**, for there is **no other name** under heaven given among men **by which we must be saved**.

Rewrite: There is no other way anyone on earth can be saved from eternal punishment but by Jesus Christ.

Application: Peter's statement that there is salvation in no one else exclusively sets Jesus and Christianity apart from the world. Peter was sure of this truth because Jesus said it Himself in John 14:6: "I am the way, and the truth, and the life. No one comes to the Father except through me." In this one bold statement, Jesus demolishes the belief that forgiveness of sins can be found in any other religion. There is no hope for anyone who is depending on another religion, or anything else, to ever be saved. When Jesus says He is the only way to the Father and we disagree with Him, we are calling Jesus a liar. When we say Mormons can be Christians as well, we are bearing false testimony. When we say we can find peace through yoga, we are lying. When we say we can have our sins forgiven by obeying sacraments, we are lying. If we say that we can have our sins forgiven through a priest, who claims to be a human mediator between man and God, we are calling Jesus a liar. "For there is one God, and there is one mediator between God and men, the man Christ Jesus" (1 Timothy 2:5). The only hope for anyone to have their sins forgiven and to have peace is through the Prince of peace and His atoning sacrifice on the cross in our place. Jesus said of Himself, "Whoever believes in him is not condemned, but whoever does not believe is condemned already, because he has not believed in the name of the only Son of God" (John 3:18). Jesus is exclusive. Christianity is exclusive. There is no other way to be saved in any other religion or by any other person. There is life in Christ and death in everything else. "Whoever has the Son has life; whoever does not have the Son of God does not have life" (1 John 5:12). It is exclusive and simple, and it is the only way to peace with God.

Day 111

When they look on me, on him whom they have pierced, they shall mourn for him

Zechariah 12:10b

Emphasis: When they **look** on me, **on Him whom they have pierced**, they shall **mourn for Him.**

Rewrite: When they look on me, whom they pierced, they shall mourn for him, as one mourns for a son.

Application: This is a prophecy about and fulfilled by Jesus. We read about it in John 19:37. When they came to Jesus and saw that He was already dead, they did not break His legs. But one of the soldiers pierced His side with a spear, and at once there came out blood and water (John 19:33-34). These things took place that the Scripture might be fulfilled: "They will look on him whom they have pierced" (John 19:36-37). After Jesus died, the people of Jerusalem wept because they realized who Jesus was through God giving them a spirit of grace and pleas for mercy (Zechariah 12:10). On that day, when the blood flowed from Jesus, a fountain was opened for the people of God to cleanse them from sin and uncleanness (Zechariah 13:1). We also see this verse referenced in Revelation 1:7, which states, "Behold, he is coming with the clouds, and every eye will see him, even those who pierced him, and all tribes of the earth will wail on account of him. Even so. Amen." The instant an unbeliever sees Jesus, he will immediately know who He is and what He did on the cross. The unbeliever will see his own sin and the fountain of blood that flowed from Immanuel's veins to cleanse him, but instead of rejoicing, he will wail on account of his fear and hatred for Jesus. He will know that all he believed was wrong. Jesus will be a terror to all who have wounded and crucified Him by their unrepentant hearts and rejection of Him. When Christ returns and all the world, pagan and Christian, sees Him, they will know that Jesus comes to take vengeance on the enemies of God. The believer will rejoice at His coming because they are greatly loved by Him and are freed from their sins by His blood (Revelation 1:5). This should cause the believer to look at his own sin. Every time the Christian sins, it should make him mourn.

Day 112 – Your Meditation

Bring the full tithe into the storehouse, that there may be food in my house. And thereby put me to the test, says the LORD of hosts, if I will not open the windows of heaven for you and pour down for you a blessing until there is no more need.

Malachi 3:10

Read: Malachi 3:6-15

Emphasis: _____

_____

_____

Rewrite: _____

_____

_____

Application: _____

_____

_____

_____

_____

_____

_____

_____

_____

_____

_____

_____

_____

_____

_____

_____

_____

_____

_____

Day 113

The Father of mercies and God of all comfort, who comforts us in all our affliction, so that we may be able to comfort those who are in any affliction.

2 Corinthians 1:3-4

Emphasis: The **Father of mercies** and God of all **comfort**, who comforts us in all **our affliction**, so that we may be **able** to comfort those who are in any affliction.

Rewrite: The Father of mercies and God of all comfort compassionately gives us comfort in our affliction, which enables us to comfort others in affliction.

Application: We must stop and praise God because He is our compassionate Father who cares for us and gives us comfort when we are in the worst pain. Psalm 34:18 says, "The LORD is near to the brokenhearted and saves the crushed in spirit." When His children are in the worst despair and crushed with grief, God manifests His presence through the comfort He gives at the moment of deep affliction. One reason that God allows us to go through affliction is so we can experience His comfort. If we always had a perfect life without problems then we would have no need to be comforted by God, and we would never experience this great gift from God. The more affliction we go through in this life, the more we will experience the mercy and comfort of God, and the more we will praise and glorify Him for His goodness to us. Another reason we are allowed to go through great affliction is so that from the experience of being comforted by God, we can, in turn, comfort others who are going through similar affliction. God often uses the woman who was raped to minister to others who have had the same horrendous experience. When you receive great comfort and peace from God after being rescued from drug abuse or suicide, you are enabled to greatly minister to those who are living in affliction from the same sins. Mercy and comfort in affliction can only come from the God of all comfort who, in His mercy, sent His Son to suffer in our place so that we can have peace with God and comfort in the Holy Spirit. Without God, there is no comfort, only affliction.

Day 114

In the beginning, God

Genesis 1:1

Emphasis: In the beginning, **God**

Rewrite: In the beginning, God

Application: The first subject of the first sentence of the Bible is God. God is the main purpose and theme of all of Scripture. We often think that Genesis chapters one and two are about creation, but really they are about God. In Genesis 1, God is mentioned 32 times. God said, God saw, God separated, God called, God made, God set, God created, and God blessed. From Genesis to Revelation we find that God is the subject and common thread woven through all of His inspired words. The book of Genesis is the foundation for all of Scripture, and therefore it is appropriate that the Author of life is the subject and theme of this foundational book. In the first two chapters of Genesis we see that God is the creator and sustainer of all life. Just from the first few words in this book, we see that God is eternal. He has always existed and is self-existent. "In the beginning" shows that God existed before the beginning because He began all of creation. Before there was a beginning, God existed. We also learn, since God created the heavens and the earth, that He is self-sufficient. God did not need anyone or anything to help Him create everything. God spoke and it came into existence. We learn that God is omniscient (Job 37:16, 1 John 3:20, Psalm 147:5, Job 23:10, Psalm 37:18), omnipresent (1 Kings 8:27, Isaiah 66:1, Acts 7:48-49, Psalm 139:7-10, Jeremiah 23:23-24, Acts 17:27-28), omnipotent (Matthew 26:64, Deuteronomy 9:29, Job 24:22, Psalm 21:13, Matthew 6:13, Romans 1:20, Revelation 4:11) and sovereign (Deuteronomy 10:17, Acts 4:24, 1 Timothy 6:15, Revelation 6:10, Proverbs 16:33). God is our creator, lord, prophet, priest, king, truth, holiness, justice, goodness, love, mercy, power, righteousness, wisdom, and our sustainer in whom we live and have our being. So if God is all of this, then He is the only true God and deserves all our worship, love, and service. What a great and worthy God we serve.

Day 115

He will declare to you a message by which you will be saved.

Acts 11:14

Emphasis: He will **declare** to you a **message** by which you **will be saved.**

Rewrite: He will audibly declare a particular message by which you will be saved.

Application: God will save all of His people before the end of the age because He sovereignly controls all things. God could save people in any way that He chooses, but He has already ordained the means by which He will save people. This verse shows us the means that God has chosen to save men. A message was spoken, people heard it and obeyed it and were saved. It is said that Francis of Assisi (1182-1226) once said, "Preach the gospel, and if necessary, use words." There is no record or proof that he actually said this, but the popular quote among today's "Christians" is attributed to him. This quote is in direct contradiction to the Scriptures in every way. It is impossible to preach the gospel without words. No one will ever understand the life, death, and resurrection of Jesus and His sin bearing atonement for His people by looking at the way you live. It would be like saying, "Please give me your phone number; if necessary use numbers." The preaching of the gospel is the means of salvation. No one on earth can ever be saved unless the gospel message is communicated to them in some way. Romans 10:14 is blatantly clear on this point; it says, "How then will they call on him in whom they have not believed? And how are they to believe in him of whom they have never heard? And how are they to hear without someone preaching?" God uses the foolishness of preaching to save men (1 Corinthians 1:21). If we read the book of Acts and then the history of the church up to modern times, we will see that the only way people have been saved, and the kingdom of Christ advanced, was by someone preaching the gospel, which led to people obeying the gospel and being saved. We must not fall into the snare of the devil, which tells us not to audibly proclaim the gospel to everyone, but to only live a moral life in the hope that dead, unregenerate sinners will figure out the gospel by our lives.

Day 116

If you do well, will you not be accepted? And if you do not do well, sin is crouching at the door. Its desire is for you, but you must rule over it.

Genesis 4:7

Emphasis: If you do well, will you not be accepted? And if you do not do well, **sin** is crouching at the door. **Its desire is for you**, but **you must rule over it.**

Rewrite: If you do what is right, will you not be lifted up? And if you do what is wrong, sin is waiting to devour you. You must mortify it.

Application: Sin is pictured here as a wild animal or lion crouched and seeking to devour its prey at any moment. It is obvious that Cain did not rule over sin but was ruled by sin when he killed his brother Abel. Every man is faced with the same challenge; he can devour sin or sin will devour him. Charles Spurgeon said, "If you will not have death unto sin, you shall have sin unto death. There is no alternative. If you do not die to sin, you shall die for sin. If you do not slay sin, sin will slay you." We have only one choice as a Christian, we must seek to mortify every sin in our lives before it destroys us. Romans 8:13 teaches the same principle. It says, "For if you live according to the flesh you will die, but if by the Spirit you put to death the deeds of the body, you will live." We are constantly in a war with our flesh and sin. We must fight against our sinful nature that longs to return to our old task master. Cain had no reason to be angry, and we see from this verse that Cain had a chance to repent and to do what is right and do it well. God was not condemning Cain for his offering but correcting him and instructing him to repent and do well. We have failed many times in our war with sin, but we have a chance to fight it. How are we fighting the battle with anger, pride, frustration, assumptions, sinful motivations, jealousy, slander, gossip, and hypocrisy? We often fight the desires of the flesh with our flesh. We were saved by grace through faith in Jesus Christ, and we trusted Him for our salvation. Often times, however, we trust in our own ability to fight sin. We must kill these sins in the same way we were delivered from the penalty of sin, by trusting in Jesus. We must trust in Jesus to lead us not into temptation, but deliver us from evil (Matthew 6:13).

Day 117

*They received the word with all eagerness, examining the Scriptures
daily to see if these things were so.*

Acts 17:11

Emphasis: They received the **word** with all **eagerness, examining** the
Scriptures **daily** to see if **these things were so.**

Rewrite: They listened attentively to the preaching with eagerness and
then examined the Scriptures each day to see if what they heard was true.

Application: This is the well known story of the Bereans and their
response to hearing Paul and Silas preach the gospel. Paul reasoned with
them from the Scriptures of the Old Testament, and the Bereans were
willing to receive it. They did not just accept the words of Paul as true;
they opened up the Scriptures and searched them to see how his words
compared to the truth. The Bereans were willing to conform to the
Scriptures if what they found Paul saying was in the Scriptures. Another
thing to notice is Paul actually used the Scriptures to preach the gospel.
The preacher who stands up and scarcely opens or references the Bible is
dangerous. The people are forced to trust the man speaking by accepting
his words as truth or to reject him. They can't open up the Bible and see
if the things are true if the things are not in the Bible. This is how so
many people are deceived by false prophets. Notice also that the
Bereans did not just listen to the sermon and then go out to lunch
afterwards and forget everything. They went away and searched the
Scriptures each day. This must be our duty as well. We must not only
gather with the church to hear the word of God preached; we must take
what we heard and examine it, study it, meditate on it, and apply it to our
lives. Like the Bereans, we must prepare our hearts to hear the word of
God, so whether we are reading the Bible in the morning or hearing it
preached on a Sunday morning, we will receive it with all eagerness and
expectation, knowing God will speak to us through His word. When
God's word is truly preached, His voice is truly heard through the words
of Scripture. We must always come to the Bible, whether hearing it or
reading it, with the expectation that something is going to happen. We
must expect and pray that we will be changed by it.

Day 118

For behold, I will bring a flood of waters upon the earth to destroy all flesh in which is the breath of life under heaven. Everything that is on the earth shall die.

Genesis 6:17

Emphasis: For behold, I will bring a **flood** of waters upon the earth to **destroy all flesh** in which is the breath of life under Heaven. **Everything that is on the earth shall die.**

Rewrite: I am going to flood the entire earth to destroy everything that breathes.

Application: We must look at the flood and see the justice and holiness of God and His hatred for sin. Often times the story of Noah and the ark is told to children as a fun little story. Sunday school walls are painted with the ark and a lot of cute, fuzzy animals entering it. This could not be further from the reality of what happened. God looked upon the earth and saw that the wickedness of man was great and that every intention of the thoughts of his heart was only evil continually (Genesis 6:5). This grieved the Lord, and He was sorry that He had made man on the earth (Genesis 6:6). In response to the wickedness of man, God said, "I will blot out man whom I have created from the face of the land, man and animals and creeping things and birds of the heavens, for I am sorry that I have made them" (Genesis 6:7). God only showed grace and mercy to Noah and made the first covenant with him (Genesis 6:18). We learn two things from this story as told by Peter in 2 Peter 2:5 and verse 9. He says, "if he did not spare the ancient world, but preserved Noah, a herald of righteousness, with seven others, when he brought a flood upon the world of the ungodly; then the Lord knows how to rescue the godly from trials, and to keep the unrighteous under punishment until the day of judgment." God hates sin and will punish the wicked according to the demands of divine justice, and God is able to rescue His people. In God's great rescue plan, He sent His son Jesus to rescue those who are perishing in their sin and misery. Jesus bore the flood of God's wrath upon His own head in the place of all those who trust in Him and repent of their wickedness. This must cause us to hate sin and love God.

Day 119 – Your Meditation

Serve the LORD with gladness!

Psalm 100:2a

Read: Psalm 100

Emphasis:_____

_____

_____

Rewrite:_____

_____

_____

Application:_____

_____

_____

_____

_____

_____

_____

_____

_____

_____

_____

_____

_____

_____

_____

_____

_____

_____

_____

Day 120

Now the LORD said to Abram, "Go from your country and your kindred and your father's house to the land that I will show you.

Genesis 12:1

Emphasis: Now the LORD said to Abram, "**Go from** your **country** and your **kindred** and your **father's house** to the land that I will show you.

Rewrite: The Lord said to Abram, "Leave your country, relatives, and your father's house to a new land that I will show you.

Application: When God called Abram, He completely uprooted him from his native land, relatives, culture, and all that was familiar to him. In Acts 7:2-3 we can read Stephen's New Testament perspective on Abram's call. He says, "The God of glory appeared to our father Abraham when he was in Mesopotamia, before he lived in Haran." The God of glory appeared to Abram to confirm his calling. Abram had a hard road ahead of him in his calling, but it was the will of God. Just because the calling for the Christian to be holy is a hard calling does not mean it is not the will of God. People often mistake God's call for being the easy road, but it is usually the hard road, the hard decision, and the hard life. When the God of glory appeared to us as the regenerating work of the Holy Spirit, we were saved from the penalty of sin and set apart, or called, to a life of holiness. When we are adopted into the family of God through faith in Christ, we, like Abram, are called to renounce our national identity and leave our association with the sinful practices of the world. We are called to renounce our identity, status, and popularity and be identified with Jesus Christ as ambassadors for Him (2 Corinthians 5:20). This is never the easy road in life, but it is the will of God, and we will receive the greatest joy from it. When our identity with the world is transferred to an identity with Christ, we no longer can be identified with a particular nation, like the United States, a particular race, a particular lineage, or a particular social status. We are now Christians, and everything the culture sinfully dictates in a nationality, race, lineage or social status must die. National pride can't exist because we are now strangers and pilgrims on this earth, making our way to the city of God. Racism, favortism and social status can't exist anymore.

Day 121

To open their eyes, so that they may turn from darkness to light and from the power of Satan to God, that they may receive forgiveness of sins

Acts 26:18

Emphasis: To **open their eyes**, so that they may turn **from darkness** to **light** and from the power of **Satan to God,** that they may receive forgiveness of sins.

Rewrite: To make them see the truth, so that they can escape from lies to the truth and from being a slave of Satan to God, so that they will have their sins forgiven.

Application: On the road to Damascus, the Pharisee Saul, had a life changing encounter with the Lord Jesus. Jesus appeared to Paul causing him to be a servant and witness among the Gentiles so their eyes would be opened to the message of the gospel and so they would escape from darkness and Satan to the light and power of God. We know that all men are born into sin and slavery. All men live in darkness, and they are blinded by the god of this age, Satan. They can't see the light of the gospel of the glory of Christ (2 Corinthians 4:4). Even when the light of Christ walked on this earth, men loved the darkness and rejected the light. Even today when the light of the gospel is preached, people love the darkness rather than the light because their works are evil (John 3:19). Mankind loves their sins more than the truth, and they do not come to the light for fear their works will be exposed as evil (John 3:20). Man cannot open his eyes nor raise himself spiritually from the dead. Because of this sinful condition of man, God had to do all the work in salvation by sending His Son Jesus to die for sinful men. The Spirit of God applies salvation to the people of God in the work of regeneration. In regeneration, we are convicted of our sin, enlightened to the truth, our wills are changed, and we are enabled to embrace Jesus Christ. God had to do everything. When we look at our unbelieving family and friends and wonder why they remain unchanged, we only have to remember this verse and their spiritual condition and pray that God would do the work of salvation in them. Unbelievers will always act like unbelievers, but there is hope. Whoever believes in Him is not condemned (John. 3:18).

Day 122

For in passing judgment on another you condemn yourself, because you, the judge, practice the very same things.

Romans 2:1

Emphasis: For in passing **judgment** on another **you condemn yourself**, because you, the judge, **practice the very same things**.

Rewrite: When you judge others for the same sin you commit yourself, you are condemning yourself.

Application: The context of this verse is ungodly men that are given up by God to their own passions which result in an ultimate display of depravity. They were filled with all manner of unrighteousness, evil, covetousness, malice. They are full of envy, murder, strife, deceit, maliciousness. They are gossips, slanderers, haters of God, insolent, haughty, boastful, inventors of evil, disobedient to parents, foolish, faithless, heartless, ruthless (Romans 1:29-31). Even though they knew that these things were wrong, they not only did them but gave approval to those who practiced them (Romans 1:32). Worse yet, they judged others for the same sins that they practiced. This resulted in God giving them up (Romans 1:24-28) and their own condemnation. Hypocritical judgment is being condemned here. We are called to judge things according to Scripture, for example: teaching (Acts 17:11), prophecy (1 Thessalonians 5:20-21), spirits (1 John 4:1), leaders (1 Timothy 3:10), other believers (1 Corinthians 5:12), the times (Luke 12:56), and ourselves (1 Corinthians 11:28). Judging becomes sinful when we judge motives, personal piety, and the same sins that we are committing (1 Corinthians 4:3-7). Sinful judging is also when we judge matters of conscience (Romans 14:1-4) and those outside the church (1 Corinthians 5:12-13). When we judge, we must judge biblically. Often times it is easy to see the sins that we struggle with the most in other people. If we are easily angered, we are quick to see and condemn others who are angry. If we gossip, we hate others who gossip. If we struggle with pride, we are quick to point out the pride of others. Whenever we find ourselves judging others, we must first look at ourselves and then ask if we are judging biblically. If not, we will fall under the discipline of God.

Day 123

Return to the Lord your God, for he is gracious and merciful, slow to anger, and abounding in steadfast love; and he relents over disaster.

Joel 2:13

Emphasis: **Return** to the LORD your **God**, for he is **gracious** and **merciful**, **slow to anger**, and abounding in **steadfast love**; and he relents over disaster.

Rewrite: Return to your God, for He is gracious, merciful, patient, and abounding in steadfast love; He is eager to relent and not punish.

Application: The prophet Joel warns the people that the great day of the Lord is coming. Judgment is coming. Sins will be exposed and dealt with. Justice will be satisfied. There is no other hope but to repent and return to the Lord. At times we fall into sin and find ourselves distant from God. In times when we are caught up in sin, we begin to not only stray from God but run from Him. If you have been running from God, you are drowning in a sea of sin. You have been treading water for a long time, but you are very weak. You can't keep hiding this forever. You are losing strength. Every day you wake up is only by the mercy of God. You will die any day. You have only one hope of rescue. There is only one Rescuer. He is Jesus. You see Him, but you don't run to Him with all your might. You ask questions like, "What will people say if they find out?" "Will this cost me my marriage?" "Will God restore me?" Fool. You're drowning. You're going to die. Nothing else matters in your life. Run to Christ. Run to Him with all your might! He is your only hope. Your only Rescuer. You're going the wrong direction and looking for another way out, but there is no other. Jesus is the only one who can deliver and restore you. Nothing else matters. He is your only chance. Everything has failed you up to this point. Run to Him while you have breath! Don't stop until He has you in His grip. He is mighty to save and promises He will never cast out all who come to Him. He is gracious and merciful, slow to anger, and abounding in steadfast love, and He relents over disaster. He doesn't want to destroy you. Confess your sin, repent of it, and cling to Jesus Christ, your only hope. He was mighty to save you and is mighty to restore you.

Day 124

For I delight in the law of God, in my inner being, but I see in my members another law waging war against the law of my mind and making me captive to the law of sin that dwells in my members.

Romans 7:22-23

Emphasis: For I **delight in the law of God**, in my inner being, but I see in my members another law **waging war** against the law of my mind and making me **captive to the law of sin** that dwells in my members.

Rewrite: I now love the law of God, but because of my sinful nature, I am always waging war against the sin that still dwells in me.

Application: When we were lost and without Christ, we were a slave to sin (Romans 6:6-20), and our only desire was to obey our master. Sin reigned in us, and we obeyed its passions. We loved the sin we wallowed in and wanted nothing else. When God saved us through the blood of Christ, we were freed from our evil-taskmaster of sin. We were no longer enslaved to sin but set free (Romans 6:6-23). The Christian now has a choice; he can obey the sinful passions of the flesh or die to sin and live to righteousness (Romans 6:14, 18, 22). We can walk in the Spirit, or we can walk in our flesh. Even though we are no longer a slave to sin, the remnants of sin still dwell in us, and they will continue to do so until we are resurrected with Christ. This is the process of sanctification or practical holiness. At our conversion we are made holy in that we are set apart from sin and the world to Christ. We are now set apart from our old master of sin to our new Master, Jesus Christ. At our deaths, we are made perfect in holiness, and there will be no more sin in us. In our lives on earth we must strive for practical holiness, which is the process of dying to sin more and more each day and conforming to the image of Christ. This practical holiness is what we must spend our lives pursuing. It seems in the Christian life that God reveals our sins and then we are enabled to repent and grow in holiness. God then reveals the next layer of sin to us, and we do the same for our whole lives. As we grow in the knowledge of holiness and our sins, we advance in the practice of holiness. We must always be diligently warring against sin and growing in holiness. We must kill sin, or it will kill us.

Day 125

The LORD is merciful and gracious, slow to anger and abounding in steadfast love.

Psalm 103:8

Emphasis: The LORD is **merciful** and **gracious**, **slow to anger** and abounding in **steadfast love**.

Rewrite: The Lord is compassionate and gracious, slow to get angry and abounding in steadfast love.

Application: This Psalm was written to remember and not take for granted the steadfast love and mercy of God. This Psalm expounds on God's own words from Exodus 34:6-7. We must thank God continually for His mercy, grace, patience, and steadfast love, which He demonstrated to us through the person and work of His precious Son. Through Christ, God was merciful, gracious, slow to anger and loving to us when we were the worst sinners on earth. He forgave our sins (Psalm 103:10), removed our transgressions from us as far as the east is from the west (v. 12), and showed compassion to us in the same way a father shows compassion to his children (v. 13). The Lord is slow to anger; He doesn't deal with us according to our sins, nor does He repay us according to our iniquities (v. 10). He does not hold a grudge against us or get frustrated with us when we don't meet His expectations. He knows how depraved we are which is why He sent His perfect Son to die in our place. He showed all of creation His unconditional, steadfast love when He saved us, who deserved only justice. We must look at these attributes of God and compare ourselves to them. How merciful are we? Do we always demand that justice be brought down on the heads of those with whom we disagree? How gracious are we? Do we show favor to those who deserve wrath? Are we slow to anger, or do we get easily irritated at the slightest offense? Are with thick skinned or thin skinned? Are we always in a conflict? Is our love steadfast and unconditional, or does it go in spurts and depend on our mood? We must strive to develop these attributes. In each day of our lives we have the opportunity to demonstrate these attributes to others in the same way God demonstrates them to us.

Day 126 – Your Meditation

...[W]e rejoice in our sufferings, knowing that suffering produces endurance, and endurance produces character, and character produces hope

Romans 5:3-4

Read: Romans 5:1-11

Emphasis:_____
_____
_____

Rewrite:_____
_____
_____

Application:_____
_____
_____
_____
_____
_____
_____
_____
_____
_____
_____
_____
_____
_____
_____
_____
_____
_____
_____
_____

Day 127

Who shall separate us from the love of Christ? Shall tribulation, or
distress, or persecution, or famine, or nakedness, or danger, or sword?

Romans 8:35

Emphasis: Who shall **separate** us from the **love of Christ**? Shall tribulation, or distress, or persecution, or famine, or nakedness, or danger, or sword?

Rewrite: Can anything separate us from Christ's love for us? Can tribulation, or distress, or persecution, or famine, or nakedness, or danger, or sword?

Application: Of course the answer to this is no one, using any means, can separate us from the love of Christ. It is not our love for Christ but Christ's love for us. "We love because he first loved us" (1 John 4:19). "In this is love, not that we have loved God but that he loved us and sent his Son to be the propitiation for our sins" (1 John 4:10). God's unfathomable love caused Him to send his precious Son to die for us. What could ever hinder this unconditional, amazing love? Nothing. Paul has no doubts as well, and in the closing verses of this chapter he boldly states: "For I am convinced that neither death, nor life, nor angels, nor principalities, nor things present, nor things to come, nor powers, nor height, nor depth, nor any other created thing, will be able to separate us from the love of God, which is in Christ Jesus our Lord" (Romans 8:38-39). When Job went through distress, tribulation, persecution, famine, nakedness, danger and sword, all his friends abandoned him, and even his own wife demanded that he curse God and die (Job 2:9). When Paul was brought to Rome, almost everyone abandoned him. When Jesus was captured in the garden, all His followers and even His closest friends abandoned Him. Unlike the weak men in this world, Christ will be with us always to the end of the age (Matthew 28:20). It is impossible for God to stop loving us because He cannot change. Going through tribulation, trial, hardship, danger and disaster is not evidence of Christ's failing love. His love is unfailing. God promises He will never leave us nor forsake us. So we can confidently say, "The Lord is my helper; I will not fear; what can man do to me?" (Hebrews 13:6).

Day 128

For behold, I create new heavens and a new earth.

Isaiah 65:17a

Emphasis: For behold, **I create** new **heavens** and a new **earth**.

Rewrite: Gaze upon this, I will create a new heavens and a new earth.

Application: Whether this is a picture of the restored Jerusalem, a millennial state, or the eternal state, we have a promise that the current heaven and earth will pass away and that God will create a new heavens and a new earth (Revelation 21:1, 2 Peter 3:13, Isaiah 66:22). Ever since the fall of Adam, the creation has been groaning under sin and longs for the day when salvation is fully realized and God restores the creation to perfection. Paul tells us, "For the creation waits with eager longing for the revealing of the sons of God. For the creation was subjected to futility, not willingly, but because of him who subjected it, in hope that the creation itself will be set free from its bondage to corruption and obtain the freedom of the glory of the children of God. For we know that the whole creation has been groaning together in the pains of childbirth until now" (Romans 8:19-22). In this fallen world we suffer, but we look forward to the day when the glory will be revealed to us. We long for a new resurrected body and the new heavens and the new or restored earth. All things will be restored (Acts 3:21). The heavens and earth will be fully renewed and restored like they were before sin entered them. No more effects of a cursed earth will be seen. Even now the creation, the heavens, and earth are declaring the glory of God. All the earth shall be filled with the glory of the *Lord* (Numbers 14:21). How much more will the fully restored and renewed heavens and earth declare the glory of the Lord. Martyn Lloyd-Jones explains what it might be like for us on the new earth: "Everything will be glorified, even nature itself. And that seems to me to be the biblical teaching about the eternal state: that what we call heaven is life in this perfect world as God intended humanity to live it."[18] Meditating on what awaits us and what it will be like on the new earth should bring us great joy and longing for Christ.

---

18 D. M. Lloyd-Jones, *The Church and the Last Things*. (Wheaton, IL: Crossway Books, 1998), 247-248.

Day 129

Then he said, "Let me go, for the day has broken." But Jacob said, "I will not let you go unless you bless me."

Genesis 32:26

Emphasis: Then he said, "Let me go, for the day has broken." But Jacob said, "**I will not let you go unless you bless me.**"

Rewrite: Let me go, we have wrestled all night. But Jacob refused to let him go until he received his blessing.

Application: Jacob persistently wrestled all night with this "man" that he came upon in a place that would be called Peniel, which means "face of God." We know that this "man" Jacob wrestled with was no man at all but the pre-incarnate Lord Jesus Christ (Genesis 32:30, Hosea 12:4). Jacob, even though he was about 97 years old at this time, struggled with all his might, weeping and seeking God's favor. This is a picture of how we should pray. Jacob's perseverance and determination to cling to Christ and not let go until his request had been granted is an example of fervent, desperate, importunate prayer. E.M. Bounds said, "Importunate prayer is a mighty movement of the soul toward God. It is a stirring of the deepest forces of the soul, toward the throne of heavenly grace. It is the ability to hold on, press on, and wait. Restless desire, restful patience, and strength of grasp are all embraced in it. It is not an incident, or a performance, but a passion of soul. It is not a want, half-needed, but a sheer necessity."[19] We must go to God in fervent, lion's den prayer, not lukewarm, routine, complacent prayer. We should be striving and struggling in prayer before the throne of grace (Romans 15:30, Colossians 4:12). It is so easy to find ourselves complacent in our prayer lives. We may go to our closet to pray, but we leave unaffected by our time. We find ourselves going through the motions out of routine and duty. It is usually at these times when God sends trials, which quickly revive our prayer lives. We must guard ourselves from being lukewarm and complacent in prayer and communion with God. We must strive to cling to Christ and not let go until our prayer has been answered.

---

19 E.M. Bounds, "The Necessity of Prayer." in *The Complete Works of E. M. Bounds.* (Radford, VA: Wilder Publications, LLC., 2008), 207. Print

Day 130

If you confess with your mouth that Jesus is Lord and believe in your heart that God raised him from the dead, you will be saved.

Romans 10:9

Emphasis: If you confess with your mouth that Jesus is Lord and believe in your heart that God raised him from the dead, you will be saved.

Rewrite: If you confess with your mouth Jesus as Lord and believe in your heart that God resurrected Him from the dead, you will be saved.

Application: This is one of the most quoted verses while evangelizing because it is emphatically clear what a person must do to be saved. Confessing that Jesus is Lord is acknowledging and submitting to Jesus as our master; the one who has all power and authority over us. It is not only an intellectual acknowledgment that Jesus is God, it is a full submission to Him as our one and only master whom we serve. We know that at the name of Jesus every knee will bow, in Heaven and on earth and under the earth, and every tongue will confess that Jesus Christ is Lord (Philippians 2:10-11). Whether we confess this while we live on earth and gain salvation or we confess it at judgment and receive our just condemnation, we will confess it one day. We learn from this verse the importance of the resurrection. We must believe the resurrection of Jesus, or we cannot be saved. To deny the resurrection is to deny Christ because the resurrection proved who Christ said He was. Without the resurrection, Christianity is vain. Belief is in contrast to Israel's unbelief. Paul says a few verses earlier that, "...Israel who pursued a law that would lead to righteousness did not succeed in reaching that law. Why? Because they did not pursue it by faith, but as if it were based on works" (Romans 9:30-32a). Like Israel, Catholics, Mormons, Muslims, Jehovah's Witnesses, Adventists, Hindus, Buddhists all base salvation on works, not faith. Every one of these religions would disagree with or add to this verse in Romans 10:9. But the Bible is clear, "For by grace you have been saved through faith. And this is not your own doing; it is the gift of God, not a result of works, so that no one may boast" (Ephesians. 2:8-9). Believe and you will have eternal life (John 3:15).

Day 131

We who are strong have an obligation to bear with the failings of the weak, and not to please ourselves.

Romans 15:1

Emphasis: We who are strong have an **obligation** to **bear with** the failings of the **weak**, and **not to please ourselves.**

Rewrite: Those who are strong must pick up, carry and endure with those who fail in their weakness, and not live selfishly to satisfy our own desires.

Application: The context of this verse is found in chapter 14 and concerns the tensions of Jewish and Gentile Christians living together in harmony. There was conflict over eating certain foods, esteeming one day as better than another and judging each other for these practices. The point of this verse is to say that we must live in peace and harmony with one another, not selfishly, for the sake of the work and glory of God (Romans 14:20). Those who are strong in the faith and more spiritually mature must help, pick up, carry, and endure with those who are weak in the faith and are still struggling with things that the strong have already overcome by the grace of God. Our lives must be marked by and focused on strengthening our brothers and sisters in Christ so that they will mature in the faith. Christ is our ultimate example of the strong bearing, or carrying the weight of, the weak. Christ never pleased Himself but bore the reproach of the weak (v. 3). Our desire must be for the glory of God and the upholding of the body of Christ in peace. Fighting, arguing, conflicts, and contention within the church bring shame to the cause of Christ, not glory. The strong in faith have a greater obligation than the weak. We are not supposed to only tolerate the weak but lift them up and strengthen them. This always will take sacrifice and self-denial. The strong person in the faith in any relationship, whether in marriage, in family, or in the church, must always take the initiative to encourage, endure, strengthen, love and strive for peace. The strong must always be the first to give up their own will for the good of others and to make the sacrifice for the strengthening of the weak. The strong must set the example of how the weak should be, just as Christ modeled.

Day 132

Let love be genuine. Abhor what is evil; hold fast to what is good.

Romans 12:9

Emphasis: Let **love** be **genuine.** Abhor what is **evil**; hold fast to what is **good.**

Rewrite: Let your love prove true. Hate what is evil and do what is good.

Application: Our love cannot be genuine until we have experienced the unfathomable love of God. We cannot understand what love is until we understand the cross. The cross is God's expression of His love for us. God demonstrates His love for us by sending His Son to be the propitiation for our sins (1 John 4:10). Understanding the love that God shows us, we also ought to love one another (1 John 4:11). Paul starts verse nine urging the church to have genuine love. He then gives a very detailed description of how love should manifest itself in the life of a believer. Evidence that you have genuine love as opposed to hypocritical love is proven by the fruit it bears. Having genuine love proves you belong to God, who is Himself love. The first evidence of genuine love is to hate evil and to do good. If you tolerate evil from time to time then you prove you have hypocritical love. The world may hate evil and do good, but they define what is evil and good themselves, and it is usually subjective to the person. The list continues in verses 10-21, and it is a good set of proofs to examine ourselves as we read through them in order to see if we really have genuine love. We should show brotherly affection and outdo one another in showing honor. We must be fervent and zealous in spirit, serving the Lord. We should rejoice in hope, be patient in tribulation, and constant in prayer. We should provide for the needs of others and show hospitality. We should treat our enemies different from the way the world treats their enemies. We must bless those who persecute us and not curse them, and if our enemy is hungry we should feed him. We must live in harmony with one another and not show favoritism, but associate with the lowly. We must be marked by humility. We must never repay evil for evil nor avenge ourselves. Finally, Paul urges us to not be overcome by evil, but overcome evil with good.

Day 133 – Your Meditation

And we know that for those who love God all things work together for good, for those who are called according to his purpose.

Romans 8:28

Read: Romans 8:18-30

Emphasis:_____

_____

_____

Rewrite:_____

_____

_____

Application:_____

_____

_____

_____

_____

_____

_____

_____

_____

_____

_____

_____

_____

_____

_____

_____

_____

_____

Day 134

God is a righteous judge, and a God who feels indignation every day.

Psalm 7:11

Emphasis: God is a **righteous** judge, and a God who feels **indignation** every day.

Rewrite: Because God is a righteous judge, He is angry with the wicked every day.

Application: God is righteous, and He is the just judge of the universe. Because God is righteous and just, He hates all evildoers and abhors the bloodthirsty and deceitful man (Psalm 5:5). God hates the wicked and the one who loves violence (Psalm 11:5). All men are depraved and wicked (Psalm 14:1-3, Romans 3:10-12). Because of God's holiness and man's wickedness, He is angry at the wicked every day. God readies His sword and bends His bow (v. 12). His deadly weapons are pointed at the wicked and ready to destroy at any moment (v. 13). How can man escape from God's righteous anger? When a man repents (v. 12) and trusts in Christ, God turns His sword and bow away from Him and aims it at the heart of His own precious Son. Because God is just, He must punish wickedness. Jesus takes our wickedness upon Himself, and God lets loose the sword and bow into the heart of the glorious Christ. Christ bears the punishment of those who trust in Him and satisfies the divine justice of God. "O Lord, our Lord, how majestic is your name in all the earth" (Psalm 8:1)! How amazing is the love of God that He would satisfy His wrath on His perfect Son instead of on us! How glorious is the Christ, who would voluntarily be treated like He was the worst sinner on earth and die as a condemned man for us! Salvation belongs to the Lord (Psalm 3:8)! When we meditate on the glorious grace of God displayed in His Son Jesus, we will have fullness of joy. "Be exalted, O Lord, in your strength! We will sing and praise your power" (Psalm 21:13). This verse brings great joy and peace to the Christian but great fear to the unrepentant sinner who has rejected Christ. Justice must be satisfied. The bow must be released on the wicked. It will either be released on you, in your unrepentant sin, or in the heart of Christ, as your substitute.

Day 135

*For the word of the cross is folly to those who are perishing, but to us
who are being saved it is the power of God.*

1 Corinthians 1:18

Emphasis: For the word of the **cross is folly** to those who are
perishing, but to **us** who are being saved it is the **power of God.**

Rewrite: The message of the gospel is foolishness to those who are
dead in their sins, but to us who are being saved it is the power of God.

Application: To the world, the gospel is the most ridiculous news that
can be spoken.   In the world's eyes, the Christian is trusting in a poor
carpenter who was murdered by Romans 2000 years ago.   To tell the
world to turn from their sins, which they love, and give their lives to this
person called Christ, is beyond absurd.   Until the Spirit of God awakens
their souls through His regenerating work, they remain blinded by this
truth (2 Corinthians 4:4), and it will never make sense.   Until they
encounter the living Christ, they will never see their sin and the need for
a Savior.   God uses the foolishness of preaching the gospel as the means
of saving men (1 Corinthians 1:21).   The message is a stumbling block
to both Jews and Gentiles (v. 22).   God chose what is foolish in the world
to shame the wise and what is weak in the world to shame the strong (v.
27).   God chooses to use the weakest of men to preach the most foolish
message to save men.   He accomplishes this so that the wisdom of this
world is made to be foolishness and so that no human being can boast in
the presence of God (v. 29).   When men put their trust in this gospel
message they are resting in the power of God instead of the wisdom of
men.   The cross of Christ alone makes our Lord Jesus the wisdom from
God.   We must not get discouraged as we share the gospel and are
rejected.   We must never be tempted to make the gospel more palatable
for unrepentant sinners in hopes that they will believe it.   We must not
lose hope in God that He will save that person in your life who you have
shared the gospel with countless times.   We do not depend on the
wisdom of this world but the power of God to save men.   We can fully
trust that when the Spirit of God awakens the spiritually dead man, the
gospel will become the power of God and that they will be saved.

Day 136

Let not the wise man boast in his wisdom, let not the mighty man boast in his might, let not the rich man boast in his riches, but let him who boasts boast in this, that he understands and knows me, that I am the LORD who practices steadfast love, justice, and righteousness in the earth. For in these things I delight, declares the LORD.

Jeremiah 9:23–24

Emphasis: **Let not the wise man boast in his wisdom**, let not the mighty man boast in **his might**, let not the rich man boast in **his riches**, but let him who boasts **boast in this**, that he understands and knows me, that I am the **LORD** who practices steadfast love, justice, and righteousness in the earth.

Rewrite: Do not boast in anything in yourself, boast in the Lord who is perfect in love, justice, and righteousness.

Application: Man has the tendency to strive to gain wisdom, power, and wealth so that he can boast in himself. These are things the world holds very high, and when a person advances in these, the world generally admires the person. How opposite does the Bible teach us to live? When we understand who God is then we will see how weak we are, and we will want to boast in God, who is worthy of boasting. God will share His glory with no man (Isaiah 42:8). To show His glory more, God chooses to use the weak things in the world. We learn this principle of boasting in God alone in 1 Corinthians 1:28-31: "God chose what is low and despised in the world, even things that are not, to bring to nothing things that are, so that no human being might boast in the presence of God. And because of him you are in Christ Jesus, who became to us wisdom from God, righteousness and sanctification and redemption, so that, as it is written, 'Let the one who boasts, boast in the Lord.'" When we understand that we can do nothing good apart from God, we will never boast in ourselves. Jesus modeled that He could do nothing on His own (John 5:30) and in turn says to us in John 15:5, "for apart from me you can do nothing." If every good gift comes from God then why do we boast as if it was apart from God? We should continually meditate on all that God gives us and boast in Him for it.

Day 137

But now I am writing to you not to associate with anyone who bears the name of brother if he is guilty of sexual immorality or greed, or is an idolater, reviler, drunkard, or swindler—not even to eat with such a one.

1 Corinthians 5:11

Emphasis: But now I am writing to you not to **associate** with anyone who **bears the name of brother** if he is **guilty** of sexual immorality or greed, or is an idolater, reviler, drunkard, or swindler—**not even to eat with such a one.**

Rewrite: Do not associate or even eat with someone who claims to be a Christian, yet lives a lifestyle of sin.

Application: The key to this verse is the phrase "Anyone who bears the name of brother." Paul is clear that he does not mean non-Christians who practice these things because they would have to leave the world to find someone who is not guilty. He says in verses 9 and 10, "I wrote to you in my letter not to associate with sexually immoral people—not at all meaning the sexually immoral of this world, or the greedy and swindlers, or idolaters, since then you would need to go out of the world." We must associate, in some way, with the world to proclaim the gospel so that people can be saved. Paul is talking about not associating with people who say they are Christians but live in a lifestyle of sin. In this letter, Paul addressed a specific sin of sexual immorality that was happening in the church (v. 1). Paul was shocked that this particular sin was being committed by someone claiming to belong to Christ, but he was even more shocked that the church was tolerating it. Paul knew the world was watching the followers of Christ for hypocrisy and how damaging it would be to tolerate sin within the church. Paul warns them to not only deal with the sin but, if it continued without repentance, to not even associate with this man. He gave strict instructions to remove the man from the church (v. 5). When we associate with people who claim to be Christians but who live in open, unrepentant sin, we show the world that we give approval of the sin and of those who practice it. We must be set apart from sin to Christ and seek to kill sin in our lives, to not tolerate it, or associate with it in any way.

Day 138

So it was not you who sent me here, but God.

Genesis 45:8a

Emphasis: So it was **not you** who sent me here, **but God**.

Rewrite: God used your evil to send me here for our good.

Application: The sovereignty and providence of God is plainly seen in this event. Joseph's brothers sold him into slavery in the land of Egypt because of their jealousy and wickedness. Joseph must have asked many questions to God about his circumstances. Why did he get sold by his own brothers as a slave when he did nothing against them? Why did he have to spend so long in prison for false charges against him? Why did the cupbearer forget about him and leave him in prison? Why were all these bad things happening to him when he only sought to do good? God blessed Joseph in Egypt and raised him from a slave in prison to the ruler of all the land of Egypt with no one above him in authority other than Pharaoh himself. God used Joseph to save all of Egypt, including his own family in the land of Canaan, from seven years of famine. Joseph recognized God's guiding hand and purpose in all his early years of hardship. When his brothers begged for forgiveness, Joseph graciously forgave them because he saw that God had ordained salvation for them all through this means. In Genesis 50:20 Joseph says, "As for you, you meant evil against me, but God meant it for good, to bring it about that many people should be kept alive, as they are today." God always uses both good and evil to accomplish His purposes. Romans 8:28 says, "And we know that for those who love God all things work together for good, for those who are called according to his purpose." This is a promise to all those who love God. No matter what circumstance we find ourselves in, no matter how evil or unjust, we can be confident that God has ordained the situation and is working it out for our good and His glory. Every person goes through hardship and trials. Everyone has a sudden event change their lives forever. How you respond to it will be determined by your understanding of God. If you are trusting in a sovereign God who controls the universe and ordains all things that come to pass for your good, you can have peace in all trials.

Day 139

He who was free when called is a bondservant of Christ. You were bought with a price; do not become bondservants of men.

1 Corinthians 7:22b-23

Emphasis: He who was free when called is a bondservant of Christ. You were bought with a price; do not become bondservants of men.

Rewrite: He who was free in the world is now a slave of Christ. You were bought with a price; do not become slaves of men.

Application: Because of the belief that Christ was coming back soon and persecution seemed inevitable, Paul urges new converts to remain as they are, not seeking to change their social or marital status just because they are converted. The word for bondservant in this passage is *doulos*, which can only mean slave. A better translation would be: *He who was free when called is now a slave of Christ. You were bought with a price; do not become slaves of men.* The man who was not a slave to men in the world is now a slave to Christ just as much as those who are slaves to men in the world. When a person is converted, he becomes a slave to one Master, the Lord Jesus Christ. He no longer has a will of his own, and he no longer does what he pleases. He must become a slave and servant of Christ with full obedience to His word. Before conversion, all men are slaves to sin, but after, they are set free and no longer enslaved (Romans 6:6). Now, having been set free from sin, we have become slaves of righteousness (Romans 6:18). Our freedom was not awarded to us for our good behavior; it was bought with a price. Jesus ransomed people to Himself by shedding His own blood on the cross. He paid the penalty for our sins. *"The Son of Man came not to be served but to serve, and to give his life as a ransom for many"* (Matthew 20:28). Because we are no longer a slave to sin, we are a slave to God (Romans 6:22). Because we are a slave to God, we must stop being slaves to men. That is, we must stop being slaves to sin, the ways of the world, and our old sinful desires. We must stop trying to please man and start pleasing our new Master. We must look at our lives and see if we reflect a life of slavery. Does the world look at us and say that we are a slave to Christ? How are we different from when we were a slave to sin?

Day 140 – Your Meditation

Put away from you crooked speech, and put devious talk far from you.

Proverbs 4:24

Read: Proverbs 4

Emphasis:_____

_____

_____

Rewrite:_____

_____

_____

Application:_____

_____

_____

_____

_____

_____

_____

_____

_____

_____

_____

_____

_____

_____

_____

_____

_____

_____

_____

_____

_____

Day 141

No temptation has overtaken you that is not common to man. God is faithful, and he will not let you be tempted beyond your ability, but with the temptation he will also provide the way of escape, that you may be able to endure it.

1 Corinthians 10:13

Emphasis: No **temptation** has overtaken you that is not **common to man.** God is faithful, and He will not let you be tempted beyond your ability, but with the temptation He will also provide the **way of escape**, that you may be able to **endure** it.

Rewrite: Your temptations are the same temptations that all people face. God is faithful, He will not let you be tempted more than you can bear, He will always give you a way out so that you can endure.

Application: Even when we think there is no other choice but to fall into temptation and sin, the Christian always has options. In every situation, there is always a right option that will glorify God instead of bring Him disgrace. Because we live in a fallen world and we still have a sinful nature, we will always be tempted in some way. We must never be so confident in ourselves to think we will not fall into a particular sin. How many pastors have committed adultery after 20 years of faithful ministry? People often say that they are not tempted by certain sins, but Paul warns, "Let anyone who thinks that he stands take heed lest he fall" (v. 12). There will always be temptations, but Paul gives verse 13 as a great encouragement to Christians. He says that God is in control and will limit temptation so there is always a way out. God promises that no matter what temptation we face in this life, it will never be so overwhelming that we have no hope. There is always a way out, and the way out is God. When we go to God in these situations, we find refuge and hope. If the temptation cannot be removed, God promises that He will give us the strength to endure it. We naturally want to fight our own battles, but every time we will find that the problem gets worse. When we trust in God and ask Him in prayer to help us, we will be delivered. When we trust in the LORD with all our heart, and do not lean on our own understanding, God will make straight our paths (Proverbs 3:5-6).

Day 142

Now therefore go, and I will be with your mouth and teach you what you shall speak.

Exodus 4:12

Emphasis: Now therefore **go**, and I **will be** with your mouth and **teach** you what you shall speak.

Rewrite: Go, trust in me; I will give you the words to speak.

Application: God gave Moses a command, but Moses did not instantly obey it, instead, he made excuses. He says, "They will not believe me or listen to my voice" (v. 1). Then he says in verse 10, "Oh, my Lord, I am not eloquent, either in the past or since you have spoken to your servant, but I am slow of speech and of tongue." Either Moses was extremely humble or he lacked faith in God to work through a weak man. God reminds Moses of His sovereignty in verse 11, stating, "Who has made man's mouth? Who makes him mute, or deaf, or seeing, or blind? Is it not I, the LORD?" Moses was trusting in his ability to speak instead of God's ability to work through him. When God called Jeremiah to a very difficult ministry at a young age, he responded in fear as well; he said, "Ah, Lord GOD! Behold, I do not know how to speak, for I am only a youth" (Jeremiah 1:6). God comforted Jeremiah by saying, "Do not be afraid of them, for I am with you to deliver you" (v. 8). Again, like Moses, Jeremiah was trusting in his ability and not in God's ability. So often we do the same thing when we have an opportunity to do something bold for the Kingdom. We instantly cower in our lack of faith in God and say we are not qualified. God knows our weakness, and He knows we are not qualified, which is why God is not depending on our ability but on His own. God does not search the earth and see who among His people are the most talented to do His work. Often times He uses the weakest person so that He will get all the glory and so that person will see God work in a mighty way, strengthening his faith. God chose what is weak in the world to shame the strong and what is low and despised in the world so that no human being might boast in His presence (1 Corinthians 1:27-29). We must repent of our self-reliance and rely fully on God and His ability to work through a broken vessel.

Day 143

And if Christ has not been raised, your faith is futile and you are still in your sins.

1 Corinthians 15:17

Emphasis: And if **Christ** has not been **raised**, your faith is **futile** and you are still in your **sins**.

Rewrite: And if Christ has not been resurrected, your faith is worthless and you must pay the penalty for your sins.

Application: What more glorious subject can we meditate on other than the resurrection? The resurrection is the cornerstone of Christianity. All of Christianity is bound tight or destroyed on the doctrine of the resurrection. The evidence that Christ was who He claimed to be and that He accomplished what He promised is proven in the resurrection. The evidence that the atonement of Christ was accepted by God as just payment for our sins is the fact that God rose Jesus from the dead. If Jesus was not fully God and fully man, He could have never bore our sins because He would have died for His own sins, not ours. If Jesus had sinned even one time then He would be in some unnamed grave this day, but he was sinless, perfect, and able to bear our sins and the wrath of God. The divine justice of God had to be satisfied by either us in Hell for all eternity or by the spotless Lamb of God dying in our place. Jesus satisfied divine justice, and the resurrection was proof of God accepting His sacrifice. If Jesus never rose from the dead like He proclaimed, it would have proven that Jesus was not God and that He died for no one but Himself. All of Christianity would crumble and be in vain. Paul said that if Christ never rose from the dead, our preaching and faith would be in vain (v. 14), we would be misrepresenting God (v. 15), we would still be in our sins (v. 17), and we would be hopeless and the most pitied of all people (v. 19). Our faith would be worthless and no different from all the other religions that vainly trust in their idols. In verse 20, however, Paul encourages us stating: "But in fact Christ has been raised from the dead." Jesus really was resurrected! Our faith is not in vain! We are not misrepresenting God, but proclaiming great news! We are no longer in our sins! Our debt has been satisfied! Glory to God!

Day 144

But as for me, I will look to the LORD; I will wait for the God of my salvation; my God will hear me.

Micah 7:7

Emphasis: But as for me, I will **look to the LORD**; I will **wait** for the God of my salvation; my **God will hear me**.

Rewrite: I will wait with expectation for the Lord; I will trust in the God of my salvation; I know my God will hear me.

Application: Israel's sin had affected all parts of society, even inside the home (vv. 5-6). The judgment of God was coming because of their refusal to repent. Micah declares despite the circumstances and the decision of the rest of Israel, he will look to the Lord and wait for the God of his salvation to deliver him. He knows that God will hear him. No matter how dark and evil the world becomes, Micah knows the Lord will be a light to him in the darkness (v. 8). Micah's complete trust and dependence are on God because He is a God of mercy, who pardons the guilt of His people and delights in showing unfailing love. God is always ready to show mercy to repentant sinners because of the person and work of His Son Jesus. Verse 19 says, "He will again have compassion on us; he will tread our iniquities underfoot. You will cast all our sins into the depths of the sea." We can always rely on the character of God. God is just and merciful. He satisfies His justice by turning His wrath toward His own Son and crushing Him in our place. He shows His mercy to us by sending His perfect Son to be the sacrifice for our sins. This work made it possible for our sins to be cast into the depths of the sea. The pardon of sin and mercy of God should leave the whole world in amazement. God saved us, and He continues to keep us. We must not only look to the Lord in the hardest circumstances, we must wait on the God of our salvation with eager expectation that He will hear our prayers. God desires to give us good gifts for His glory. Matthew 7:11 says, "If you then, who are evil, know how to give good gifts to your children, how much more will your Father who is in heaven give good things to those who ask him!" We must always look to the Lord and wait for Him confident that He will hear us.

Day 145

If I give away all I have, and if I deliver up my body to be burned, but have not love, I gain nothing.

1 Corinthians 13:3

Emphasis: If I give away all I have, and if I deliver up my body to be burned, but have not **love**, I gain **nothing.**

Rewrite: If I give away all I have to the poor, and even sacrifice my body, but do not have love, it profits me nothing.

Application: Often times we seek to develop many other gifts before love. Love sometimes gets put on the back burner. We want to be sound in doctrine, able to teach the Bible, evangelize, show hospitality, and demonstrate great faith, but in this chapter Paul argues that love is essential. We can have all gifts, but if we do not have love we have nothing. Of course the opposite is true as well. If we have love but no understanding of God or His Word, then we can't really understand love. Often times we can know the truth very well, and we can explain it very well, but if it is not done in love, it becomes a hindrance. Many arguments among Christians and in the church could be resolved if people had the pure motivation of love. Paul goes on to tell us what love is. He says in verses 4 through 7 that, "Love is patient and kind; love does not envy or boast; it is not arrogant or rude. It does not insist on its own way; it is not irritable or resentful; it does not rejoice at wrongdoing, but rejoices with the truth. Love bears all things, believes all things, hopes all things, endures all things." A person can be sound in doctrine and at the same time be lost. Love is a fruit of the Spirit and must be an attribute of someone who is truly a Christian. "...Love is from God, and whoever loves has been born of God and knows God. Anyone who does not love does not know God, because God is love" (1 John 4:7-8). The ultimate display of love is Jesus Christ Himself, and He left us an example so that we can follow in His steps. In Colossians 3:12-14, Paul urges believers to have "compassionate hearts, kindness, humility, meekness, and patience... and above all these to put on love, which binds everything together in perfect harmony." In our sinful natures we can say the right thing in the wrong way. We must seek love above all things.

Day 146

Open my eyes, that I may behold wondrous things out of your law.

Psalm 119:18

Emphasis: Open my eyes, that I may behold wondrous things out of your law.

Rewrite: Open my eyes so I can see wonderful things from your instructions.

Application: In this longest chapter in the Bible, we find great praise to God for His Word, the Bible. Psalm 119 has 176 verses with a primary focus on the greatness of the law, testimonies, precepts, statutes, commandments, rules, and words of God. It is an immense work that can be meditated on for a lifetime without exhausting its content. Charles Spurgeon wrote 349 pages on this Psalm alone in his *Treasury of David*. In the eighteenth verse of this Psalm, the Psalmist begs for his eyes to be opened so that he may behold wondrous things out of the law of God. He has a passion in his pursuit to know God through His Word. His soul is consumed with longing for the Word (v. 20), he delights in his testimonies and seeks counsel from them (v. 24), his soul longs for the words of life (v. 25), he meditates on the wondrous works of God (v. 27), and he clings to the testimonies of God (v. 31). He begs God to teach him (v. 33), give him understanding (v. 34), lead him (v. 35), incline his heart (v. 36), turn his eyes from worthless things (v. 37), confirm his promise (v. 38), and to turn away reproach (v. 39). He longs for the precepts of God and the life that comes from them. His attitude toward the Word of God leads him to trust in the Word. Is this our attitude toward the Word of God? Do we hunger and thirst for it? Do we long to read it the moment we wake up each morning? How different would our lives be if our attitude was like the Psalmist's? How much would we be transformed to the Bible if we passionately pursed understanding it. Meditating on the Word should drive us deeper into the Word. The more we read the Bible, the more we will desire to continue. Today we must be resolved to cry out to God to open our eyes, to give us a longing for the Word so that we delight in it and are changed by it. Our souls must long for the very words of life more than our body longs for food.

Day 147 – Your Meditation

Do not be deceived: neither the sexually immoral, nor idolaters, nor adulterers, nor men who practice homosexuality, nor thieves, nor the greedy, nor drunkards, nor revilers, nor swindlers will inherit the kingdom of God. And such were some of you. But you were washed, you were sanctified, you were justified in the name of the Lord Jesus Christ and by the Spirit of our God.

1 Corinthians 6:9b-11

Read: 1 Corinthians 6:1-11

Emphasis:_____

_____

_____

Rewrite:_____

_____

_____

Application:_____

_____

_____

_____

_____

_____

_____

_____

_____

_____

_____

_____

_____

_____

_____

Day 148

So we do not lose heart. Though our outer self is wasting away, our inner self is being renewed day by day.

2 Corinthians 4:16

Emphasis: So we do not lose heart. Though our **outer self** is **wasting away**, our **inner self** is being **renewed** day by day.

Rewrite: We should not lose heart. Even though our physical body is wasting away, we are being revived spiritually day by day.

Application: In the preceding verses, Paul gives reasons why he does not lose heart amidst all his hardship. The glorious God preserved Paul's life in every tribulation. He suffered a lot through these tribulations, but God sustained him to the end. Even though Paul poured out his life for the sake of the gospel, and his body was wasting away because of the abuse that it took, he was being sustained inwardly in his spirit. Physically, Paul was dying, but spiritually he was living. His body deteriorated each day while his spiritual life grew and revived each day. We too are called to pour out our lives for the sake of Christ and His Kingdom, and even though we may suffer physically from this great task, we will reap great spiritual benefits from it at the same time. We must live for eternity not our lives on earth. What good would it do to live a safe, comfortable, Christian life of ease if we are not being renewed spiritually. We grow the most spiritually during times of great distress, not during the times when our lives are easy. When we behold the living Christ and know that He who raised the Lord Jesus will raise us also with Jesus (v. 14), we have great hope in life after death. We can suffer any hardship knowing that when we die we will be raised to life again. This is the inner peace that only a child of God can attain. If in the latter years of our lives we are suffering in our bodies because of age, cancer, disease, handicap or because we wore out our bodies in service to God, we can rest in spiritual comfort and contentment because God will renew us spiritually each day. His mercies will come afresh to us each morning, and we can use our peace in suffering as a testimony to the God who sustains us. We can say in the deepest pain, "Though our outer self is wasting away, our inner self is being renewed day by day."

Day 149

I was glad when they said to me, "Let us go to the house of the LORD!"

Psalm 122:1

Emphasis: I was **glad** when they said to me, "Let us **go** to the **house of the LORD!"**

Rewrite: I was excited when they invited me to go to the house of God.

Application: Psalm 122 is a song of ascent which was sung as the people of God went up to Jerusalem to worship God. The Psalmist says that he was glad when they invited him to go to the house of the Lord. He longed to be with the people of God. When you are gone or isolated from your home country for many years, you rejoice at the opportunity to return for a visit. You begin to long to see all the things you have missed over the years. Your years of longing break forth in pure joy when you are en route to return home. It was like this for the Psalmist when he was invited to go up to the house of the Lord. He longed to return to the house of God. He was burdened when he was away from the people of God. He was grieved that he was isolated for a time, but when he was invited, he broke forth in gladness. He was returning to the house of the Lord to worship God with his people. There was nothing that could bring him more joy than this. Is this our attitude when we meet with the church each Sunday? Are we longing to be with the people of God when we are away? Does it gladden our hearts when we are on our way to worship God? Are we singing praises to God because of our excitement to go up to the house of the Lord? Often times we are quite the opposite. We find reasons or excuses to justify not joining the people of God in worship on Sunday. When we do attend worship, we sleep in late and then rush out the door, which causes irritation and dread to be with the people of God. When we get there our hearts are so far from being prepared to worship God that we get nothing out of the whole service, and we give nothing to God in our worship. Our worship is in vain. How different would our experience in a church service be if we prepared our hearts and were overjoyed to meet with the church? How much would we be changed by the Word of God if we went expecting to hear from God through the Word?

Day 150

Unless the LORD builds the house, those who build it labor in vain.

Psalm 127:1

Emphasis: Unless the LORD **builds** the house, those who build it labor in **vain**.

Rewrite: Unless the Lord is in the work, those who work build in vain.

Application: The verse does not say to not build or to stop building. We are encouraged to work. The verse is saying that if we work hard and try to accomplish something without God, we labor, toil, and work in vain. Unless God is in the work, we labor in vain. It is in vain that you rise up early and go late to rest, eating the bread of anxious toil (v. 2). When we labor, independently from God, to build a family, a church, a home, a marriage, a career, or a ministry, we labor in vain. We face many struggles that result in anxiety, toil, and loss of sleep instead of finding hope and trust in God. We are not called to be idle or careless in our work, but we are called to labor with all our might and trust in God since all depends on Him anyway. An example of building without God is the tower of Babel. The people set out to accomplish something apart from God, and it resulted in mass confusion and destruction (Genesis 11:1-9). An example of building something with God is the construction of Solomon's temple as well as the rebuilding of Jerusalem, the wall, and the temple. When God is in something there is nothing anyone in the world can do to stop it. Jesus said, "...apart from me you can do nothing" (John 15:5). We must ask what is our motivation for work? Why do we toil in this life? The average person works 2,080 hours per year. If a person starts work at the age of 21 and ends when he is 65 then he works about 91,520 hours in his life. Why do we work so hard? What are we working for? Are we trying to build our own little empire? Are we trying to achieve the American dream? Unless the Lord builds the house, we labor in vain. We must labor many hours in our lives, but if God is not in our labor then we are laying another foundation which is not Jesus Christ (1 Corinthians 3:11). "For every house is built by someone, but the builder of all things is God" (Hebrews 3:4). Today we must meditate on what we are building and on whether God is in it.

Day 151

For they gave according to their means, as I can testify, and beyond their means, of their own accord.

2 Corinthians 8:3

Emphasis: For they gave according to their means, as I can testify, and **beyond their means**, of their **own accord**.

Rewrite: They gave by and beyond their means, of their own will.

Application: We read in the first two verses that in a severe test of affliction, their abundance of joy and their extreme poverty have overflowed in a wealth of generosity. This is amazing! These people were severely afflicted but had an abundance of joy. They were extremely poor but were more generous than the rich. They gave to the suffering Christians in Jerusalem above and beyond what they had. It seems it has always been, with few exceptions, that the poor are far more generous with their money than the rich. The Macedonians were like the widow that gave two small copper coins. She gave all that she had to live on. Jesus responded to her faith, "Truly, I say to you, this poor widow has put in more than all those who are contributing to the offering box. For they all contributed out of their abundance, but she out of her poverty has put in everything she had, all she had to live on" (Mark 12:43-44). The churches in Macedonia not only gave beyond their means, they begged for the opportunity to take part in supporting those in Jerusalem (2 Corinthians 8:4). Paul urged the Corinthians to give like the Macedonians so they could give proof to the churches of their true love (v. 24). Giving is evidence that you truly love. When you hear of a need but don't give, it shows you don't really care. Love initiates actions. If you love, you will act. Paul goes on to teach about giving in chapter nine; he says, "whoever sows sparingly will also reap sparingly, and whoever sows bountifully will also reap bountifully (2 Corinthians 9:6). You can't out give God. We must ask, do we give out of our abundance like a Macedonian? Do you want to see God? Give beyond your means and you will see how my God will supply every need of yours according to His riches in glory in Christ Jesus (Philippians 4:19). If you want to see much of God in provision, then give radically.

Day 152

Behold, how good and pleasant it is when brothers dwell in unity!

Psalm 133:1

Emphasis: Behold, how good and pleasant it is when **brothers** dwell in **unity**!

Rewrite: How good and delightful it is when Christians are united.

Application: We see so much disunity in the world today that we need to get a glimpse of what it would be like if there was unity. How good and beautiful would it be to have unity in the church, unity in marriage, unity in families, schools, jobs and among the nations. Sin separates, causes division, and brings disruption and disunity among brothers. Because we are sinful, we divide. Look at the church you are in now; is there complete unity? It seems that every church has some disunity in it, but hopefully every church has experienced a season of spiritual unity within it. At these times of unity, fellowship is so sweet, there is so much joy within the body of Christ, and the church body is really one big family. Christ is what binds us together in unity. God is pleased with unity, not discord. One of the things the Lord absolutely hates is the person who sows discord among brothers (Proverbs 6:19). Jesus wants Christians to be united in the same way that the Father, Son, and Holy Spirit are united. Jesus calls for Christians to become perfectly one so that the world will look at the unity and see that God loves them (John 17:21-23). Paul urges us to walk in a manner worthy of our calling, with all humility and gentleness, with patience, bearing with one another in love, eager to maintain the unity of the Spirit in the bond of peace because there is one body and one Spirit which should bring unity (Ephesians 4:1-4). Peter calls us to have "unity of mind, sympathy, brotherly love, a tender heart, and a humble mind" (1 Peter 3:8). How pleasant and peaceful is life when brothers dwell in unity. Even if the world is continually trying to crush the church family, if there is unity among believers, there is no trial that cannot be endured. When there is unity, the body of Christ functions correctly and the brothers are encouraged, sharpened, strengthened in the faith and are able to model to the world that which is the true body of Christ.

Day 153

But I am afraid that as the serpent deceived Eve by his cunning, your thoughts will be led astray from a sincere and pure devotion to Christ.

2 Corinthians 11:3

Emphasis: But I am afraid that as the serpent deceived Eve by his cunning, your thoughts will be **led astray** from a **sincere and pure devotion to Christ.**

Rewrite: I'm afraid that just as the serpent deceived Eve, your thoughts will be corrupted, and you will be led away from your simple and pure devotion to Christ.

Application: With a fatherly care for the flock, Paul was afraid the Corinthians would be deceived by false prophets that would lead them away from their simple and pure devotion to Christ. Paul writes that he has a daily burden for all the churches (v. 28) because he knew there were false prophets within the church causing division by criticizing him. Paul says, they are "false apostles, deceitful workmen, disguising themselves as apostles of Christ. And no wonder, for even Satan disguises himself as an angel of light. So it is no surprise if his servants, also, disguise themselves as servants of righteousness. Their end will correspond to their deeds." (2 Corinthians 11:13-15). It seems that when Satan loses a soul to Christ, he does what he is allowed to destroy or lead astray that soul. When God first saves us, we have a simple and pure faith. We don't know much doctrine, but we know Christ, and we are filled with joy. Everything seems so simple. As we grow in our faith, the devil comes to us as an angel of light to deceive us. A teacher who teaches bad doctrine and brings confusion, books, and teachings are the means that the devil uses to lead us astray. We must guard ourselves from deception by comparing every teaching to the Bible. We must not take other people's words for granted and accept them as true. We must renew our simple, childlike trust and faith in God and strive to have pure devotion to Christ so others will see a pure reflection of Christ in us. The glory of God can be evidenced in us when all else is removed and devotion to Christ is reflected.

Day 154 – Your Meditation

For you have exalted above all things your name and your word.

Psalm 138:2b

Read: Psalm 138

Emphasis:_____

_____

_____

Rewrite:_____

_____

_____

Application:_____

_____

_____

_____

_____

_____

_____

_____

_____

_____

_____

_____

_____

_____

_____

_____

_____

_____

_____

_____

Day 155

The blood shall be a sign for you, on the houses where you are. And
when I see the blood, I will pass over you, and no plague will befall you
to destroy you, when I strike the land of Egypt.

Exodus 12:13

Emphasis: The **blood** shall be a **sign** for you, on the houses where you are. And when I see the blood, I will **pass over** you, and no plague will befall you to destroy you, when I strike the land of Egypt.

Rewrite: The blood on your house is a sign for you so that when I see it, I will pass over you, and you will be spared from death.

Application: From this event came the Passover, which is still celebrated by Jews today. The Passover was a time of great deliverance, when God delivered the Jews from Egyptian slavery. God judged Egypt with ten plagues; the last of the plagues being the killing of every first born son in the land of Egypt. The Jews were spared from the judgment of these plagues, but they were only spared their first born by offering a substitutionary lamb to die in their place. The blood on the doorpost of each family gave them a constant reminder that a sacrifice of life had to occur to save their own lives. Israel was supposed to keep the Passover each year as a reminder of what God did. When their children asked about the meaning of the Passover, they were instructed to tell them, "It is the sacrifice of the LORD's Passover, for he passed over the houses of the people of Israel in Egypt, when he struck the Egyptians but spared our houses" (Exodus 12:27). The interesting thing about the Passover is that the substitutionary lamb could not be an ordinary lamb. The Passover lamb had to be a male without blemish, killed at twilight (v. 5), and none of its bones could be broken (v. 46). This event of the Passover was a shadow of the substitutionary atonement of Jesus Christ. None of His bones were broken (John 19:33), and He was a male without blemish (Hebrews 9:14). When Jesus, the Lamb of God who takes away the sin of the world, died as a substitute in our place, the sword and justice of God passed over us and was unleashed on Christ, fulfilling the ultimate Passover. Redemption has come to us by the shedding of the precious blood of Christ. We must meditate on our redemption through Christ.

Day 156

Give thanks to the God of heaven, for his steadfast love endures forever.

Psalm 136:26

Emphasis: Give thanks to the God of Heaven, for His **steadfast love endures** forever.

Rewrite: Thank the God of Heaven because His faithful, loyal, and pure love is everlasting.

Application: Each verse of this Psalm is a reason to praise God, and the response to each reason is an expression of God's motive for doing these great things. His steadfast love endures forever. God's motivation for all His actions is His steadfast love. He shows His steadfast love in that He is the only true God and Lord over all His creation. His steadfast love is revealed in His wonders and His creation. His steadfast love is revealed in His provision of a substitute for Isaac. His steadfast love is revealed in His sustaining of Israel in the famine of Egypt. His steadfast love is revealed in His deliverance of Israel from the land of Egypt. His steadfast love is revealed in His removal of great kings and empires. His steadfast love is revealed in the provision and sustaining of His people throughout all ages. His steadfast love is revealed in His mercy shown to Israel through all their sin and rebellion. His ultimate demonstration of His steadfast love is in the sending of His own perfect Son as our Savior to free us from the bondage of sin and bring reconciliation. Because of the steadfast love of God, we don't have to face the justice of God; Christ paid the penalty for our sins. Because of the steadfast love of God, He sent the Helper to dwell in us so that we can die to sin and walk in the Spirit. God shows His steadfast love by giving us His Word in writing so that the following generations after Christ may read it and discover who God is, who we are, and how we must be saved. In His steadfast love, God gave us the body of Christ so we can have fellowship with the people of God even though we are strangers and pilgrims on this earth. The steadfast love of God is His motivation for everything He does. How does this differ from our motivation? Is steadfast love the motivation of our Christian walk, raising a family, our marriage, relationships, and all our actions?

Day 157

Grace to you and peace from God our Father and the Lord Jesus Christ,
who gave himself for our sins to deliver us from the present evil age,
according to the will of our God and Father.

Galatians 1:3-4

Emphasis: The Lord **Jesus Christ**, who gave himself for **our sins** to deliver us from the **present evil age**, according to the will of our God and Father.

Rewrite: The Lord Jesus Christ, who gave His life for our sins to rescue us from the evil age we live in, according to the plan of God.

Application: The Lord Jesus Christ gave Himself for our sins. This will be the theme of meditation for all eternity. The perfect Son of God lived a perfect life in a world of sin; He died on a cross as a sacrifice for our sins, and He then rose from the dead three days later to validate that His sacrifice was accepted by the Father. Why would Christ give Himself for our sins? Because He loves us. Why does He love us? I have no idea because there is nothing lovable in us, only sin and rebellion against God. This is the great mystery of God - His unconditional love for us. The cross of Christ not only has freed us from the penalty of sin but also the power of sin in this present evil age. When we were lost, without Christ, and without hope, we were a slave to the devil and his schemes. Paul says in 2 Corinthians 4:4 that "...the god of this world has blinded the minds of the unbelievers, to keep them from seeing the light of the gospel of the glory of Christ, who is the image of God." When Christ gave His life for us, He delivered us from this evil age, although not in the sense that we are removed from the world but that the evil present age, the devil, and sin do not have power over us anymore. Jesus prayed, "I do not ask that you take them out of the world, but that you keep them from the evil one" (John 17:15). Now that we have been purchased by the blood of Christ, we no longer live for ourselves but for Christ. Paul says, "I have been crucified with Christ. It is no longer I who live, but Christ who lives in me. And the life I now live in the flesh I live by faith in the Son of God, who loved me and gave himself for me" (Galatians 2:20). We must never give into this present evil age.

Day 158

I cry to you, O LORD; I say, "You are my refuge, my portion in the land of the living."

Psalm 142:5

Emphasis: I cry to you, O LORD; I say, "You are my **refuge**, my **portion** in the land of the living."

Rewrite: I go to you, O Lord, because you are my only hope, my only refuge, and you are all I have in this life.

Application: This Psalm is an individual lament. David was the individual, and he was lamenting to God about his current situation. David found himself in a situation that seemed without hope. After David killed Goliath, he entered into military service under king Saul. Saul soon became jealous of David, which caused David to flee for his life into the desert. David had no provisions, security, nor any place to go. He finally found himself hiding from Saul in a cave, which is where he cried out to God for help and wrote this Psalm. David knew that everyone had abandoned him and that his only hope was his God. He knew that God was his only refuge, option, and hope. We all go through trials, difficult situations, and at times we suffer greatly. Just because we are a Christian does not remove these hardships; in fact, being a Christian often brings more suffering. In these times of desperation and suffering, we draw close to God. God uses these times of suffering to conform us to Christ far more than He uses our health and prosperity. In these times we learn that it is vain to trust in man and that our only hope and refuge is in Christ. Everything in this life will fail us at some point. Our friends, spouse, children, money, health, beauty, and security will fail us. In the end, our only hope is the one who will never leave us or forsake us, Jesus Christ. Christ is not only our only refuge, He is our only hope. He is not the best option, He is the only option. He cannot ever fail us; it is not possible in His character and promise. This Psalm enables us to go to God, our only refuge, with confidence in prayer that He will deliver us from this present evil age and sin and eventually bring us to live with Him for all eternity. Christ is our portion in this life and the life to come. We must stop going to men and go to God, our refuge.

Day 159

Great is the LORD, and greatly to be praised, and his greatness is unsearchable.

Psalm 145:3

Emphasis: Great is the **LORD**, and greatly to be praised, and His **greatness is unsearchable.**

Rewrite: The Lord is great, and He should be greatly praised. His greatness is unfathomable.

Application: The more we catch a glimpse of the greatness of God, the more we will respond to Him in worship and praise. God is worthy of all praise and worship because of His greatness and His wondrous works, but ultimately all praise is due to Him for sending of His Son to die in the place of His enemies. After we spend a billion years in eternity with God, we will still be amazed and dumbfounded at the greatness of God. His greatness in unsearchable. We can never exhaust our discovery of God's greatness. God shows His greatness to us in His person, His glorious splendor and majesty. He also shows His greatness in His wondrous works (v. 5). God shows His greatness in His grace, mercy, and patience that He shows to unworthy people (vv. 8-9). The Lord shows His greatness in upholding all who are falling (v. 14), and He satisfies our desires (vv. 15-16). God continually shows His greatness in creation (Romans 1:20). James Montgomery Boice said, "If you can look at the surge of the ocean, the glory of the mountains, or the splendor of the sky on a cloudless night and not be moved to praise God, you are more to be pitied than a person who has lost his or her physical sight."[20] How should we respond to God's unfathomable greatness? The first two verses tell us: they say, "I will extol you, my God and King, and bless your name forever and ever. Every day I will bless you and praise your name forever and ever (vv. 1- 2)." We should also respond by meditating on His word and works (v. 5). We should speak of His glory and greatness and tell everyone of His power and mighty deeds (vv. 11-12).

---

20 J.M Boice, *Psalms 107–150: An Expositional Commentary.* (Grand Rapids, MI: Baker Books, 2005), 1251.

Day 160

Your grumbling is not against us but against the LORD.

Exodus 16:8

Emphasis: Your grumbling is not against us but against the LORD.

Rewrite: When you complain, you are complaining about the Lord.

Application: After being delivered by God from slavery in the land of Egypt, crossing the Red Sea on dry ground while watching the entire Egyptian army being consumed, the Israelites are found grumbling because they were hungry. It had only been fifteen days since they left Egypt, and they were already complaining about Moses and Aaron in the wilderness. God answered their grumbling by giving them manna from Heaven so that He could test them (v. 4), so that they would know He is the Lord their God (v. 12), and so that they could see their grumbling was not against Moses and Aaron but against God Almighty Himself. We learn from this text that God not only hears our grumbling and complaining about our lives or situations, but when we grumble and complain we are doing it against God. God is sovereign and ordains everything that comes to pass. When we complain and grumble about something God has ordained for His glory and our good, we complain that God is wrong and we are right. How blasphemous! How often do we complain about everything? We complain that the weather is too hot or cold, too rainy or dry, too windy or too much snow, but we know that God commands the snow and rain to fall on the earth (Job 37:6). God sends it for our good and we complain. We go through hardship and trials and complain the whole time, but trials are ultimately for our good. Trials and hardship are either the consequences of our sins or they are brought about by God to conform us to Christ. Like the Israelites in the wilderness, we even complain about the food that God provides for us or if our coffee is not made just right. Meditating on how we grumble and complain on a daily basis and how our sovereign God is in control of all things should make us take note of what we are doing. We are grumbling against God. We think God is wrong and we are right. We must discover our grumblings, repent, and fight to mortify these complaints and grumblings against God.

Day 161 – Your Meditation

Examine yourselves, to see whether you are in the faith. Test yourselves. Or do you not realize this about yourselves, that Jesus Christ is in you?—unless indeed you fail to meet the test!

2 Corinthians 13:5

Read: 2 Corinthians 13:1-10

Emphasis:_____

_____

_____

Rewrite:_____

_____

_____

Application:_____

_____

_____

_____

_____

_____

_____

_____

_____

_____

_____

_____

_____

_____

_____

_____

_____

Day 162

But you say, 'What a weariness this is,' and you snort at it, says the LORD of hosts. You bring what has been taken by violence or is lame or sick, and this you bring as your offering!

Malachi 1:13

Emphasis: But you say, '**What a weariness this is**,' and you snort at it, says the LORD of hosts. **You bring** what has been taken by **violence or is lame or sick**, and this you bring as your offering!

Rewrite: You say, "It is too hard to serve the Lord." You offer me your half-hearted service.

Application: The people at the time of Malachi became lukewarm in their worship. They gave their offerings out of obligation, even though they despised giving them. They gave animals taken by violence, the lame, and the sick because they kept the best for themselves. They were no different from Cain, who did not offer an acceptable offering by faith, but he gave an unacceptable offering out of obligation (Hebrews 11:4). When we do what God requires out of obligation instead of pure worship, we become a hypocrite and receive no spiritual benefit. The work of the ministry and worship become boring, empty, and annoying. This will lead to doing only what is required. If worshiping God with the church, serving, giving, singing, reading, and praying become boring and a nuisance, it is a clear sign that we are not worshiping God in spirit and truth, but only out of our preconceived obligation. Even our offering of money should be done with a pure heart and pure motives. 2 Corinthians 9:7 says, "Each one must give as he has decided in his heart, not reluctantly or under compulsion, for God loves a cheerful giver." Giving pocket change when you have a wallet full of money is an offering you will receive nothing from. You will receive no joy, contentment, or satisfaction. Verse 14 tells us this, "Cursed be the cheat who has a male in his flock, and vows it, and yet sacrifices to the Lord what is blemished." Giving less than our best will result in resentment, not joy. God will accept nothing less than our best because His name will be great among the nations. God gets no glory when the world looks at His followers and yet sees no difference in those who claim His name.

Day 163

So you are no longer a slave, but a son, and if a son, then an heir through God.

Galatians 4:7

Emphasis: So you are no longer a **slave**, but a **son**, and if a son, then an **heir** through God.

Rewrite: You are no longer a slave, but an adopted son of God and heir through Him.

Application: When God saves us we turn from sin to God, from darkness to light, from Hell to Heaven, from slavery to sin to freedom, from death to life, from the power of Satan to the power of God, from an enemy of God to His friend, and from a child of the devil to a child of God. These great dichotomies are brought about by Jesus Christ. We become an heir through God, that is, through the person and work of Christ on the cross. We were enslaved to the elementary principles of the world. But when the fullness of time had come, God sent forth his Son, born of woman, born under the law, to redeem those who were under the law, so that we might receive adoption as sons (vv. 3-5). Faith in Christ's perfect life, death, and resurrection enable a slave to become an adopted son and heir. In love He predestined us for adoption as sons through Jesus Christ (Ephesians 1:4-5). According to the *Westminster Shorter Catechism of 1647*, "Adoption is an act of God's free grace, whereby we are received into the number, and have a right to all the privileges, of the sons of God."[21] How incredible is it that we not only become a child of God, we become heirs—heirs of God and fellow heirs with Christ (Romans 8:17). Christ was appointed the heir of all things (Hebrews 1:2), and because we are fellow heirs with Christ, we receive all things. We inherit the kingdom of God (James 2:5), eternal life (Titus 3:7), membership into the body of Christ (Ephesians 3:6), and all the privileges of the sons of God. We once were enslaved to a harsh taskmaster, and now, through Christ, we are not only freed from slavery, but adopted into God's family and given the same benefits as a son of God. We are now kids of the King.

---

21 *The Westminster Shorter Catechism*, 1647. Question 34

Day 164

I lay down and slept; I woke again, for the LORD sustained me.

Psalm 3:5

Emphasis: I lay down and slept; I woke again, for the LORD **sustained** me.

Rewrite: I went to sleep and woke again because the Lord sustained me.

Application: David wrote this Psalm about the time when he fled from Absalom his son. He was in a very desperate situation, but he modeled faith in God by always trusting Him. Due to his situation, David had much cause to be anxious, but he was able to sleep. Instead of worrying all night, he rested in God's comfort. It says that he woke again because the Lord sustained him. David woke with a renewed confidence and trust in God. He said, "I will not be afraid of many thousands of people who have set themselves against me all around." Like David, we can go to sleep with a confidence in God that will let us rest calmly in His care. Psalm 4:8 says, "In peace I will both lie down and sleep; for you alone, O Lord, make me dwell in safety." We can have a holy confidence that we dwell in safety because God is our protector and sustainer. Not only did David sleep in confidence, he woke up. God woke him because He sustained him. We need the mercy of God each day. The mercies of yesterday will not be sufficient for today. "The steadfast love of the LORD never ceases; his mercies never come to an end; they are new every morning" (Lamentations 3:22-23). Every day we wake up by the mercy of God because He has sustained us through the night. We should thank God for each day that He has given us another day on this earth to live for Him. Anxiety is a lack of trust in our sovereign God who sustains everything by the word of His power. God upholds and governs the universe with more ease than us making coffee. How can we not trust Him to sustain us and awaken us each morning? The God who orders all of creation will never give us more than we can bear but always gives us a way out by His sustaining grace. What does our faith look like when it is being tested in a difficult trial? Do we have enough confidence in God that we can sleep easy during tribulation, or do we worry all night?

Day 165

And let us not grow weary of doing good, for in due season we will reap,
if we do not give up.

Galatians 6:9

Emphasis: And let us not grow **weary** of doing **good**, for in due season we will reap, if we **do not give up**.

Rewrite: We must not grow tired of doing good, for we will reap what we sow in due time, if we do not quit.

Application: We make many decisions each day. In every circumstance we have the opportunity to do good or to do evil. We can make a worldly, sinful decision in our flesh, or we can make a good decision in the Spirit. However, every decision has consequences. Whatever one sows, that will he also reap (v. 7). For the one who sows to his own flesh will from the flesh reap corruption, but the one who sows to the Spirit will from the Spirit reap eternal life (v. 8). The verse says that we should not grow weary of doing good. Sometimes it can be discouraging when we are wearing ourselves out doing good without any recognition nor visible results from it. However, we must examine our motives to see if we are doing good out of love and obedience to God or because we want to get something out of it. Our motives should never be to do good in order to be rewarded by men or to gain praise for our own ego. The Pharisees did this, and Jesus rebuked them. Our primary purpose in life is to do all to the glory of God (1 Corinthians 10:31). Our priority is the Kingdom of God, and our allegiance is to Christ. We must serve God by doing good, even if we never see any results. Jeremiah the prophet preached for 40 years and saw no fruit. David Livingstone, the great missionary explorer in Africa, did not weary of doing good. He would push through the jungles with malaria when others could not move. He lost his wife and child due to malaria. He persevered by God's grace through constant trials. Through all this he pushed on to spread the gospel. He sacrificed all for the gospel and never ceased from doing good. His one convert died, but his life's work opened the door wide to thousands of missionaries who reaped millions of souls. If we do not give up doing good, God will use what we did to bear fruit.

Day 166

You shall be my treasured possession among all peoples, for all the earth is mine; and you shall be to me a kingdom of priests and a holy nation.

Exodus 19:5-6

Emphasis: You shall be my **treasured possession** among all peoples, for all the earth is mine; and you shall be to me a **kingdom of priests** and a **holy nation.**

Rewrite: You will be my valuable possession among all people on earth, which is mine; and you will be a kingdom of priests and a holy nation.

Application: The Lord told Moses on Mount Sinai that if the people of Israel would obey His voice and keep His covenant, they would become His treasured possession, a kingdom of priests, and the holy nation of God. This would be fulfilled sometime in the future. Amazingly, Peter writes to primarily Gentile Christians (1 Peter 1:1) and states, "But you are a chosen race, a royal priesthood, a holy nation, a people for his own possession" (1 Peter 2:9). Peter takes the special privileges and titles reserved for Old Testament Israel and applies them freely to the New Testament church. Peter views the church as the true Israel. Because Christ fulfilled the covenant, the promise is for him and the true people of God through faith in Christ. Again John, in the book of Revelation, applies this verse in Exodus to the church, which is made up of believing Jews and Gentiles. He says, "And made us a kingdom, priests to his God and Father" (Revelation 1:6). Again he says, "and you have made them a kingdom and priests to our God, and they shall reign on the earth" (Revelation 5:10). Because of Jesus Christ and His work of reconciliation on the cross, there is no distinction between Jew and Greek; for the same Lord is Lord of all (Romans 10:12). There is only one people of God, the Church, comprised of believing Jews and believing Gentiles. This is amazing news for the Christian. It is not Israel that is God's treasured possession; you are. You are part of the kingdom of priests and a holy nation made up of all those bought by the blood of Jesus Christ. You are set apart from the rest of the world because of Christ. Your redemption is set, and your future is secure. What a glorious promise to meditate on today.

Day 167

For you were called to freedom, brothers. Only do not use your freedom as an opportunity for the flesh, but through love serve one another.

Galatians 5:13

Emphasis: For you were called to **freedom**, brothers. Only do not use your freedom as an **opportunity for the flesh**, but through love **serve** one another.

Rewrite: You were set free, brothers. Do not use your freedom to satisfy your sinful desires, but use it to love and serve others.

Application: Today, we often see people use "freedom" as a way to justify their sinful practices. They search the Scriptures to find ways to justify their sin, instead of searching the Scriptures to conform to what they teach. The Christian is not under the law but under grace (Romans 6:14). "For the law was given through Moses; grace and truth came through Jesus Christ" (John 1:17). Christ redeemed us from the curse of the law, not from our obligation to follow the moral law. As Christians, when we lie, steal, kill, or commit adultery, we sin, and we must pay consequences for sins in this life. We will never be eternally condemned for sinning (Romans 8:1), but we do fall under the discipline of the Lord and we must repent. We are free from the dietary and ceremonial laws but we are not free to sin. Paul says clearly in this verse that we must not use our freedom in Christ as an opportunity for the flesh. He says in verse 16, "But I say, walk by the Spirit, and you will not gratify the desires of the flesh." As Christians, we are obligated to mortify the sin in our lives. We must constantly battle with the sinful desires of our flesh and walk in the Spirit. Some people use their freedom in Christ to justify cussing, watching movies that God hates, drinking in the bars, and a variety of other sins that the world participates in on a daily basis. If we are free in Christ, why would we ever go back to our sinful, worldly practices? Even though a Christian won't be condemned because of sin, since Christ bore our condemnation on the cross, he will cause others to stumble and cause division and controversy in the church. We are free to do good, imitate Christ and love and serve others. We must use our freedom for good, not evil.

Day 168 – Your Meditation

For the sake of Christ, then, I am content with weaknesses, insults, hardships, persecutions, and calamities. For when I am weak, then I am strong.

2 Corinthians 12:10

Read: 2 Corinthians 12:1-10

Emphasis:_____
_____
_____

Rewrite:_____
_____
_____

Application:_____
_____
_____
_____
_____
_____
_____
_____
_____
_____
_____
_____
_____
_____
_____
_____
_____
_____
_____

Day 169

In him you also, when you heard the word of truth, the gospel of your salvation, and believed in him, were sealed with the promised Holy Spirit, who is the guarantee of our inheritance until we acquire possession of it, to the praise of his glory.

Ephesians 1:13-14

Emphasis: In Him you also, when you **heard** the word of truth, the gospel of your salvation, and **believed** in Him, were **sealed** with the promised Holy Spirit, who is the **guarantee** of our inheritance until we acquire possession of it, to the praise of His glory.

Rewrite: In Christ, when you heard and believed the gospel, you were sealed with the Holy Spirit, which guarantees your salvation.

Application: We have many spiritual blessings because of our union with Christ. God chose us in Him before the foundation of the world (v. 4). Because of God's love, He predestined us for adoption as sons through Jesus Christ (v. 5). We are redeemed by the blood of Christ (v. 7). As adopted sons, we have obtained an inheritance (v. 11). Finally, we are sealed with the Holy Spirit, who is the guarantee of our salvation and our inheritance (vv. 13-14). The Father chose us for salvation. The Son gained our salvation and redeemed us. The Holy Spirit secures and preserves our salvation. We see the work of all three persons of the Trinity in salvation. When we heard the word of God, which is necessary to be saved (Romans 10:17), and believed what we heard, which is also necessary to be saved (John 1:12), we were converted. At conversion the Spirit of God comes to dwell in us; we are sealed by Him, and we receive the guarantee, or the down payment, of our inheritance, which is eternal life. It is so encouraging to see the sovereign work of God in salvation because we see that He did it all, and all depends on Him. Just as we never earned our salvation, we can't keep it. However, because God earned our salvation, He keeps us and guarantees that we will inherit eternal life. Jesus confirms this in John 10:28, saying, "I give them eternal life, and they will never perish, and no one will snatch them out of my hand." It is impossible to lose our salvation. The evidence that you are in Christ is that you continue to believe and repent.

Day 170

Let the words of my mouth and the meditation of my heart be acceptable in your sight, O LORD, my rock and my redeemer.

Psalm 19:14

Emphasis: Let the **words** of my mouth and the **meditation** of my heart be **acceptable** in your sight, O LORD, my rock and my redeemer.

Rewrite: O Lord, let my speech and my thoughts be acceptable to you.

Application: The words that come out of our mouths are what is rooted in our hearts. When people say something cruel in their anger and realize their foolishness, they often say they are sorry and really didn't mean it. However, what came out of their mouth reveals what was in the meditation of their heart when they spoke. Their words revealed what was in their heart. "The good person out of the good treasure of his heart produces good, and the evil person out of his evil treasure produces evil, for out of the abundance of the heart his mouth speaks" (Luke 6:45). The words of our mouths reveal our hearts. An adulterer reveals the lust in his heart when he commits the act of adultery (Matthew 5:28). The meditations of his heart were not pure, and then one day he fell into adultery. The act of adultery reveals prolonged lustful meditations in the heart. Murder reveals the hateful meditations in the heart (1 John 3:15). We must train our hearts in meditating on the pure word of God. The more we can meditate and obey the word of God, the more we will conform to the image of Christ in our character and thought life. As ambassadors of Christ, we are His representatives (2 Corinthians 5:20), and our words and actions reflect on Christ. Our motivation for everything is Christ. We are not necessarily supposed to glorify God, as in giving something to God that we don't possess. Rather, we are to reflect God's glory. When our words and meditations are acceptable to God, we reflect Christ's character and glory. We show the world a glimpse of Christ as His character is reflected. We must reflect on our own words and meditations. Have they been acceptable in God's sight? We must fill ourselves each morning with the words of life and meditate on them all day so that our meditations will produce acceptable actions.

Day 171

...the mystery of Christ, which was not made known to the sons of men in other generations as it has now been revealed to his holy apostles and prophets by the Spirit.

Ephesians 3:4-5

Emphasis: The **mystery of Christ**, which was not **made known** to the sons of men in other generations as it has now been **revealed** to His holy apostles and prophets by the Spirit.

Rewrite: The salvation of God, which was not made known to other generations, has now been revealed to us by the Spirit.

Application: The mystery which was revealed to Paul by God was the unbelievable fact that the Gentiles are fellow heirs with the believing Jews. They would now become members of the same body and partakers of the same promise in Christ through the gospel. The mystery is that there is no more distinction between Jew and Greek, but all are part of the one Body of Christ (Romans 10:12). This one body, the Church, is made up of all believers, whether Jew or Gentile. This mystery of Christ was not made known to men in other generations as it has now been revealed to His holy apostles and prophets by the Spirit. We read hints of this in the Old Testament, but the readers never put it fully together. When Christ came, He made it clear that in the new covenant there is only one body, and the Gentiles are included. Often people will say that they would believe in God if He just revealed Himself in the same way He did in the Old Testament. They say that these people in the Old Testament had a greater advantage than themselves. The fact is: "Long ago, at many times and in many ways, God spoke to our fathers by the prophets, but in these last days he has spoken to us by his Son" (Hebrews 1:1-2). God has revealed Himself to us far more than anyone. Now that we have the written Word of God and the work of Christ on the cross has been accomplished, we have a greater revelation than anyone in the Old Testament. The progressive revelation of salvation is revealed to us more clearly than at any other time in history. We know more now about salvation through Christ than any other generation. What we do with this knowledge will determine our eternal destiny.

Day 172

Lift up your heads, O gates! And be lifted up, O ancient doors, that the King of glory may come in.

Psalm 24:7

Emphasis: Lift up your heads, O gates! And be lifted up, O ancient doors, that the **King of glory** may come in.

Rewrite: Open, O gates!   Open up, you ancient doors and let the King of glory enter.

Application: This Psalm of David is a procession Psalm, which is a picture of Christ ascending to the gates of Heaven after His resurrection. Verses 3 and 4 say, "Who shall ascend the hill of the LORD? And who shall stand in his holy place? He who has clean hands and a pure heart, who does not lift up his soul to what is false and does not swear deceitfully."   This is a picture of coming into the presence of God. Because all men are sinful and no man is righteous before God, no one can stand in His holy place.   There are none who have clean hands and a pure heart, who are not liars and deceivers.   There is only one who meets this criteria.   He is the same worthy one who we see opening the scroll in the book of Revelation (Revelation 5).   He is the Lion of the tribe of Judah, the Root of David, the one who has conquered by His death on the cross and resurrection from the grave.   As this worthy one, the Christ, ascends to Heaven, the ancient gates that have never let any man pass are now called to open up so the King of glory may enter in!   All of Heaven stands watching this event unfold.   These personified gates respond to this bold man who stands before them, saying, "Who is this King of glory?"   The response is, "The Lord, strong and mighty, the Lord, mighty in battle!" (v. 8)   The gates are called to open up again so that the King of glory can enter (v. 9).   For the first time in history, they open up to a man because this was no ordinary man.   This is the Christ, the spotless lamb, He who conquered and who can boast of clean hands and a pure heart.   The glorious Christ enters the gates and sits down at the right hand of the Majesty on high, and He reigns until His enemies are made a footstool for His feet (Hebrews 1:3,13).   Meditating on this glorious event will give us a glimpse of Christ that will change us forever.

Day 173

My eyes are ever toward the LORD, for he will pluck my feet out of the net.

Psalm 25:15

Emphasis: My **eyes** are ever **toward the LORD**, for He will pluck my feet out of the net.

Rewrite: My eyes are always on the Lord, for He will deliver me my from my troubles.

Application: David resolves to keep his eyes on the Lord because he is certain that God will deliver him from the enemy's net. David knows that God is his only refuge (Psalm 31:4). When the righteous cry for help, the Lord hears and delivers them out of all their troubles (Psalm 34:17). When our eyes are fixed on the excellencies of Jesus Christ, we avoid and are delivered from sin. Often times when a Christian is seeking to get victory over a sin, they are focusing so much on the sin that the sin begins to consume them. How we must fight sin in our lives is by turning our back to the sin and putting our eyes on Christ. When we truly behold the beauty and excellencies of Christ, we will be focused on the amazing love of Christ and not on sin and its hold on us. When we are truly blown away by our incredible Christ, we won't be struggling with lust at the moment. When we truly get a glimpse of the glorious Christ, we don't turn around and commit adultery. When we truly behold the beauty of Christ we will stop adorning ourselves to impress and fit into the world's standards. When we are meditating on the majesty of Christ, we are not gossiping about our co-worker. Christ is our solution and motivation for everything. Often times we try to fight sin with ten step programs and countless barriers, but we can never get victory over sin without putting and keeping our eyes on the perfect Christ. If we want to be delivered from the snares of the devil, we must run to Christ. "Let us also lay aside every weight, and sin which clings so closely, and let us run with endurance the race that is set before us, looking to Jesus, the founder and perfecter of our faith..." (Hebrews 12:1-2). Our thoughts should be according to the old hymn which says: "Turn your eyes upon Jesus, Look full in His wonderful face; And the things of earth will grow strangely dim In the light of His glory and grace."

Day 174

May have strength to comprehend with all the saints what is the breadth and length and height and depth, and to know the love of Christ that surpasses knowledge.

Ephesians 3:18-19

Emphasis: May have strength to **comprehend** with all the saints what is the **breadth** and **length** and **height** and **depth**, and to know the **love** of Christ that surpasses knowledge.

Rewrite: May we be able to comprehend what is the breadth and length and height and depth, and know the love of Christ that is unsearchable.

Application: Paul is praying (v. 14) for the indwelling power of the Holy Spirit in the believer (v. 16). The Spirit of God that lives in us enlightens our mind in the knowledge of the truth through the Scriptures. Paul prays that, through the Spirit, we will have the strength to comprehend, with all the saints, God and the unsearchable riches of Christ (v. 8). The unsearchable riches of Christ cannot be measured in breadth, length, height, nor depth. We can never exhaust our meditation on this theme. In 1977 the Voyager 1 spacecraft was launched to study the outer planets, but then it just kept going. On August 25, 2012, the Voyager became the first man-made object to leave the Solar System. The Voyager is now 12 billion miles from Earth, which is 121 times the separation between the Earth and the Sun. Amazingly the Voyager has been traveling 100,000 mph and will not reach another star for almost 40,000 years. We cannot even comprehend the breadth, length, height, and depth of the universe, let alone the love of Christ. It is amazing that the universe proclaims the glory of God, and no human has ever seen even a tiny speck of it. The love of Christ and the riches of Christ are far more vast than the universe. Even if we could grasp fully the depth and grandeur of the universe, we would still have minimal knowledge of the riches of Christ because the love of Christ surpasses knowledge. Oh, how amazing is the love of Christ and how vast are His riches. How unsearchable are His ways, His works, and His love. After a billion years in eternity with Christ, we will not even understand one-hundredth of the riches of His love.

Day 175 – Your Meditation

Look carefully then how you walk, not as unwise but as wise, making the best use of the time, because the days are evil.

Ephesians 5:15-16

Read: Ephesians 5:1-21

Emphasis:_____

_____

_____

Rewrite:_____

_____

_____

Application:_____

_____

_____

_____

_____

_____

_____

_____

_____

_____

_____

_____

_____

_____

_____

_____

_____

_____

_____

Day 176

The next day Moses said to the people, "You have sinned a great sin. And now I will go up to the LORD; perhaps I can make atonement for your sin."

Exodus 32:30

Emphasis: The next day Moses said to the people, "You have **sinned** a great sin. And now **I will go up to the LORD**; perhaps I can make **atonement** for your sin."

Rewrite: Moses said to the people, You have committed a horrible sin. I will intercede to the Lord for you; perhaps I can make atonement.

Application: Because the Israelites were sinners, like us, they were quick to turn their backs on the Lord and serve other gods. This is the pattern we see throughout their entire history. Moses was a little delayed coming down from the mountain so the Israelites told Aaron to make new gods for them. Aaron, in his foolish sin, obeyed their demand and made a golden calf. By our nature, when we did not have salvation in Christ, we had no desire to seek the living God, but to invent a god to suit our sin. We see our innate desire to turn away from God illustrated in the parable of the sower (Matthew 13:18-23). Three of the four people in the parable seem to follow God, but they soon turn from God. With the first man, the evil one comes and snatches away what has been sown in his heart. The second man hears the word and immediately receives it with joy, but when tribulation or persecution arises on account of the word, immediately he falls away. The third man hears the word, but the cares of the world and the deceitfulness of riches choke the word, and it proves unfruitful. Because we are by nature enemies of God, we, like Israel, need someone to intercede for us and atone for our sin. Moses was the person to intercede for the Israelites, and he even went as far as making himself a substitute to bear the penalty for their sin (v. 32). Moses, offering himself as a substitute to make atonement for the sin of Israel, prefigures Christ's substitutionary atonement for his people. Because we have sinned great sins, we need a Savior to stand in our place and make atonement for our sin. Only Jesus can fulfill this role. Today we should think of our sin and wanderings and thank our Savior.

Day 177

Put on the new self, created after the likeness of God in true
righteousness and holiness.

Ephesians 4:24

Emphasis: Put on the **new self**, **created** after the likeness of God in true
righteousness and holiness.

Rewrite: Put on your new self, which was created in true righteousness
and holiness after the likeness of God.

Application: When the Spirit of God regenerated us, we received a new
heart and a new nature. Though our old self still lingers, we are not
slaves to it and sin any longer. We now can walk in our new self, as
children of light. When we were lost and without Christ, we walked in
the futility of our minds (v. 17). Our love for sin caused our hearts to be
hardened, which developed an ignorance within us, which alienated us
from a life with God, and darkened our understanding (v. 18). As our
hearts became more hardened, we gave in to sensuality, greed, and we
practiced every kind of impurity (v. 19). We loved the darkness rather
than the light because our works were evil (John 3:19). Knowing this,
Paul exhorts the Ephesians to put off their old self, which belonged to
their former manner of life and to be renewed in the spirit of their minds
(v. 22). In Christ, our renewed mind is marked by telling the truth as
opposed to lying (v. 25), by controlled anger (v. 26), by doing honest
work instead of stealing (v. 28), by giving to those in need (v. 28), by
clean, uplifting speech instead of corrupt talk (v. 29). Paul says, "Let
there be no filthiness nor foolish talk nor crude joking, which are out of
place, but instead let there be thanksgiving" (Ephesians 5:4). We are
urged to let all bitterness and wrath and anger and clamor and slander to
be put away from us, along with all malice and to be kind to one another,
tenderhearted, forgiving one another, as God in Christ forgave us (vv.
31-32). As a new creation in Christ we are urged to be imitators of God
(Ephesians 5:1), and to walk in love as Christ loved us and gave Himself
up for us, a fragrant offering and sacrifice to God (v. 5:2). Today we
must focus on walking as children of light and take no part in the
unfruitful works of darkness, but instead expose them (Ephesians 5:11).

Day 178

Let each one of you love his wife as himself, and let the wife see that she respects her husband.

Ephesians 5:33

Emphasis: Let each one of you **love his wife** as himself, and let the wife see that she **respects her husband**.

Rewrite: The husband must love his wife as himself, and the wife must respect her husband.

Application: What is marriage but a picture of the relationship between Christ and the church. Paul explains the purpose of submission and the role of a husband and wife in verses 22-31 and then goes on to say in verse 32 that, "This mystery is profound, and I am saying that it refers to Christ and the church." In marriage the husband plays the part of Christ and therefore is the head of the wife, just as Christ is the head of the church (v. 23). Just as the church submits to Christ, so the wife should submit to her husband (v. 24). The husband has the responsibility of leading his wife, and he is called to love her in the same way that Christ loved the church and gave Himself up for her (v. 25). The husband must love his wife when she is fulfilling her role or when she is failing miserably. It is not a conditional love but an unconditional love. The husband must lay down his life for his wife, teach her the word of God, and present her to God as holy (vv. 26-27). The wife is called to respect her husband in the same way she should respect Christ. It is very easy to see a person's relationship with God through marriage. If the husband does not love his wife unconditionally, it is clear he is treating God in the same way. If he loved God, he would love his wife. If the wife does not submit to and respect her husband as the leader of the household, it is because she does not submit to and respect God. Because marriage is a picture of Christ and the church, couples have an enormous responsibility to model their marriage to the outside world and their children in a way that when the world looks at their relationship, they will see Christ and the Church. Even though men and women are equal, they have different roles, and if they fail at fulfilling their roles, they will not only be miserable, but they will bring shame to Christ.

Day 179

You cannot see my face, for man shall not see me and live.

Exodus 33:20

Emphasis: You cannot see my face, for **man shall not see me and live**.

Rewrite: Because of my holiness, no man shall be in my presence and live.

Application: God is holy, incomparable, incomprehensible, and unapproachable to sinful man. God is separated from sin and the corruption of the fallen world. God's holiness is the attribute from which all His attributes flow and belongs to Him alone. In this verse we see that Moses could not stand before God and see His face or he would die. God will not tolerate sin in His presence. Psalm 5:4 says, "For you are not a God who delights in wickedness; evil may not dwell with you." In Exodus 33:5, God says to Israel, "You are a stiff-necked people; if for a single moment I should go up among you, I would consume you." In Habakkuk 1:13, it says, "You who are of purer eyes than to see evil and cannot look at wrong." It is not that God cannot look at sin as if He feared it, rather He hates sin and will not tolerate it. For Moses to stand in the presence of God, he had to be shielded from seeing the face of God. In verses 22-23 God said, "and while my glory passes by I will put you in a cleft of the rock, and I will cover you with my hand until I have passed by. Then I will take away my hand, and you shall see my back, but my face shall not be seen." Because Moses is sinful, he cannot see God. What hope do we have, being far more sinful than Moses? We have the same hope and the only hope of any sinful man on earth. We have the hope of Christ. When Christ took our sins upon Himself and bore the wrath of God that was directed toward us, He stood in our place as our shield. Christ shielded us from the wrath of God by bearing it. Jesus became the propitiation for our sins (1 John 4:10). The word propitiation means appeasement or satisfaction. Jesus appeased the wrath of God's holiness. Jesus shielded us and absorbed all of God's wrath that was due to us, and He satisfied the divine justice of God. Oh what a Savior! We must meditate on our need for Christ to shield us from God's holiness. We need a Savior.

Day 180

For we do not wrestle against flesh and blood, but against the rulers, against the authorities, against the cosmic powers over this present darkness, against the spiritual forces of evil in the heavenly places.

Ephesians 6:12

Emphasis: For we do not wrestle against **flesh and blood**, but against the **rulers**, against the **authorities**, against the **cosmic powers** over this present darkness, against the **spiritual forces of evil** in the heavenly places.

Rewrite: Our battle is not against what we can see, but against the spiritual forces of evil in the spiritual world.

Application: The Puritan William Gurnall, in the late 1600s, wrote a nearly 1,300 page book about spiritual warfare by expounding Ephesians 6:10-20. The book is titled, *A Treatise of the Whole Armour of God, The Christian in Complete Armour, A Treatise of the Saints War against the Devil.* His extensive writing on this subject demonstrates the high importance that he put on the subject. Often times we forget that we are in a spiritual battle, and we are quick to think our circumstances are fleshly instead of spiritual. Paul exhorts us otherwise. He says in verses 10 and 11 that we must be strong in the Lord and in the strength of His might and that we must put on the whole armor of God, so that we can stand against the schemes of the devil. Whether we can see the battle with our eyes or not, we are in a great war with the devil and his forces. The devil and demons are described by their government, strength, kingdom or territories, and their nature. This war is occuring in the heavenly places. It is important to understand that the devil can do nothing to a Christian without permission. He is restrained by God. He is not omnipotent like God. He is like a dog on a leash. How do we fight this spiritual battle? We are told to fight it with truth, righteousness, the gospel of peace, faith, salvation, and the Word of God (vv. 14-17). We are to fight this battle, not necessarily by doing things in our flesh, but by praying at all times in the Spirit (v. 18). The battle is not ours, but the Lord's. The victory has been won already. Now we must stand, pray, and fight until the victory is complete.

Day 181

And I am sure of this, that he who began a good work in you will bring it to completion at the day of Jesus Christ.

Philippians 1:6

Emphasis: And I am sure of this, that **He who began** a good work in you will bring it to **completion** at the **day of Jesus Christ**.

Rewrite: I am certain that God, who began the good work in you, will finish it at the day of Jesus Christ.

Application: What a comforting and assuring verse. The same God who saved us, will keep us and finish the work that He has started. God started the work of salvation, and He will complete it. The Father ordained that we would be saved (Ephesians 1:4-5), the Spirit of God enlightened our mind to the truth and regenerated us, and at conversion, we put our trust in Christ and repented of our sins. Salvation was obtained through the death and resurrection of Christ. Even though we are saved, the fullness of salvation is not yet complete. When Christ returns and we are raised to life, we will inherit our eternal reward, and our salvation will be complete. From this verse we can be confident that if God has begun a good work in us by granting us eternal life through Christ, then He will complete it when Christ returns. We have been saved from the penalty of sin, we are being saved from the power of sin each day, and we will be eternally saved at the day of Jesus Christ. This means that if you are truly a Christian, sanctification is not an option. If you are in Christ, you will persevere to the end. You will continue to repent and believe until death itself. We are saved by the work of Christ, not our own. We are kept by Christ, not ourselves. A true Christian will be approved as excellent, pure, and blameless on Judgment Day only because he is filled with the fruit of righteousness that comes from and through Christ (vv. 10-11). This fact is a great comfort. We did not earn our salvation, and we have no power to keep it. We must rest in God and trust that He will keep us and conform us to Christ. God guarantees that He will finish the work He has started in us through Christ. We will have eternal life and be raised in the last day (John 6:40). No matter how difficult our lives may be, we will persevere to the end.

Day 182 – Your Meditation

Weeping may tarry for the night,
but joy comes with the morning.

Psalm 30:5

Read: Psalm 30

Emphasis:_____
_____
_____

Rewrite:_____
_____
_____

Application:_____
_____
_____
_____
_____
_____
_____
_____
_____
_____
_____
_____
_____
_____
_____
_____
_____
_____
_____

Day 183

I want you to know, brothers, that what has happened to me has really served to advance the gospel.

Philippians 1:12

Emphasis: I want you to know, brothers, that what has happened to me has really **served to advance the gospel**.

Rewrite: I want you to know that my suffering served to advance the Kingdom of Jesus Christ.

Application: The apostle Paul, who is writing this letter from prison, is comforting the believers by assuring them that his imprisonment and suffering has really been used to advance the gospel. He says in verse 14 that the brothers have become confident in the Lord through his imprisonment and now are much more bold to speak the word without fear. Throughout the history of the Church, God has used persecution and suffering far more than health and prosperity to advance His Kingdom. Because suffering for the sake of the gospel and the advancement of the gospel go hand in hand, we should be, not only willing to suffer for Christ, but to die for Him if it will advance the Kingdom. Whether we must physically suffer for the gospel or not, we should have the attitude of Paul, who said in verse 20, "...Christ will be honored in my body, whether by life or by death." God will get glory out of your life and often times more glory out of your death. Jesus said, "Truly, truly, I say to you, unless a grain of wheat falls into the earth and dies, it remains alone; but if it dies, it bears much fruit. Whoever loves his life loses it" (John 12:24-25). Paul was content to live or to die for Jesus Christ, which is why he said in Philippians 1:21, "For to me to live is Christ, and to die is gain." Because the gospel is often times advanced through suffering, Paul exhorts the Philippians to let their manner of life be worthy of the gospel of Christ (v. 27). We must look at our current situation, hardship, or trial and know that it has been ordained by God. No matter how difficult it is and no matter how much we are suffering, God will use it to advance the Kingdom for His glory and our good. In every trial, we have the opportunity to glorify God in the way we respond to it, and when we do, the Kingdom advances another step.

Day 184

Oh, fear the LORD, you his saints, for those who fear him have no lack!

Psalm 34:9

Emphasis: Oh, **fear** the LORD, you His saints, for those who fear Him have **no lack**!

Rewrite: Fear the Lord and you will lack no good thing.

Application: When we fear the Lord, we will have a high view of God, we will revere His holy name, we will seek to follow His law and do His will, we will hate evil and desire a holy life, and we will seek to be like Christ in all things.   "The fear of the Lord is the beginning of knowledge" (Proverbs 1:7).   When we really fear the Lord, we will turn away from all evil and hate it with a passion (Proverbs 3:7).   We will not seek to justify our sins or continue to indulge in worldliness and sin under the banner of Christian freedom.   If a man does not fear the Lord, he will not seek a holy life, and he will eventually harden his heart and fall into sin.   "Blessed is the one who fears the LORD always, but whoever hardens his heart will fall into calamity" (Proverbs 28:14).   Bad doctrine can be fixed and wrong decisions can be corrected, but if a man does not fear the Lord, he cannot be taught holiness.   There is more hope for a fool than him (Proverbs 26:12b).   A good way for us to examine our lives to determine if we fear the Lord is to examine our relationship with sin.   Do we read the Bible to find ways to justify our behavior, or do we read the Bible and conform our behavior to what it teaches?   Do we justify things we know are wrong because other Christians we know do the same thing, or do we seek to do what is right, no matter who is doing it?   If we are finding ways to justify doing things we know are wrong, or if we are following the lead of other Christians who are justifying sin, we have no fear of God.   If we find a lack of fear of God in us, we must repent and seek a life of holiness before sin destroys us.   Those who fear the Lord will have no lack.   "The reward for humility and fear of the LORD is riches and honor and life" (Proverbs 22:4).   This does not mean money, fame, and a long life, but spiritual riches, heavenly honor, and eternal life.   As we seek a holy life with a fear of God, He will bless us with sweet communion, and He will always provide for us.

Day 185

Though he was in the form of God, did not count equality with God a thing to be grasped, but emptied himself, by taking the form of a servant, being born in the likeness of men.

Philippians 2:6-7

Emphasis: Though He was in the **form of God**, did not count **equality** with God a thing to be **grasped**, but **emptied** Himself, by taking the **form of a servant**, being born in the likeness of men.

Rewrite: Although He was God, He did not count equality with God something that could be grasped. He emptied Himself of His rights and privileges in Heaven, by taking the form of a humble human servant.

Application: There is an old theory called the k*enosis* theory which states that Christ gave up some of His divine attributes when He became a man and lived on earth. Not only did no Greek scholar of the time understand this emptying to mean that Christ gave up any divine attributes, this teaching is absolutely contrary to the rest of Scripture. Colossians 1:19 says: "For in him all the fullness of God was pleased to dwell." If Jesus gave up any of His divine attributes then He would not have been fully God. If Jesus was not fully God then He could have never satisfied the divine justice of God in our place. If Jesus was not fully God then we are still in our sins and our faith is in vain. The *kenosis* theory is heresy because it denies the deity of Christ and ultimately the atonement. What Paul was explaining to the Philippians is that Christ gave up His rights, His privileges, and His status in Heaven so that He could enter the world, born of a woman, and live as a humble, fully human servant. Being found in human form, He humbled Himself by becoming obedient to the point of death on a cross. This emptying Himself was part of becoming fully human while still holding all of His divine attributes as one who is fully God. Jesus never entered the world as a conquering king, as the Jews expected; He entered as a humble carpenter. Though He was rich, yet for your sake He became poor (2 Corinthians 8:9b). This emptying was a change of role and status, not divine attributes. Meditating on this act of emptying Himself should leave us in amazement of the love and sacrifice of Jesus for us.

Day 186

Indeed, I count everything as loss because of the surpassing worth of knowing Christ Jesus my Lord.

Philippians 3:8

Emphasis: Indeed, I count everything as **loss** because of the **surpassing worth** of knowing **Christ Jesus** my Lord.

Rewrite: I count everything that I gained in this world as loss because of the infinite value of knowing Christ as my Lord.

Application: Paul had gained much in the world before God saved him. He tells of his worldly gain and the worthlessness of it in the previous verses. He says "though I myself have reason for confidence in the flesh also. If anyone else thinks he has reason for confidence in the flesh, I have more: circumcised on the eighth day, of the people of Israel, of the tribe of Benjamin, a Hebrew of Hebrews; as to the law, a Pharisee; as to zeal, a persecutor of the church; as to righteousness under the law, blameless. But whatever gain I had, I counted as loss for the sake of Christ" (vv. 4-7). Jesus describes the kingdom of Heaven in the same way. In Matthew 13:45–46 Jesus says, "Again, the kingdom of heaven is like a merchant in search of fine pearls, who, on finding one pearl of great value, went and sold all that he had and bought it." When we were lost in the world and without Christ, we sought to build up our own empires and gain the world for ourselves. Even as Christians, we sometimes hold high our social status, our wealth, our education, or our business skills. Paul did the same thing, but after he was enlightened to the knowledge of the truth, he counted all of his worldly gain as a loss because of the surpassing worth of knowing Christ Jesus as his Lord. When we encounter the living God through faith in Jesus Christ, we will want nothing else in this world but Him. We will gladly give all we have gained in this life for a glimpse of Christ. Jesus is the pearl of great price that we abandon everything to gain. The strong words, "surpassing worth of knowing Christ" are words to meditate on today. If we gained the whole universe as a gift, it would be infinitely inferior to the gift of knowing Christ. What are we doing with this privilege and gift?

Day 187

He shall lay his hand on the head of the burnt offering, and it shall be accepted for him to make atonement for him.

Leviticus 1:4

Emphasis: He shall lay his hand on the head of the **burnt offering**, and it shall be **accepted** for him to make **atonement** for him.

Rewrite: Lay your hand on the head of the burnt offering, and God will accept its death in your place to make atonement for you.

Application: By reading Leviticus we can see the holiness of God and the great cost of atonement and forgiveness. The whole sacrificial system that we see in Leviticus foreshadows what Jesus Christ did on the cross. The animal sacrifices look forward to the sacrifice of the Lamb of God offering Himself up for a one time atonement. The burnt offering needed to be a male without blemish (v. 3). It had to be offered by free will, and it had to be killed to make atonement (v. 4). The burnt offering was killed before the Lord (v. 2) and publicly (v. 3). Jesus Christ met the requirements of the burnt offering. He was a male without blemish (1 Peter 1:19). He went to the cross by His own free will (John 10:17). He was killed to make atonement (Romans 5:11). He was killed before the Lord (Isaiah 53), and He was killed publicly (Luke 24:18). The man bringing the offering before the Lord first placed his hand on the animal's head, identifying himself with the victim. This symbolized the transfer of sin to the offering. We see this act in Jesus as well; 2 Corinthians 5:21 says, "For our sake he made him to be sin who knew no sin." The burnt offering was accepted as pardon for sin. The death of the burnt offering pardons the guilty man. It says in Hebrews 2:17 that Jesus, as our high priest, made propitiation for sin. Jesus made a one time sacrifice of Himself to atone for the sins of the people. Hebrews 10:11-12 give great insight to the failings of these offering but the perfection of Christ's offering: "And every priest stands daily at his service, offering repeatedly the same sacrifices, which can never take away sins. But when Christ had offered for all time a single sacrifice for sins, he sat down at the right hand of God." In a single offering of Himself, Christ made a permanent atonement for the sins of His people.

Day 188

For it is God who works in you, both to will and to work for his good pleasure.

Philippians 2:13

Emphasis: For it is **God** who works in you, both **to will** and **to work** for His good pleasure.

Rewrite: God gives you both the desire and ability to serve Him, because He is pleased to do so.

Application: God causes us to work for Him as His slaves. He also changes our wills so that our desire is to be His slave. When the Spirit of God regenerates us and gives us a new heart and new desires, we become willing slaves of God to do His work. Since God gives us the desire and ability to work for Him, are we doing anything? I once heard an illustration about this verse. A father gave his children some money so they could buy him a gift. The father participated in this work by giving the money, driving the children to the store, and enabling them in many ways. The children participated when they bought the gift with their father's money and when they gave the gift to him. Both the father and the children participated in the work. Even though the father could have bought his own gift apart from the children, for his good pleasure, he allowed his children to participate and do this work with him. Is it not the same with God? God can do His work without our help, but because of His good pleasure, He gives us the desire and ability to participate in this work with Him. God calls us and enables us to do His work in a crooked and twisted generation. God gives His children the desire and the ability to live opposite of the world and to stand out as lights in the darkness (v. 15). The disgruntled businessman grumbles at his boss and company when he works. We work for the Lord, so we are called to do all things without grumbling or disputing (v. 14). "Whatever you do, work heartily, as for the Lord and not for men, knowing that from the Lord you will receive the inheritance as your reward. You are serving the Lord Christ" (Colossians 3:23–24). Today we must examine our attitudes about doing any kind of work, since all work is serving Christ. Have we been grumbling or disputing over the work God has given us?

Day 189 – Your Meditation

Do nothing from selfish ambition or conceit, but in humility count others more significant than yourselves

Philippians 2:3

Read: Philippians 2:1-11

Emphasis:_____

_____

_____

Rewrite:_____

_____

_____

Application:_____

_____

_____

_____

_____

_____

_____

_____

_____

_____

_____

_____

_____

_____

_____

_____

_____

_____

_____

_____

Day 190

Delight yourself in the LORD,
and he will give you the desires of your heart.

Psalm 37:4

Emphasis: **Delight** yourself in the **LORD**, and He will give you the **desires** of your heart.

Rewrite: As you delight in the Lord, He will change your desires to become His desires and then give them to you.

Application: To delight in something is to have extreme satisfaction in it. We should have extreme satisfaction in every attribute, word, and work of God. We should delight in the will of God because it is perfect, and it is working out all things for His glory and our good. One way to delight in God is to mediate on His Word, His work, and His person. As we delight in God, our desires will be pure, and we will only desire things that are pleasing to God. Often times people twist this verse and think that God will give them the desires of their heart no matter what. This is horrifying when you understand the depravity of the human heart. I'm so glad God did not give me the desires of my heart because I would have destroyed my life a long time ago. If your desires are carnal and not glorifying to God then you can be sure you are not delighting in God. The amazing thing is that God changes the heart, and when He does, we get more joy out of delighting in God and doing His will than we have ever received from fulfilling any carnal desire. We are instructed in this Psalm that if we are to delight in God then we must trust in Him (v. 3), commit our ways to Him (v. 5), wait patiently for Him (v. 6), and refrain from anger (v. 8). When we practice these things our hearts begin to conform to the will of God. When we delight in His way, our steps are established by Him (v. 23). When our steps are established in the way of the Lord, we are promised that the Lord will uphold us (v. 24), supply our needs (v. 25), and preserve us forever (v. 28). Today, as we meditate on this verse, we must examine our own hearts to see what we delight in. Are we delighting in carnal, worldly pleasures, or are we delighting in the person, work, and will of God? Does our joy come from the things of God or from worldly gain and carnal experiences?

Day 191

And my God will supply every need of yours according to his riches in glory in Christ Jesus.

Philippians 4:19

Emphasis: And my God will **supply** every **need** of yours according to His **riches in glory in Christ Jesus.**

Rewrite: My God will provide your needs from His riches in glory that we have in Christ Jesus.

Application: For two years the church in Philippi had lost touch with Paul. They did not know where he was after he had been arrested in Jerusalem and then put in prison. They apologized to him for not having contact with him and for not supporting him during those years. Paul excused them by rejoicing in the Lord for their concern for him (v. 10). Verse 19 has often been misunderstood. It does not tell us that God's people will never experience a need, but it tells us God will supply the needs of His people. God sometimes does this by meeting the need and sometimes by giving His people the strength to face the need. Paul speaks of this in verse 13, stating, "I can do all things through him who strengthens me." When God supplies what we need in amazing ways, and when He gives us the strength to persevere through hardship and need, both are a gift from God and a glorious answer to prayer. Hudson Taylor often said that when God's work is done in God's way for God's glory, it will not lack for God's supply. The Philippians gave sacrificially to support the ministry of the missionary Paul, and Paul assures them that they can't out give God. It is often true that the more you give, the more God enables you to give. It is easy to trust in a budget, but God calls us to give and trust in Him. We must not trust in men or the world for our needs; we must trust God alone. We must go to Him in prayer and expect Him to supply everything we need to do His will. We must cry out with the hymn writer, who said: "I need thee, O I need thee, Ev'ry hour I need thee, O bless me now, my Saviour, I come to thee."[22] If God gave us the ultimate gift of His Son, will He not supply all our little needs? Is your giving sacrificial or comfortable?

---

22 Lowry, Robert, S. J. Vail, *I Need Thee Every Hour Sacred.* Columbia, 1909. Web

Day 192

But our citizenship is in heaven, and from it we await a Savior, the Lord Jesus Christ.

Philippians 3:20

Emphasis: But our **citizenship** is in **Heaven**, and from it we await a Savior, the Lord **Jesus Christ.**

Rewrite: We are citizens of Heaven, from where we wait for our Savior, the Lord Jesus Christ.

Application: Through Jesus Christ we have access to the Father and we are "no longer strangers and aliens, but [we] are fellow citizens with the saints and members of the household of God in Heaven" (Ephesians 2:19). The earth is not our home; Heaven is. We are no longer citizens of the country we were born in. Our citizenship is in Heaven. When we become a Christian, we are no longer an American, Peruvian, or European. We are Christians, and our culture is now a heavenly culture based on the Scripture. As citizens of Heaven, we are under Heaven's government, and Christ is our King. We receive the rights to all the benefits of the children of God because we are heirs of God and fellow heirs with Christ (Romans 8:17). We are pilgrims passing through the land on our way to Heaven. This life on earth is filled with sin and misery, so we must not focus on storing up treasures on earth. The one with the most toys still dies. We must not look at our time on this earth as the end. We must endure the hardships and trials of this life as we look forward to a perfect life in Heaven. Because of our citizenship in Heaven, we must have the attitude of John Newton, who wrote, "He is a pilgrim and a stranger here, and a citizen of Heaven. As people of fortune sometimes, in traveling, submit cheerfully to inconvenient accommodations, very different from their homes, and comfort themselves with thinking they are not always to live so; so the Christian is not greatly solicitous about externals. If he has them, he will use them moderately. If he has but little of them, he can make a good shift without them: he is but upon a journey, and will soon be at home."[23]

---

23 John Newton & Richard Cecil, *The Works of the Reverend John Newton, Volume 1* (London: Hamilton, Adams & Co., 1824), 539.

Day 193

All the rest of the bull—he shall carry outside the camp to a clean place,
to the ash heap, and shall burn it up on a fire of wood.

Leviticus 4:12

Emphasis: All the rest of the bull—he shall carry outside the camp to a clean place, to the ash heap, and shall burn it up on a fire of wood.

Rewrite: The rest of the sin offering shall be burned on the ash heap outside the camp.

Application: This section in Leviticus teaches how to deal with the sins of the priest and the congregation under the old covenant. Sometimes we may ask what the book of Leviticus has to do with Christians under the new covenant in the twenty-first century. Even though we are no longer under the ceremonial, dietary, and sacrificial laws, the principles of the laws and the shadows that point to Christ are very relevant and applicable to us. When we read that the sin offering must be taken away from the tabernacle and carried outside the camp to be burned in the ash heap, we see the prefigurement of the crucifixion of Christ, who is our sin offering, outside the camp. Hebrews 13:11-12 expounds this verse of Scripture in Leviticus. It says, "For the bodies of those animals whose blood is brought into the holy places by the high priest as a sacrifice for sin are burned outside the camp. So Jesus also suffered outside the gate in order to sanctify the people through his own blood." The New Testament explains this verse in light of the new covenant and the work of Christ. The entire Bible points to Christ. We also see that the sprinkling of blood is an act of purifying, (v. 6) which foreshadows Christ sprinkling His own blood to sanctify us. Not only does the author of Hebrews explain what this verse in Leviticus means regarding Christ, he explains how it applies to believers. He says in Hebrews 13:13-14, "Therefore let us go to him outside the camp and bear the reproach he endured. For here we have no lasting city, but we seek the city that is to come." We must go to Christ outside the camp and bear the reproach that comes with being His servant. We must leave behind our love of the world and our desire to be accepted by the world and embrace the approach of Christ.

Day 194

He has delivered us from the domain of darkness and transferred us to the kingdom of his beloved Son, in whom we have redemption, the forgiveness of sins.

Colossians 1:13-14

Emphasis: He has **delivered** us from the **domain** of darkness and **transferred** us to the kingdom of His **beloved Son**, in whom we have **redemption**, the **forgiveness** of sins.

Rewrite: He has delivered us from the authority of darkness and brought us into the kingdom of Jesus, in whom we have redemption.

Application: We were once a slave to sin (Romans 6:17), and our minds were once blinded by the god of this age. We could not see the light of the gospel of the glory of Christ, who is the image of God. (2 Corinthians 4:4). Jesus said that anyone who commits sin is a slave to sin (John 8:34). We were under the bondage of a harsh taskmaster. But thanks be to God through Jesus Christ our Lord, He delivered us from that body of death and gave us life (Romans 7:24-25). We have been delivered out of darkness into the kingdom of Jesus Christ, the beloved Son of the Father. "In him we have redemption through his blood, the forgiveness of our trespasses, according to the riches of his grace" (Ephesians 1:7). What an amazing work to meditate on for all eternity. Today it would be helpful to meditate on our lives in the darkness and where we would be now if God did not deliver us through Christ. That thought should be terrifying. We can rejoice greatly because we are not in darkness any longer. We have been delivered by the precious blood of the Lamb and have been brought into His kingdom. Our sins are forgiven; we have been redeemed. We have been bought with a price. Our souls have been ransomed by the blood of Christ. We were like the notorious prisoner, Barabbas, who was condemned but then released because Jesus stood in his place. Jesus should have been released, but the wretched Barabbas was allowed to go free instead. What a high price our salvation cost Jesus. He took all our sin and bore all our punishment so we could go free. The innocent died for the guilty. What an amazing salvation and what a worthy and amazing God we have.

Day 195

And he is before all things, and in him all things hold together.

Colossians 1:17

Emphasis: And He is **before** all things, and in Him all things **hold together.**

Rewrite: He Himself is before all things, and He holds everything together.

Application: Jesus Christ is sustaining everything that exists. He upholds the universe by the word of His power (Hebrews 1:3). The planets stay in orbit because Christ is upholding them. The earth remains the perfect distance from the sun to make tomatoes ripen, all because Jesus is upholding the earth. The reason that asteroids, the sun, floods, storms, droughts, and volcanoes do not destroy the earth is because Jesus is upholding them. The reason we are still alive and we can breathe is because we are being upheld by Jesus. All things were created by Jesus, and all things were created for Him (v. 16). Jesus is before all things, that is, He is preeminent. He is first in rank, dignity, honor, and power over all creation. Jesus is the head of the body, which is the Church. All the fullness of God dwells in Jesus because He is fully God (v. 19). The "whole fullness of deity dwells bodily" (Colossians 2:9) in Him. Amazingly we see that the Father is given credit for creating all things as well. Revelation 4:11 says, "Worthy are you, our Lord and God, to receive glory and honor and power, for you created all things, and by your will they existed and were created." We know this is the Father because He is holding the scroll, and Jesus is the person who takes the scroll from the Father and opens it (Revelation 5). Since both the Father and Jesus are credited with creating all things, this is either a contradiction or Jesus is God. Colossians 1:19 proves that Jesus is fully God. Jesus will also reconcile all things to Himself (v. 20), and He will judge all things for Himself. Ultimately, all things will glorify Jesus. Because of all this, Jesus is worthy to be worshiped. An amazing thought to meditate on concerning Jesus holding all things together is that when the Romans were killing Him on the cross, Jesus was upholding them and giving them life and the strength to kill Him.

Day 196 – Your Meditation

Do not be anxious about anything, but in everything by prayer and supplication with thanksgiving let your requests be made known to God. And the peace of God, which surpasses all understanding, will guard your hearts and your minds in Christ Jesus.

Philippians 4:6-7

Read: Philippians 4:1-9

Emphasis:_____
_____
_____

Rewrite:_____
_____
_____

Application:_____
_____
_____
_____
_____
_____
_____
_____
_____
_____
_____
_____
_____
_____
_____
_____
_____
_____
_____

Day 197

As a deer pants for flowing streams, so pants my soul for you, O God.
My soul thirsts for God, for the living God.

Psalm 42:1-2

Emphasis: As a deer pants for flowing streams, **so pants my soul for you, O God.**

Rewrite: As a deer thirsts for water, my soul thirsts for you, O God.

Application: This Psalm is about a man with depression (v. 5). He is not depressed because he does not have friends, nor because he is having family problems, nor because he keeps falling into sin, nor because of the variety of reasons that people are depressed today. He is depressed because he is unable to gather with the congregation and worship God. He has a hunger and thirst for God and because he is unable to gather with the people of God, he is desperately depressed. He questions: "When shall I come and appear before God? My tears have been my food day and night" (vv. 2-3). To make matters worse, others are mocking him because of his separation. The Psalmist says, "As with a deadly wound in my bones, my adversaries taunt me, while they say to me all the day long, 'Where is your God?'" (v. 10) All this man wants to do is get to the place of worship and worship God with the people of God. This song was sung corporately so that the congregation would develop a longing for corporate worship. Do we have the same attitude when we are hindered from gathering with the body of Christ? Are we thinking about worshiping God with the church throughout the week? Is Sunday the highlight of our week? Do we mourn when we are separated from the people of God? How different are our attitudes in this age? Often times people only gather with the church if they can't find an excuse to be absent. Their attitude is that going to worship God with the church is not really necessary. We must ask, "Why? Why don't we have the same attitude about worshiping God with the church as the Psalmist does?" I believe it comes down to our relationship with God. The reason we don't have a desperate longing to gather with the church to worship is because we don't have a desperate longing for God. We don't thirst for corporate worship because we don't thirst for God.

Day 198

And fire came out from before the LORD and consumed the burnt offering and the pieces of fat on the altar, and when all the people saw it, they shouted and fell on their faces.

Leviticus 9:24

Emphasis: And **fire** came out from before the LORD and **consumed** the burnt offering and the pieces of fat on the altar, and when all the people saw it, they shouted and **fell on their faces**.

Rewrite: Fire came from the Lord and consumed the offering, and when the people saw it, they fell on their faces in fear.

Application: The fire for the first burnt offering was not started by man, rather it came from Heaven. From this point on the fire was to be kept burning on the altar continually and never go out (Leviticus 6:13). The same thing happened when Solomon offered the first burnt offering from the Temple (2 Chronicles 7:1) and with Elijah's offering before the prophets of Baal (1 Kings 18:38). This continual burning shows that continual sacrifices must be made because of the continual committing of sin. Christ would later come and offer Himself as the one-time, perfect sacrifice that would end all sacrifices. Hebrews 10:11-14 says, "And every priest stands daily at his service, offering repeatedly the same sacrifices, which can never take away sins. But when Christ had offered for all time a single sacrifice for sins, he sat down at the right hand of God, waiting from that time until his enemies should be made a footstool for his feet. For by a single offering he has perfected for all time those who are being sanctified." Just as God demonstrated that He accepted Aaron's offering by sending fire from Heaven to consume it, God also demonstrated that He accepted Jesus' self-sacrificial offering by consuming Him and three days later raising Him from the dead. It says in Leviticus 9:23 that when the fire came down from Heaven, "the glory of the Lord appeared to all the people." Their reaction to this was to shout and fall on their faces with fear and reverence. When the glory of the Lord appeared at Calvary in the death of Christ, the fear of God also fell on the people. If God accepted Christ's sacrifice, should we not fall on our face in fear and reverence when we encounter the living Christ?

Day 199

See to it that no one takes you captive by philosophy and empty deceit, according to human tradition, according to the elemental spirits of the world, and not according to Christ.

Colossians 2:8

Emphasis: See to it that no one takes you **captive** by **philosophy** and empty deceit, according to **human tradition**, according to the elemental spirits of the world, and not according to **Christ.**

Rewrite: Don't let anyone deceive you by their worldly philosophy and human traditions which are from the spirits of the world and not Christ.

Application: Just as there were false teachers in Colossae who were spreading their deceitful philosophies and making people hold to their human traditions, there are false teachers today, and there will be false teachers until Christ returns. Today, inside the Church, we see worldly philosophies that seek to conform the Church to the world, which is a deceitful scheme that can be traced back to the spirits of the world. We also see human tradition that is equally deceptive. In 1545, the Catholic Church deemed their traditions to have equal authority with the Scriptures. This is grossly deceitful and allows people to make their own rules to suit themselves, apart from the very words of God. The results of this heretical doctrine are seen in the year 1562 when the Catholic Church changed the Ten Commandments to remove the commandment to not worship graven images. Later in 1872, the pope was declared to be infallible, and human tradition holds this to be truth today. All of these philosophies and human traditions are in direct contradiction to Christ and the Scriptures. Paul declared that Christ is the treasure of all wisdom and knowledge (Colossians 2:3). All wisdom and truth comes from Christ, who claimed He was the Truth (John 14:6). Whenever we develop ideas or listen to the ideas of others that do not come from Christ or are in contradiction to Christ, they are deceitful lies that can ultimately only come from the influence of demonic forces. Therefore, we must always weigh all our thoughts and the thoughts of others against the infallible Scriptures. If the Bible is in contradiction with someone's idea or teaching, the Bible is always correct and the teaching is wrong.

Day 200

You shall therefore be holy, for I am holy.

Leviticus 11:45b

Emphasis: You shall therefore be **holy**, for I am holy.

Rewrite: Because I am holy, you must be holy.

Application: God gave the law to Israel to teach them that which is holy. They were to learn how to discern between good and evil. Because God is holy, perfect, and set apart from sin, He will not tolerate unholiness and sin in His people. The Lord calls His people to dedicate their lives to holiness. Without being perfectly separate from sin, it is impossible to have a relationship or communion with God. In the book of Hebrews, we are called to strive for the holiness without which no one will see the Lord (Hebrews 12:14). Though we must strive for holiness and separate ourselves from sin, we realize that it is impossible to be perfectly holy in this life on earth for the law shows us our depravity. The need to be perfectly holy and our sinful inability to be holy points to the fact that we need a perfectly holy Savior. Hebrews 7:26–28 explains this, "For it was indeed fitting that we should have such a high priest, holy, innocent, unstained, separated from sinners, and exalted above the Heavens. He has no need, like those high priests, to offer sacrifices daily, first for his own sins and then for those of the people, since he did this once for all when he offered up himself. For the law appoints men in their weakness as high priests, but the word of the oath, which came later than the law, appoints a Son who has been made perfect forever." We need the perfect Son to be our substitute, savior, and high priest forever. The law points us to Christ as the only way to be reconciled to God. We tried to be perfect ourselves but failed miserably. When God saves us we are set apart from sin to Christ. When we die as a Christian, we will be made perfectly holy, however, we have not attained it yet. In this life, because we still have a sinful nature and struggle with sin, we must be constantly examining ourselves, repenting of our sin, and striving to mortify sin in our lives. As we grow in the knowledge of holiness, we must grow in practical holiness and never justify or be content with sin. Be holy as God is holy.

Day 201

Set your minds on things that are above, not on things that are on earth.

Colossians 3:2

Emphasis: Set your **minds** on things that are **above**, not on things that are on **earth.**

Rewrite: Be thinking continually on the things of Heaven, not on earthly things.

Application: The theme of the letter to the Colossians is Christ and His glory. In chapter 3 Paul exhorts the believers in the church to place their focus rightly upon Christ. He says in verse one that if you have been raised with Christ, if you are really a Christian, then you should seek the things that are above, where Christ is, seated at the right hand of God. Christ should be the focus of our thinking because our lives are hidden with Christ (v. 3), and Christ Himself is our life (v. 4). All sin starts in our minds. Before we sin, we first think about it. James makes this clear: "You desire and do not have, so you murder. You covet and cannot obtain, so you fight and quarrel" (James 4:2). In Matthew 5, Jesus teaches that what we focus on in our mind will be judged as sin. He says that lusting is considered adultery in the heart. Because sin starts in the heart, Paul exhorts the Colossians to put to death what is earthly in them, which is sexual immorality, impurity, passion, evil desire, and covetousness, which is idolatry (v. 5). He adds anger, wrath, malice, slander, obscene talk, and lying to the list of sins in which they once walked (v. 8). Paul says that the Christian has put off his old way of life and now has a new way of life in Christ that is being renewed in knowledge after the image of Christ (v. 10). This is sanctification, which is not an option for the believer. If you are in Christ, you will die more and more to these sins and conform more and more to Christ. Your thinking will change from earthly minded to heavenly minded. After Paul teaches what the Christian should put to death in themselves, he exhorts them positively with what they should "put on." He says the Christian must put on a compassionate heart, kindness, humility, meekness, and patience, along with forgiveness and love, which binds everything together in perfect harmony. The word of Christ must dwell in us richly.

Day 202

Continue steadfastly in prayer, being watchful in it with thanksgiving.

Colossians 4:2

Emphasis: Continue **steadfastly** in **prayer**, being **watchful** in it with **thanksgiving.**

Rewrite: Devote yourself to prayer, stay awake, and be thankful.

Application: Paul must exhort the Colossians to continue steadfastly in prayer because prayer seems to be something with which most Christians struggle. In prayer, we have the privilege of going before the throne of grace and offering up our desires to God with a thankful acknowledgment of His mercies. Prayer is the means that God uses to accomplish His will. Going to God in prayer is more effectual than doing a thousand things. It is not necessarily that there is power in prayer itself, like is so commonly said, but there is power in the God to whom we pray. Knowing all of this, it is surprising that Christians struggle with prayer. Our sinful natures make prayer difficult because we would rather be doing something physically in our own strength. Also in our nature, we struggle with laziness, lack of zeal, faith and love, which prevent us from praying effectually. There is also an enormous spiritual battle when a believer locks himself away, alone with God to pour out his supplications. Often our minds are so preoccupied with the worries of the world or the thoughts of the day that the first half hour of prayer is ineffectual. Because God answers prayers, the devil tries to hinder them. John Wesley insisted that continual employment should always accompany watchfulness and prayer. For grace fills a vacuum as well as nature; and the devil fills whatever God does not fill. When we are not praying, we will be doing something less productive. We must be watchful in prayer so that we know what to pray for. We must not be vague but specific in our prayers. We are to also be thankful in our prayers. The reason we are to be thankful is because God really does answer our prayers, and He deserves our thanks. If an answered prayer was like winning the lottery, we would have reason to lose hope. But God answers prayers continually, and the more that we pray, the more we will see answered prayers, and the more we will be thankful to God.

Day 203 – Your Meditation

...we have been approved by God to be entrusted with the gospel, so we speak, not to please man, but to please God who tests our hearts.

1 Thessalonians 2:4

Read: 1 Thessalonians 2:1-12

Emphasis:_____

_____

_____

Rewrite:_____

_____

_____

Application:_____

_____

_____

_____

_____

_____

_____

_____

_____

_____

_____

_____

_____

_____

_____

_____

_____

Day 204

For we know, brothers loved by God, that he has chosen you, because our gospel came to you not only in word, but also in power and in the Holy Spirit and with full conviction.

1 Thessalonians 1:4-5

Emphasis: For **we know**, brothers loved by God, that He has **chosen** you, **because** our gospel came to you not only in word, but also in **power** and in the Holy Spirit and with **full conviction**.

Rewrite: Brothers loved by God, we know that God has chosen you because the gospel, in its power and in the Holy Spirit with conviction, has changed you.

Application: People sometimes ask how they know if they are the elect, chosen by God for salvation. In Paul's letter to the Thessalonians, he explains that there is evidence. Paul is confident that these Thessalonian Christians have been chosen by God for several reasons. One reason was that when they preached the gospel, something happened. They did not only hear the words of life, they responded. The Holy Spirit made the gospel effectual to their hearing with power and conviction of sin. The Thessalonians heard and then responded in repentance and faith in Jesus Christ. They turned to God from idols to serve the living and true God (v. 9) and put their trust in Jesus to deliver them from the wrath to come (v. 10). Their election was evidenced by a changed life. The Thessalonians became imitators of the Lord by receiving the Word in much affliction but with pure joy of the Holy Spirit (v. 6). The election of the Thessalonian Christians was further evidenced by what they did with the gospel. They took the gospel and proclaimed it everywhere in faith (v.8). Conviction of sin, repentance, faith, a changed life-style, evangelism, and pure joy in affliction was the evidence of the Thessalonians' election and salvation. Has this been your experience as well? Have these changes been evidenced in your life? These are the marks of true salvation and evidence of your election. If these are not present in your life, then there is no evidence of your salvation or election. Thinking you are a Christian does not make you a Christian. We must examine ourselves to see if we are in the faith.

Day 205

For every beast of the forest is mine, the cattle on a thousand hills.
I know all the birds of the hills, and all that moves in the field is mine.

Psalm 50:10-11

Emphasis: For **every beast** of the forest is mine, the **cattle** on a thousand hills. I know all the **birds** of the hills, and **all that moves** in the field is **mine.**

Rewrite: Every animal in the forest, every cattle and bird in the hills, and everything that moves in the field is mine.

Application: This Psalm of Asaph is a picture of God summoning all the earth to judgment (v. 1). God calls out Israel for their meaningless rituals. Israel fell into the rut of going through the motions in their sacrifices and offerings. Their hearts were far from where they should have been. The sacrifices that they continually offered to God should have made them think of their continual sin and the need for a sacrifice, but they thought by offering sacrifices they were doing God a favor. God rebukes them by saying that He needs nothing from them because every beast of the forest is His, even the cattle on a thousand hills. God knows all the birds of the hills, and all that moves in the field is His. In fact, the world and its fullness are His. God even says, "If I were hungry, I would not tell you" (v. 12), to make the point that He owns everything and they are only giving Him something that is His already. God wants a broken and contrite spirit, not a bull. These rituals remind us that we are sinners who constantly sin and need a Savior to be reconciled to God and draw near to Him. We are required to do what God calls us to do in the Scriptures, but if we only check things off a list, we could be in sin. We can be in horrible sin yet we gather with the church, we tithe, we pray, we read our Bible, and we do good to others. The Pharisees fell into this trap and became legalists by outwardly following the law while inwardly being wicked. God calls us to do these things, but He does not need them. He is not more satisfied or content when we do them. He owns everything, and all of creation was made to glorify Him. The reality is that God needs nothing from us, but we need everything from God. We must know this reality to serve God with a pure heart.

Day 206

When you received the word of God, which you heard from us, you accepted it not as the word of men but as what it really is, the word of God, which is at work in you believers.

1 Thessalonians 2:13

Emphasis: When you received the **word of God**, which you heard from us, you **accepted it** not as the word of men but as **what it really is**, the word of God, which is at work in you believers.

Rewrite: When you received the word of God from us, you accepted our words, not as simply our own ideas, but as the very words of God, which it truly is and which is effectually working in you.

Application: Paul is claiming that the words he spoke to the Thessalonians are the very words of God. The words were not the words of men but the very words of God. Paul claims that his words came from God and had absolute divine authority. This is a bold statement, but Peter validated this claim when he said that Paul's teachings were equal with the other Scriptures (2 Peter 3:15-16). The Bible was written by men who were inspired by God, and every word in the Scripture was ordained to be in the Canon of Scripture. "[No] prophecy of Scripture comes from someone's own interpretation. For no prophecy was ever produced by the will of man, but men spoke from God as they were carried along by the Holy Spirit" (2 Peter 1:20–21). The Bible was written over a period of 1,600 years by more than 40 writers from three different continents, who wrote in three different languages, yet they wrote with harmony. The Bible was the first book ever printed, and since then it has been printed and read more than any other book. The Bible has been translated into more than 1,400 languages. Over the years the Bible has survived, unlike other ancient books. No other book has as many copies of the ancient manuscripts as the Bible. There are over 24,000 copies of New Testament manuscripts, some written within 35 years of the writer's death. The Bible has been attacked more than any book in history, yet it still stands strong, and each year science, history, archaeology, and prophecy prove that the Bible is powerful, inspired, eternal, and sufficient. We can trust, rely, and depend on it.

Day 207

For this is the will of God, your sanctification

1 Thessalonians 4:3

Emphasis: For this is the **will of God**, your **sanctification.**

Rewrite: The will of God is for you to be holy.

Application: As Christians we must strive for practical holiness each day. We must die to sin more and more and live to righteousness. We must become less like our old selves and more like Christ in our character and actions. We must look less like the world and more like Christ. Paul contrasts the lives of pagans to the lives of Christians and urges the Thessalonians to walk in a manner worthy of God (1 Thessalonians 2:12). He gives brief instructions concerning sanctification in verses 3 through 12. He urges them to abstain from sexual immorality, control their own bodies in holiness and honor, to love one another, to live a quiet life, to mind their own affairs, and to work hard. The world does the opposite of these things; so as we are sanctified, we die to these things and live like Christ. Many people struggle with finding the will of God for their lives, but the Scripture is clear what the will of God is for a believer. The will of God is our sanctification, "[f]or God has not called us for impurity, but in holiness (1 Thessalonians 4:3-7). We can never justify being unholy. As we learn more of what holiness is, we examine our lives, repent, and conform to Christ. This is a continual process that we will never achieve perfectly until we die and are made holy because of Christ. Living a holy life is pleasing to God, and we are called to please God, not men (v. 1). Sanctification is a gift, a command, and a guarantee. If you are truly a Christian, sanctification is not an option. God will complete the work He has started in you. Even though God will never be more pleased with us than He is now, because His pleasure in us is based on the righteousness of Christ, we are still called to please God. It is His will that we walk in holiness. If the will of God is our sanctification, we should never be content with where we are in our spiritual walk, and we should always be striving for holiness and to become more like Christ.

Day 208

Then we who are alive, who are left, will be caught up together with them in the clouds to meet the Lord in the air, and so we will always be with the Lord.

1 Thessalonians 4:17

Emphasis: Then we who are alive, who are left, will be caught up together with them in the clouds to **meet the Lord** in the air, and so we **will always be with the Lord**.

Rewrite: We who are still alive will be caught up together with them to meet the Lord in the air, and then we will be with the Lord forever.

Application: Paul's purpose in teaching the Thessalonians about the second coming of Christ was to encourage, not divide. Paul says, "Therefore encourage one another with these words" (v. 18). When we read about the return of Christ, we should be comforted and encouraged to press on. We should not have fear or be divided. We should not take the details of Christ's return and use it as a point of division between Christians. It is sinful to cause division in the body of Christ over unclear details, and if we find ourselves in a divisive argument over this subject, then we have missed the purpose of Paul's teaching. Paul's point in this teaching is to comfort the believers who are still alive assuring them that their dead loved ones who have died in Christ will be with Him in His second coming. At the second coming of Christ, the dead in Christ will rise first. Then all who are still alive on earth will be caught up together with them to meet the Lord in the air (vv. 16-17). The greatest hope and encouragement is that we will forever be with Christ (v. 17). The Puritan Richard Sibbes (1577-1635), said, "Heaven is not Heaven without Christ. It is better to be in any place with Christ than to be in Heaven itself without him."[24] To meditate on the fact that we will be with Christ for all eternity should give us tremendous encouragement to press on through any hardship that we will face in this life. We look forward to this day, and we should always encourage others to do the same.

---

24 Richard Sibbes, "Christ Is Best Or St.Paul's Strait," in The Complete Works of Richard Sibbes (Edinburgh: James Nichol, 1862), 1:339.

Day 209

Mankind will say, "Surely there is a reward for the righteous; surely there is a God who judges on earth."

Psalm 58:11

Emphasis: Mankind will say, "Surely there is a **reward** for the righteous; surely there is a **God who judges** on earth."

Rewrite: Everyone will say that there is a reward for those who do what is right and there is a God who judges all.

Application: This Psalm brings comfort to all those who are struggling with the injustice and corruption of leaders in their jobs, communities, or nations. Often times it seems that wicked people with wealth and power prosper and are never brought to justice. It seems that our efforts to do good and live righteously are unrewarded. This Psalm gives us two points of encouragement; namely, there is a God who will judge everything, and there is a reward for those who live for God. The wicked who are prospering on the earth will eventually stand before the living God and will know that there is a God who judges on earth and will bring forth justice. James gives this same warning to the rich oppressors who were gaining wealth by their injustice. He says, "You have lived on the earth in luxury and in self-indulgence. You have fattened your hearts in a day of slaughter. You have condemned and murdered the righteous person. He does not resist you" (James 5:5-6). Everything will catch up to you in the end. Sin always finds you out. You can't get away with injustice and sin forever. There will be a day of reckoning. God will judge the ungodly and the corrupt rulers. There is much to be said about persevering in living an upright life even when it seems that everyone around you is doing the opposite. This verse encourages us to press on toward the prize and finish the race, knowing that there is a reward for the righteous. All the corruption in politics, wicked men, and unjust gain will be brought to the end one day, and it will greatly benefit us on the day of judgment to be standing on the side of righteousness instead of wickedness. "The Lord redeems the life of his servants; none of those who take refuge in him will be condemned" (Psalm 34:22).

Day 210 – Your Meditation

In God I trust; I shall not be afraid. What can man do to me?

Psalm 56:11

Read: Psalm 56

Emphasis:_____

_____

_____

Rewrite:_____

_____

_____

Application:_____

_____

_____

_____

_____

_____

_____

_____

_____

_____

_____

_____

_____

_____

_____

_____

_____

_____

_____

_____

Day 211

We ask you, brothers, to respect those who labor among you and are over you in the Lord and admonish you, and to esteem them very highly in love because of their work.

1 Thessalonians 5:12-13a

Emphasis: We ask you, brothers, to **respect** those who labor among you and are **over you in the Lord** and admonish you, and to **esteem** them very highly in **love** because of their **work**.

Rewrite: Brothers, respect, honor, and esteem those who are your leaders in the Lord's work.

Application: Christians are exhorted to respect and esteem their leaders highly. The elders in the church have an overwhelming responsibility to shepherd the flock of God. They work tirelessly for little pay. They not only have their own troubles and burdens, but they share in the troubles and burdens of the entire congregation. They must pour their whole life into the people in the congregation so that they can present them mature in Christ (Colossians 1:28). The leaders, who are the teachers of the church, will be judged more strictly (James 3:1) for what they teach and their responsibilities, so they have constant pressure on them. They have given up the world for God, and they care greatly for souls entrusted to their care. The leaders don't need people to show up to service with a critical spirit and pick apart the sermon that they just spent the whole week preparing. They are entrusted with your spiritual growth which should earn them respect, honor, and esteem. Hebrews 13:17 says, "Obey your leaders and submit to them, for they are keeping watch over your souls, as those who will have to give an account. Let them do this with joy and not with groaning, for that would be of no advantage to you." We must not be the person that continually makes the pastor groan because of our prideful, critical attitudes that stir up contention in the church and make the pastor's life miserable. We must respect, honor, and esteem our leaders and imitate them as they imitate Christ. Again the author of Hebrews exhorts us, "Remember your leaders, those who spoke to you the word of God. Consider the outcome of their way of life, and imitate their faith" (Hebrews 13:7).

Day 212

Whoever blasphemes the name of the LORD shall surely be put to death.

Leviticus 24:16a

Emphasis: Whoever **blasphemes** the **name** of the **LORD** shall surely be put to **death.**

Rewrite: Whoever blasphemes the name of the Lord must die.

Application: Whoever speaks of God or His name in an impious or irreverent way is in sin. Exodus 20:7 says, "You shall not take the name of the LORD your God in vain, for the LORD will not hold him guiltless who takes his name in vain." When we speak of God and His name in vain, we are guilty, and we will give an account for this blasphemy. The Westminster Shorter Catechism says that the Third Commandment "requires the holy and reverent use of God's names, titles, attributes, ordinances, Word, and works" and that it is forbidden to profane or abuse anything by which God makes Himself known.[25] In this passage, an Israelite woman's son blasphemed the name of God and cursed. They brought him to Moses and stoned him because "whoever curses his God shall bear his sin. Whoever blasphemes the name of the LORD shall surely be put to death" (Leviticus 24:15–16). God is holy and His name is holy. He is the High and Lofty One Who inhabits eternity, whose name is Holy (Isaiah 57:15). The Jewish people have held the name of God with high reverence throughout the centuries. The Hebrew name for God, YHWH, is never pronounced out loud in Judaism. When it appears in Scripture, the reader substitutes the Hebrew word "*adonai*" which means "my lord." Any book that contains this name written in Hebrew is treated with reverence. The name is never destroyed nor erased, and any writings containing the name cannot be thrown away according to Jewish law. We know God holds His name high in reverence and does not tolerate the blasphemy of His name. We know that when we use His name irreverently or as a cuss word, we are guilty of sin, and we will be held accountable. The question is, why do we take this so lightly? Why do we use the holiest name that exists in a way that God hates? We must examine how we blaspheme God, repent, and radically change our lives.

---

25 *The Westminster Shorter Catechism*, 1647. Questions 54 and 55

Day 213

When the Lord Jesus is revealed from heaven with his mighty angels in flaming fire, inflicting vengeance on those who do not know God and on those who do not obey the gospel of our Lord Jesus.

2 Thessalonians 1:7-8

Emphasis: When the **Lord Jesus** is **revealed** from Heaven with His mighty angels in flaming fire, inflicting **vengeance** on those who **do not know God** and on those who **do not obey the gospel** of our Lord Jesus.

Rewrite: When the Lord Jesus appears from Heaven with His mighty angels in flaming fire, bringing judgment and wrath on those who do not know God and on those who rejected the gospel.

Application: Just as with the letter of 1 Thessalonians, the return of Christ is the main theme in 2 Thessalonians. We see from this verse that relief will come to the Christians who are being afflicted and persecuted when Jesus returns. The Lord Jesus will leave Heaven and return to earth visibly with His mighty angels in flaming fire. Jesus will not return as a humble carpenter who came to seek and save the lost; He will be in His resurrected body, full of glory, striking fear and awe in every unbeliever. His purpose for returning is to inflict vengeance on those who do not know God and on those who have not obeyed His gospel. "They will suffer the punishment of eternal destruction, away from the presence of the Lord and from the glory of his might" (v. 9). The enemies of God will not necessarily be away from the presence of Christ. Revelation 14:10-11 describes the torment of the enemies of God. They "will drink the wine of God's wrath, poured full strength into the cup of his anger, and he will be tormented with fire and sulfur in the presence of the holy angels and in the presence of the Lamb. And the smoke of their torment goes up forever and ever, and they have no rest, day or night." They will be punished in the presence of the Lamb but away from the presence of the Lord's saving grace. These enemies are those who did not obey the gospel. Obeying the gospel is not an option. God commands all men everywhere to repent and obey the gospel. For those who rebel, this is their fate. Jesus is coming soon, and whether you die and stand before Him or He returns, all must stand before Him.

Day 214

A soft answer turns away wrath, but a harsh word stirs up anger.

Proverbs 15:1

Emphasis: A **soft** answer **turns away** wrath, but a **harsh** word **stirs up** anger.

Rewrite: A gentle answer calms an angry man, but a harsh word infuriates him.

Application: This is a verse that can be tested and proved to be true. How often is an argument intensified when tempers flare from both parties involved.   An old saying is that when emotions run high, discernment runs low.   When anger runs high, irrationality is soon to follow. It is amazing to see a furious man, venting all his frustrations on his wife, humbled and calmed by one soft word. He expects her to be furious, and he wants her to blow up and act as irrational as he, but when she responds with a gentle, loving word, he very quickly realizes his foolishness and calms down. As we meditate on this verse today, we will probably be presented with an opportunity to test it. As Christians, we must always be the people who respond to any conflict with a gentle, calm, rational, and discerning answer. If every Christian in church obeyed this verse, there would be few conflicts and many joys. The Proverbs are filled with wise sayings concerning this verse. "There is one whose rash words are like sword thrusts, but the tongue of the wise brings healing" (Proverbs 12:18). "The tongue of the wise commends knowledge, but the mouths of fools pour out folly" (Proverbs 15:2). "A gentle tongue is a tree of life, but perverseness in it breaks the spirit" (Proverbs 15:4). James 3:6 says, "And the tongue is a fire, a world of unrighteousness. The tongue is set among our members, staining the whole body, setting on fire the entire course of life, and set on fire by hell." Although no human can tame the tongue (James 3:8), a soft word can turn away its wrath for a moment. This would be a good verse to memorize and meditate on every day because it is very practical, frequently tested, and the practice of it will end most conflicts before they are out of control.

Day 215

And then the lawless one will be revealed, whom the Lord Jesus will kill with the breath of his mouth and bring to nothing by the appearance of his coming.

2 Thessalonians 2:8

Emphasis: And then the lawless one will be revealed, whom the **Lord Jesus** will **kill** with the breath of His **mouth** and bring to nothing by the appearance of **His coming.**

Rewrite: And then the lawless one will appear, who the Lord Jesus will utterly destroy with the breath of His mouth by the appearance of Himself.

Application: The lawless one, who will come by the activity of Satan, deceives many people with false signs and wonders (v. 9). These people knew the truth but refused to embrace and love the truth and be saved (v. 10) and have condemned themselves because they chose the pleasure of sin instead of believing the truth (v. 12). They are condemned already because they have not believed in the name of the only Son of God (John 3:18). These people "will not endure sound teaching, but having itching ears they accumulate for themselves teachers to suit their own passions, and turn away from listening to the truth and wander off into myths" (2 Timothy 4:3–4). They cling to Satan instead of Jesus because they think the victory is theirs, but when Jesus comes back to earth and appears in all His glory, He will kill this lawless one with the breath of His mouth, and this lawless one will come to nothing. It is a false idea and teaching that says there is a great cosmic battle between God and the devil and that the outcome is uncertain. The devil has no power over God. He is a gnat fighting against one of the granite peaks of the Andes. Even if he gathered all the fallen angels and every wicked man who has ever lived, he would have no more power against God than a candle has to fight the sun. He is a defeated foe. Like the game of chess, there are moves left on the board, but checkmate is inevitable. Jesus does not have to battle with force, one simple word utterly destroys him. If you are in Christ, the battle has already been won.

Day 216

And the anger of the LORD was kindled against Uzzah, and God struck him down there because of his error, and he died there beside the ark of God.

2 Samuel 6:7

Emphasis: And the **anger of the LORD** was kindled against Uzzah, and God struck him down there because of his **error**, and he died there beside the ark of God.

Rewrite: Uzzah made a great error which caused the anger of the Lord to be kindled against him, and God killed him beside the ark.

Application: In the world today, the average person reads this verse and is furious that God would strike down Uzzah when he was only trying to stabilize the ark when it was falling. Because of the complete disregard for holiness today, it is hard for most people to comprehend why God in His holiness would be so strict. The ark was a symbol of God's presence and the holiest object in the tabernacle. God gave very clear and implicit instructions concerning the ark and its transport. Death was promised to anyone who approached, let alone touched, this holy object unless you were an Aaronic priest (Numbers 4:15). Uzzah was not a priest and had no authority to touch it, so God killed him instantly. God is absolutely holy. He will set the standard for His work, and it will be done His way. By God killing Uzzah in His wrath, He was showing that holiness was necessary to approach Him. It was as if God was saying that He would rather have the ark hit the ground, which was infinitely more holy than Uzzah, than to allow Uzzah, who was unholy and breaking God's clear instructions, to even touch the ark. The piece of earth never sinned or rebelled against God, nor broke His laws, nor treated God in an irreverent way. We see the same thing when Moses approached the burning bush; God called out to him and said, "Do not come near; take your sandals off your feet, for the place on which you are standing is holy ground" (Exodus 3:5). Dirt is more holy than a person born into sin. This should make us see our need for Christ's imputed holiness, the seriousness of being practically holy in our daily lives as ambassadors of Christ, and to examine how we conduct our worship of God.

Day 217 – Your Meditation

As for you, brothers, do not grow weary in doing good.

2 Thessalonians 3:13

Read: 2 Thessalonians 3

Emphasis:_____
_____
_____

Rewrite:_____
_____
_____

Application:_____
_____
_____
_____
_____
_____
_____
_____
_____
_____
_____
_____
_____
_____
_____
_____
_____
_____
_____

Day 218

The aim of our charge is love that issues from a pure heart and a good conscience and a sincere faith.

1 Timothy 1:5

Emphasis: The aim of our charge is **love** that issues from a **pure heart** and a **good conscience** and a **sincere faith.**

Rewrite: The purpose of our teaching is to produce love from a pure heart and a good conscience and a true faith.

Application: Paul's charge is in context of warning Timothy about false teachers. The aim of Paul's charge is love from a pure heart, good conscience, and true faith. This is in contrast with the aim of false teachers producing division, a sinful heart, a guilty conscience, and hypocrisy. The only way that the conscience can be restored and awakened is by the Scriptures, namely the preaching of the Scriptures. The Scriptures speak to the conscience and inform it of the law of God. The Puritans spoke much about the conscience and the importance of having a good conscience that has been restored and awakened. They spoke of the different conditions of the conscience in unbelievers. Some people have a conscience that convicts of sin and threatens punishment but never gives the peace that can only come by Christ. Others have a moral conscience that causes them to do good works but that has no spiritual good because it is not motivated by the love of God. Some people have an erring conscience that misapplies the Scripture and causes wrong actions. Human traditions and false doctrine are birthed from this conscience. Others have a conscience that is asleep and dead to a sense of evil and it is ignorant of the judgment that is coming and the punishment of Hell. The worst conscience is a seared conscience that removes feeling and remorse from committing wicked sins. This conscience brings people to an almost hopeless point of ever being saved.[26] The true, regenerate conscience is shaped by Scripture and becomes more tender with sanctification. We must examine our conscience and then renew our minds in the Scripture to develop it.

---

26 Joel R. Beeke and Mark Jones, A Puritan Theology: Doctrine for Life (Grand Rapids, MI: Reformation Heritage, 2012), 916-919.

Day 219

Father of the fatherless and protector of widows is God in his holy habitation.

Psalm 68:5

Emphasis: **Father of the fatherless** and **protector of widows** is God in His holy habitation.

Rewrite: God, in His holy dwelling, is a father to orphans and a protector of widows.

Application: God is kind to people who the world generally has dismissed. God cares for the helpless. The Lord watches over the sojourners; he upholds the widow and the fatherless" (Psalm 146:9a). "He executes justice for the fatherless and the widow, and loves the sojourner, giving him food and clothing" (Deuteronomy 10:18). When someone loses their spouse or parents they will be taken care of by a loving God. God cares for the widow and orphan, and He will be for them what they lost in their parents or spouse but far better. God is the perfect Father, in contrast with the many worthless fathers on this earth, and He is the perfect protector, unlike all those who abuse the helpless in the world. The reason there are orphanages today and widows are no longer burned, abused, or forsaken, is because of the teachings of Christianity. This is what James says that true religion must include. "Religion that is pure and undefiled before God, the Father, is this: to visit orphans and widows in their affliction" (James 1:27). We must compare what the Bible teaches that we should be doing as Christians with what Christians are actually doing today. Were rest homes, nursing homes, and retirement homes (mostly in the United States) started because children, relatives, and the church stopped caring for widows? Were state run orphanages started because the church was not doing what God called it to do? We must really examine ourselves and see what we are doing personally to help widows and orphans. Taking care of the elderly, doing chores, and visiting are a great way to start fulfilling our Christian duties and modeling Christ. Adopting, visiting, or spending time with orphans may change the lives of the ones who God cares for so much.

Day 220

The saying is trustworthy and deserving of full acceptance, that Christ Jesus came into the world to save sinners, of whom I am the foremost.

1 Timothy 1:15

Emphasis: The saying is trustworthy and deserving of full acceptance, that **Christ Jesus came** into the world **to save sinners**, of whom I am the foremost.

Rewrite: This saying is true and deserves acceptance, that Christ Jesus came into the world to save sinners, and I am the worst of all.

Application: It is a comforting thought to know that Jesus did not come to earth to find righteous people. He could search the earth over all time and never find one righteous person. The cities of Sodom and Gomorrah could not even produce ten righteous people to save the city (Genesis 18:32). Before God destroyed the whole world with the flood, He saw that: "the wickedness of man was great in the earth, and that every intention of the thoughts of his heart was only evil continually" (Genesis 6:5). If our only hope of Heaven was based on our righteousness, Heaven would be empty of all people. The good news is that Jesus came to seek and save the lost (Luke 19:10). Jesus said, "Those who are well have no need of a physician, but those who are sick. I came not to call the righteous, but sinners" (Mark 2:17). Jesus came to seek and save sinners by dying a death that they deserved and living a perfect life that they were unable to live. This is the good news of the gospel. We have a loving Savior who seeks sinners. "God shows his love for us in that while we were still sinners, Christ died for us" (Romans 5:8). We have a glorious Savior and an eternal Mediator. "For there is one God, and there is one mediator between God and men, the man Christ Jesus, who gave himself as a ransom for all" (1 Timothy 2:5–6). Even if you are the worst sinner in all the world, like Paul claimed he was, there is hope for you. If you are perfectly righteous then you have no need for the Savior Jesus, but if you are a sinner then you are qualified to be saved. When we meditate on our sins and how depraved we really are, we can find great comfort in knowing that Jesus came to save sinners like us.

Day 221

...that we may lead a peaceful and quiet life, godly and dignified in every way.

1 Timothy 2:2

Emphasis: That we may lead a **peaceful** and quiet life, **godly** and **dignified** in every way.

Rewrite: Our lives must be marked by peace, quietness, godliness and dignity in every way.

Application: Paul speaks about the theme of godliness throughout this letter to Timothy. Paul wrote to Timothy so that he would know how the church should function and how people should behave in the church (1 Timothy 3:14-15). The life of a Christian must be marked by godliness. In this chapter we see what godliness should include. Prayer is a mark of godliness. A godly man or woman should be pouring out supplications, prayers, intercessions, and thanksgivings for all people. We must pray all sorts of prayers for all sorts of people. Another mark of godliness is a peaceful and quiet life, dignified in every way. We must not be marked by controversy and as one who is always arguing or stirring up trouble. Our lives should be above reproach, and we should be well thought of by those outside of the church. We must have a godly fear which drives us to active obedience to the Scriptures. Another mark of godliness is to live without anger or quarreling (1 Timothy 2:8). A mark of godliness in women is that they adorn themselves in respectable apparel, with modesty and self-control, as well as good works, love, holiness, and submissiveness (vv. 9-15). Why do we want to be marked by godliness? Because it is good, and it is pleasing in the sight of God our Savior (v. 3). When the whole congregation is seeking holiness and a godly life, the Church will function in a biblical way that glorifies God, and many conflicts will be eliminated. We must meditate on this verse and examine our lives to see what they are marked by. Would other people describe us as a man or woman of prayer who is peaceful, dignified, and obedient to the Scriptures? Or do people know us as the angry person who craves controversy and is always stirring up trouble? We are ambassadors of Jesus Christ and must strive to reflect His glory.

Day 222

Jesus Christ, who gave himself for us to redeem us from all lawlessness and to purify for himself a people for his own possession who are zealous for good works.

Titus 2:14

Emphasis: Jesus Christ, who gave Himself for us to redeem us from all lawlessness and to **purify** for Himself **a people** for His own possession who are **zealous** for good works.

Rewrite: Jesus Christ gave Himself for us to redeem us from sin and to purify for Himself a zealous people.

Application: Zeal is a consuming, constant passion for the glory of God and everything pertaining to the advancement of the Kingdom of Christ. When we understand zeal in such a way, and then look into the Christian community, we will see that zeal is most definitely lacking. At times we may see temporary zeal, fake zeal, blind zeal, and jealous zeal, but true biblical, God-centered, sacrificial zeal is a rarity. Everyone is zealous for what they love or what they hate. People are zealous for sports, politics, freedom, and television shows, but not God. The problem is not a lack of zeal but a lack of zeal for God. The reason people are not dedicated to the church, missions, holiness, and evangelism is because they lack a zeal and love for God. Jesus Christ gave Himself to redeem His people and to purify a people who are zealous for Him and for doing His will. When true, biblical zeal is planted deep into your soul by a love for Christ, you are consumed with Jesus and will do anything He has directed in the Scriptures. When Jesus says, "Go" in the Great Commission, you can do nothing but obey with a passionate excitement. You cannot love God and be lukewarm because complacently loving God is not really loving Him at all. How can we understand the gospel of a zealous Christ and call ourselves followers of Him, but not have His zeal? Christianity and zeal cannot be separated. We must examine our zeal. There can be no sitting on the fence. You either live your life zealously or lukewarm. The lukewarm will be spit out of the mouth of Jesus. Jesus calls us to be zealous and repent (Revelation 3:19). We must wake up! We must reform our zeal for God and be active in obedience.

Day 223

The household of God, which is the church of the living God, a pillar and buttress of the truth.

1 Timothy 3:15

Emphasis: The household of God, which is **the Church** of the **living God**, a **pillar** and **buttress** of the **truth.**

Rewrite: The household of God is the Church of the living God, a pillar and support of the truth.

Application: In verses 14 and 15, Paul explains to Timothy the purpose of his writing. He says, "I hope to come to you soon, but I am writing these things to you so that, if I delay, you may know how one ought to behave in the household of God, which is the church of the living God, a pillar and buttress of the truth." First we must notice that the Church is described as the household of God or as a sizable family of believers under the single headship of God. The local church is a group of people, not a building, where the presence of God is manifested through the preaching of the Word and the partaking in the ordinances. Each true church is also the Church of the living God. The Church does not belong to man, but God Himself. It is also a pillar and buttress of the truth. A pillar is a column or support that holds up the building or roof. A buttress is also a supporting structure that brings stability or strengthens the building or wall. God has entrusted and ordered the Church to proclaim and protect the truth of Scripture. The Church holds up, protects, and defends the truth. It is important to note that all the authority to be a pillar and buttress of the truth has been given to the Church and not to other types of organizations. We have all the truth we will ever have on this earth contained in the Bible, and it is the Church's duty to promote and protect this truth. The Church is a primary part of God's plan, and He reveals Himself and His glory through the Church. Even angels learn about God by watching the Church. Ephesians 3:10 says, "...through the church the manifold wisdom of God might now be made known to the rulers and authorities in the heavenly places." We must meditate on the important role of the church in God's ordained plan and our role in it.

Day 224 – Your Meditation

Whoever isolates himself seeks his own desire; he breaks out against all sound judgment.

Proverbs 18:1

Read: Proverbs 18:1-2

Emphasis:_____

_____

_____

Rewrite:_____

_____

_____

Application:_____

_____

_____

_____

_____

_____

_____

_____

_____

_____

_____

_____

_____

_____

_____

_____

_____

_____

_____

_____

Day 225

...set the believers an example in speech, in conduct, in love, in faith, in purity.

1 Timothy 4:12

Emphasis: Set the **believers** an **example** in speech, in conduct, in love, in faith, in purity.

Rewrite: Be an example to other believers in the way you speak, in the way you live, in love, in faith, and in purity.

Application: Paul gives this exhortation to Timothy so that he, despite his youth, could prove his doctrine by his actions. What we truly believe is what drives our actions. Our theology drives our practice. Whether you are a leader in the church or a member of the body of Christ, this exhortation is for all believers. People are always watching our actions, and God always knows perfectly our actions, words, thoughts, and motivations. We are called to be an example and to set a pattern for the people around us so that they will imitate us as we imitate Christ. As parents, it seems that our children imitate us closely, and sadly they pick up or imitate our bad behavior more than our good behavior. The same thing happens when a young Christian is mentored by a more mature Christian. The young Christian may violate his conscience because his mentor sets a bad example for him. We are a new creation in Christ; therefore, the way we talk, live, love, believe and our morality should be radically different from when we were an enemy of God. We must set an example in our speech. That is, we should not be cussing anymore nor using the Lord's name in vain. We should be careful to show an example in the way we say things and what we talk about. Our conversations should be edifying and Christ-saturated. We talk about what we love, so how much more should Christ be in our conversations? Our conduct should be Christ-like, always striving for holiness. We should grow in our love for Christ and others. We should be an example in our faith, encouraging others to believe and trust, rather than doubt. We also must set an example of what moral purity is, guarding our heart and teaching others to do the same. Paul encourages Timothy to immerse himself in these things (v. 15). We must do the same.

Day 226

Now the man Moses was very meek, more than all people who were on the face of the earth.

Numbers 12:3

Emphasis: Now the man Moses was very **meek**, more than all people who were on the face of the earth.

Rewrite: Moses was more humble than anyone on earth.

Application: Moses was an example of meekness, humility, and gentleness. These are the same qualities of Christ that we must strive for in our pursuit of holiness. In Colossians 3:12-14, Paul urges believers to have compassionate hearts, kindness, humility, meekness, and patience, and above all these to put on love, which binds everything together in perfect harmony. Becoming more meek in character is part of the process of becoming more like Christ in His character. Meekness is surrendering your will and having a broken will, as opposed to being self-willed. Meekness is walking in humility and not abusing the authority that God has given. Meekness is being a servant and willingly submitting to the authority that is over you. A proud, immature man criticizes everyone but himself because he has a problem with authority and God. A meek man looks more at the log in his eye than he does at others. A meek man does not need to always be right or insert his opinion in every argument. A meek man can keep quiet and not get in every vain argument. A meek man does not crave controversy or for his voice to be heard. A meek man can patiently take criticism and careful examine it without losing his temper or getting defensive. A meek man is secure in Christ and is not driven by insecurity or emotions. Meek men do not have to criticize and tear others down to make themselves look good. A meek man does not need to defend his reputation, but he trusts in the sovereignty of God. Sadly, a meek person is rare, but when he is found, he gives off the "aroma of Christ to God among those who are being saved and among those who are perishing" (2 Corinthians 2:15). We must imitate Moses as he imitates Christ. We have an example of meekness in the Scriptures, so we must examine ourselves and strive to be marked as a meek person for the glory of God.

Day 227

But if anyone does not provide for his relatives, and especially for members of his household, he has denied the faith and is worse than an unbeliever.

1 Timothy 5:8

Emphasis: But if **anyone** does not **provide** for his **relatives**, and especially for members of his **household**, he has denied the faith and is worse than an unbeliever.

Rewrite: If anyone does not take care of his relatives, especially of his own household, he has denied the faith and is worse than an unbeliever.

Application: This is a sharp rebuke to those who have given up caring for their aged parents and selfishly put them in a nursing home. There may be reasons for a nursing home, but if the children of a widow put her in a nursing home, there should be a biblical and not self-serving motivation. The context of this verse is how the gospel should shape the caring for widows by the church. There were criteria for caring for widows. If the widow did not have any family to care for her, if she was over sixty years old, and if the widow was a godly woman (vv. 4-10), then the church was required to care for the widow. It was first the job of the children and the relatives to take care of their widow relative. Even among non-Christian cultures, the value of family is usually high. Therefore, it is a bad testimony to claim to be a Christian and then not take care of your parents when they get old. It is a bad witness when the church is taking care of your aging parents because you chose not to honor your parents and fulfill this biblical mandate. This is why Paul strongly says that if anyone does not provide for his relatives, and especially for members of his household, he has denied the faith and is worse than an unbeliever. Our parents brought us into the world, cared for us when we where helpless, guided us in life, provided for all our needs. When our parents become aged, and sometimes helpless, it is the duty of their children to take care of them. To neglect this duty is to deny Christian love and even faith in Jesus Christ. The person who neglects the care of his own parents is worse than an unbeliever.

Day 228

The LORD is slow to anger and abounding in steadfast love, forgiving iniquity and transgression, but he will by no means clear the guilty.

Numbers 14:18

Emphasis: The LORD is slow to anger and abounding in **steadfast love**, **forgiving** iniquity and transgression, but He will by no means clear the **guilty.**

Rewrite: The Lord is slow to anger, His love never fails, He forgives sin, but He will never excuse the guilty.

Application: Many times Christians and unbelievers like to focus on what they would consider the good attributes of God but ignore what they would consider His harsh attributes. It is easy to say that God is slow to anger, He has unfailing love, and He forgives us when we sin against Him. However, God will not clear the guilty. All of God's attributes are perfect and glorious, even His wrath, anger, justice, and jealousy. If we choose to believe that God has some attributes and not others, we have stopped worshiping the true and living God and have begun worshiping an idol we have invented in our minds to suit our sins. This verse says the Lord is slow to anger and abounding in steadfast love, forgiving iniquity and transgression, but He will by no means clear the guilty. God does forgive sin, but it is conditioned on whether you are in Christ. God does not forgive the sins of unbelievers. God forgives our sins by faith in the perfect Savior Jesus Christ and repentance of our sins. God is both just and loving. In order for God to lovingly save His people and forgive their sins, He must first lovingly crush His own Son in the place of His people to satisfy divine justice. God clears the guilty by placing our guilt on Christ. Christ took the punishment that is due to us from our guilt and sin. This great act of love demonstrates that God is slow to anger, abounding in steadfast love, and forgiving. When Jesus Christ satisfied divine justice by bearing our sins and paying our debts, God freely forgave His people. "As far as the east is from the west, so far does he remove our transgressions from us" (Psalm 103:12). We must praise God for His steadfast love, patience, forgiveness, and His justice demonstrated at Calvary.

Day 229

But godliness with contentment is great gain, for we brought nothing into the world, and we cannot take anything out of the world.

1 Timothy 6:6-7

Emphasis: But godliness with **contentment** is great gain, for we **brought nothing** into the world, and we **cannot take anything** out of the world.

Rewrite: Godliness with contentment is great gain, after all, we brought nothing into this world, and we cannot take anything out of it.

Application: Paul instructed Timothy about godliness throughout this letter, and now he exhorts him to add contentment to godliness, saying it will be of great benefit to him. Paul wants Timothy to have an eternal perspective while living his short life on earth. He wants Timothy to put his mind on the things of Heaven instead of the things of earth. He gives a warning about the danger of desire. He says in the ninth verse that those who desire to be rich fall into temptation, into a snare, into many senseless and harmful desires that plunge people into ruin and destruction. Paul calls the love of money the root of all kinds of evils (v. 10), and that this craving for money drives some men way from the faith, proving their unbelief. Money is not the problem. The love of money is the problem that causes men to set their hopes on the uncertainty of riches instead of on God (v. 17). Paul exhorts Timothy and us to be content with our food and clothing and not to desire to be rich (v. 8). We are called not to be rich in worldly wealth but to be rich in good works, to be generous and ready to share (v. 18). We are called to flee from these desires to accumulate wealth and to pursue righteousness, godliness, faith, love, steadfastness, and gentleness (v. 11). By pursuing these things we are storing up treasure as a good foundation for the future in eternity (v. 19). Because we still have a sinful nature, it is difficult at times to not fall into this snare. That is why Paul urges Timothy to war against these desires. He says in verse 12 to "Fight the good fight of faith." Godliness with contentment is great gain. We must meditate on our contentment and what it means to be content.

Day 230

*And he stood between the dead and the living, and the plague was
stopped.*

Numbers 16:48

Emphasis: And he **stood between** the **dead** and the **living**, and the
plague was stopped.

Rewrite: He stood between the dead and the living, and the destruction
was stopped.

Application: The men of Korah, Dathan, and Abiram stirred up a
rebellion against Moses and Aaron because they were tired of their
leadership. Really they were rebelling against God. They stood on one
side, and Moses and Aaron stood on the other side. God opened up the
ground, and these rebellious men were swallowed up. God sent fire
down and consumed the other 250 men who were in rebellion (vv. 1-35).
As a new day arose, amazingly, the congregation of the people of Israel
grumbled against Moses and Aaron (v. 41). They had no fear of God
even after they saw the judgment of the previous day. Once again, God
appeared and was ready to consume them, but Moses and Aaron fell on
their faces and interceded for the rebellious people. Moses instructed
Aaron to quickly take his censer and carry it to the congregation and
make atonement for them because the wrath of God was being poured
out on the congregation as a plague (vv. 42-47). Aaron stood between
the dead and the living, and the plague was stopped. Aaron, as the priest
interceding for the people, turned away the wrath of God. This event
prefigures Christ's propitiation for our sins. Because of our rebellion
against God, the wrath and fury of God was about to be poured out on us,
but because of God's great love for us, He sent His Son, Jesus Christ, to
stand in between Himself and us. Jesus absorbed the full fury and wrath
of God that was due to us because of our sins, and He stopped the plague
of death that we deserve. Jesus, our great high priest, not only stopped
the plague of death, He gives eternal life to all who believe in Him. God
did this so that He might be just and the justifier of the one who has faith
in Jesus (Romans 3:26). Where would we be today if Jesus never stood
in the gap?

Day 231 – Your Meditation

...for God gave us a spirit not of fear but of power and love and self-control.

2 Timothy 1:7

Read: 1 Timothy 1:3-7

Emphasis:_____

_____

_____

Rewrite:_____

_____

_____

Application:_____

_____

_____

_____

_____

_____

_____

_____

_____

_____

_____

_____

_____

_____

_____

_____

_____

_____

_____

_____

_____

_____

Day 232

...by the power of God, who saved us and called us to a holy calling.

2 Timothy 1:8b-9a

Emphasis: ...by the power of **God**, who **saved** us and **called** us to a holy calling.

Rewrite: By God's power, He saved us and called us to live a holy life.

Application: It was by the power of God, not our power to believe or decide, that we were saved. Why did God save us and not others? Verse nine says it was "not because of our works but because of his own purpose and grace, which he gave us in Christ Jesus before the ages began." Ephesians 2:8-9 says the same: "For by grace you have been saved through faith. And this is not your own doing; it is the gift of God, not a result of works, so that no one may boast." God saved us for His own good pleasure and purpose because He loves us. He gave us grace in and through Jesus Christ and His work on the cross. Jesus earned our salvation by paying the penalty for our sins and giving us His perfect righteousness. The amazing thing is that God gave us this grace before the ages began. Paul teaches the same thing in Ephesians 1:4-5. He says "...he chose us in him before the foundation of the world, that we should be holy and blameless before him. In love he predestined us for adoption as sons through Jesus Christ, according to the purpose of his will." This grace "has been manifested through the appearing of our Savior Christ Jesus, who abolished death and brought life and immortality to light through the gospel" (2 Timothy 1:10). How should we live our lives considering this verse? Death has been abolished, which means that even though we must die, death no longer has a stronghold on the Christian. We have nothing to fear any longer. We have a holy calling, and part of this calling is that we suffer for the gospel (v. 8). Because we have no fear of death, we can suffer for the cause of Christ. God gave us "a spirit not of fear but of power and love and self-control" (v. 7). Because our past is redeemed, our present mission is clear, and our future is secure. We can set our gait toward the heavenly city and press on to the prize of eternal life. God has a plan, and it has never changed since the foundation of the world. We can trust in His plan and His purposes.

Day 233

And the LORD said to Moses, "Make a fiery serpent and set it on a pole, and everyone who is bitten, when he sees it, shall live."

Numbers 21:8

Emphasis: And the LORD said to Moses, "Make a fiery serpent and set it on a pole, and everyone who is **bitten**, when he **sees it**, shall **live**."

Rewrite: The Lord told Moses to make a bronze serpent and put it on a pole so that everyone who was bitten would see it and live.

Application: There are consequences for our actions. The Israelites became impatient in the desert. They took out their frustrations on God and Moses and blamed them for their trouble. They complained there was no food or water in the desert and that they were tired of the manna God provided for them each day. They longed to return to Egypt as slaves. Their sinful actions reaped the consequence of death. Verse six says, "Then the LORD sent fiery serpents among the people, and they bit the people, so that many people of Israel died." The people who survived came to Moses and acknowledged their sin and begged him to pray to God to take away the serpents. Moses interceded for them. God responded to Moses and said, "Make a fiery serpent and set it on a pole, and everyone who is bitten, when he sees it, shall live." So Moses made a bronze serpent and set it on a pole. And if a serpent bit anyone, he would look at the bronze serpent and live (vv. 8-9). We can learn a lot from this story. The wages of sin is death (Romans 6:23). The people's sin and rebellion against God resulted in death, and sin still does today. The Israelites longed to return to their bondage of sin in Egypt and to be away from God. By nature, the sinful man longs to live in sin and rebellion instead of in obedience to God. Sin brings consequences, but because of God's great love for us, He provides a way of escape. God is both just and loving. God had Moses make a bronze serpent so that those who were bitten would look at it and live. In the same way, God sent His perfect Son Jesus to be lifted up on a cross so that all who look to Him, will live. Jesus said this about Himself in John 3:14-15, "And as Moses lifted up the serpent in the wilderness, so must the Son of Man be lifted up, that whoever believes in him may have eternal life."

Day 234

"Truly, I say to you, if you have faith and do not doubt, you will not only do what has been done to the fig tree, but even if you say to this mountain, 'Be taken up and thrown into the sea,' it will happen. And whatever you ask in prayer, you will receive, if you have faith."

Matthew 21:21-22

Emphasis: "Truly, I say to you, if you have **faith** and do not **doubt**, you will not only do what has been done to the fig tree, but even if you say to this mountain, 'Be taken up and thrown into the sea,' **it will happen**.

Rewrite: If you have faith and do not doubt, through the means of prayer, God will do things that are impossible for man.

Application: Matthew Henry said: "Faith, if it be right, will excite prayer; and prayer is not right, if it does not spring from faith. This is the condition of our receiving—we must *ask in prayer, believing.*"[27] We know from Hebrews 11:6 that without faith it is impossible to please God. We must pray in faith and never doubt God and His ability to do the impossible. The impossible will be made possible. Moving a mountain was a Jewish saying that meant doing something impossible. "Whatever you ask in prayer, you will receive, if you have faith" assumes you are praying and requesting according to the will of God. The source of all faith is God, and if the faith that God gives us is from Him, then it can't fail. Only from God-given faith will there be no doubt. The more you know the Bible, the glory of God, the depravity of man, and the way God works in the world, the more you will understand His will. The Holy Spirit will use this to teach you to pray rightly. God uses the means of prayer to accomplish His will, and He will burden you to pray for particular things. When this happens, pray in faith and you will see God work in amazing ways. Pray consistently, pray in faith, pray according to the will of God and pray fervently.

---

27 Matthew Henry, *Matthew Henry's Commentary on the Whole Bible: Complete and Unabridged in One Volume.* (Peabody: Hendrickson, 1994), Mt 21:18–22.

Day 235

If a man vows a vow to the LORD, or swears an oath to bind himself by a pledge, he shall not break his word. He shall do according to all that proceeds out of his mouth.

Numbers 30:2

Emphasis: If a man vows a **vow** to the LORD, or **swears an oath** to bind himself by a pledge, he **shall not break** his word. He shall do according to all that proceeds out of his mouth.

Rewrite: A man who makes a vow to the Lord or swears an oath that he will do something, shall never break his word, but do exactly as he said.

Application: This verse should make us think before we speak. If we are not sure that we can fulfill our promises, we should not make them. A vow is a solemn promise made to God. There was no requirement on any Israelite to make vows, but once made, they were binding and had to be kept. To make a vow is to bind yourself in an oath that cannot be broken, which is why vows should not be made hastily. If you make a vow and then do not fulfill it, it is sin. Deuteronomy 23:21 says, "If you make a vow to the LORD your God, you shall not delay fulfilling it, for the LORD your God will surely require it of you, and you will be guilty of sin." God takes your promises seriously. Ecclesiastes 5:4-5 says, "When you vow a vow to God, do not delay paying it, for he has no pleasure in fools. Pay what you vow. It is better that you should not vow than that you should vow and not pay." The New Testament goes even further concerning vows. James exhorts us to "not swear, either by heaven or by earth or by any other oath, but let your 'yes' be yes and your 'no' be no, so that you may not fall under condemnation" (James 5:12). It is far better to never make a promise than to make one and break it. Countless people ignore these warnings concerning vows, and it is evident when people say, "I swear to God that I will do it." Jesus teaches that we should not swear to God. He says let what you say be "simply 'Yes' or 'No'; anything more than this comes from evil" (Matthew 5:34-37). We must repent of this sin of making vows that we do not fulfill, and we must start taking what we say more seriously. Do you have unfulfilled promises? Have you broken your word?

Day 236

Have nothing to do with foolish, ignorant controversies; you know that they breed quarrels.

2 Timothy 2:23

Emphasis: Have nothing to do with foolish, ignorant **controversies**; you know that they breed **quarrels**.

Rewrite: Avoid foolish and ignorant arguments that will only start fights.

Application: The context of these foolish and ignorant controversies is false teaching. False teaching always breeds quarrels instead of unity. Often false teaching starts with stressing a view on a minor, misunderstood teaching, and then, because of the argument, the minor point turns into a major point causing division. The focus of these controversies are foolish and ignorant. Paul exhorts Timothy to "Not quarrel about words" (v. 14), to "Rightly handle the word of truth" (v. 15), to "avoid irreverent babble" which leads people to ungodliness (v. 16), and to "Have nothing to do with foolish, ignorant controversies" which will only breed quarrels (v. 23). Why is this so applicable? Because this is happening in countless churches everywhere. Paul explains the motive for avoiding these foolish, ignorant controversies. In verses 24-26, he says: "And the Lord's servant must not be quarrelsome but kind to everyone, able to teach, patiently enduring evil, correcting his opponents with gentleness. God may perhaps grant them repentance leading to a knowledge of the truth, and they may come to their senses and escape from the snare of the devil, after being captured by him to do his will." A servant of our Master Jesus Christ must model Him. A servant must be marked as a kind, patient, and gentle man who is able to teach and does not crave controversy (1 Timothy 6:4). If we apply this verse to every aspect of our lives, even our marriages, we would avoid many problems. If we handled everyone with kindness, gentleness, patience, and did not get in fights over things that do not matter, every relationship would change. If we trusted in God instead of wanting to force our point and went to Him in prayer, our opponents may be led to the truth and come to their senses. Are we fighting or trusting in God?

Day 237

Preach the word; be ready in season and out of season; reprove, rebuke, and exhort, with complete patience and teaching.

2 Timothy 4:2

Emphasis: **Preach** the word; **be ready** in season and out of season; **reprove, rebuke, and exhort**, with complete **patience** and teaching.

Rewrite: Preach the word when it is convenient or inconvenient; patiently correct error, rebuke, and strongly urge others through teaching.

Application: Paul charges Timothy in the presence of God and of Christ Jesus, who will judge all people, to spend his ministry doing five essential things. Timothy must preach the word. The word is the Word of God, the Scriptures, that make men wise for salvation through faith in Christ Jesus (2 Timothy 3:15). Because the Scriptures are breathed out by God, profitable for teaching, reproof, correction, and training in righteousness (2 Timothy 3:16), they must be preached. Timothy was not called to preach anything but the Word itself. He was not called to tickle ears or tell people what they wanted to hear so that he could be popular. He was to preach the Word of God alone. Paul also charges Timothy to be ready to preach the Word in season and out of season, that is, when it is easy and convenient and when it is hard and inconvenient. It is often the times when sharing the gospel is most difficult and inconvenient that God uses it the most. We must not be fair weather Christians who only fulfill our duties when it is convenient. Paul charges Timothy to patiently reprove, or correct, those who are in error in their understanding of the Scriptures. The Lord's servant must correct his opponents with gentleness so that "God may perhaps grant them repentance leading to a knowledge of the truth" (2 Timothy 2:25). Timothy must rebuke those who persist in sin. He must rebuke them sharply, that they may be sound in the faith (Titus 1:13). Finally, he must exhort, or strongly urge and encourage the people to press on in the faith, endure suffering, and to grow in the grace and knowledge of the Lord Jesus Christ. Every Christian is charged one way or another with these five duties. We should meditate on these duties and examine if we are, through teaching and patience, living out these charges.

Day 238 – Your Meditation

*...the sacred writings, which are able to make you wise for salvation
through faith in Christ Jesus.*

2 Timothy 3:15

Read: 1 Timothy 3:10-17

Emphasis:_____

_____

_____

Rewrite:_____

_____

_____

Application:_____

_____

_____

_____

_____

_____

_____

_____

_____

_____

_____

_____

_____

_____

_____

_____

_____

_____

_____

Day 239

They profess to know God, but they deny him by their works. They are detestable, disobedient, unfit for any good work.

Titus 1:16

Emphasis: They **profess** to know God, but they **deny** Him **by their works**. They are detestable, disobedient, **unfit** for any good work.

Rewrite: Some people say they know God, but they really deny Him by how they live their lives. They are detestable, disobedient, and unfit.

Application: There are many people who claim to be Christians but are not. They deceive themselves, or they are deceived by others. They profess to know God with their mouths, but they live in complete contradiction to the Scriptures. They are only hearers of the Word, not doers. They can tell you what the Bible says, but they don't obey what they know to be true. They can preach truth from the pulpit, but show their disbelief and hypocrisy by their disobedience. They can teach their children how to live, but they don't model it. They teach their children to be hypocrites by their contradictory life. James 1:22-25 speaks clearly on this: "But be doers of the word, and not hearers only, deceiving yourselves. For if anyone is a hearer of the word and not a doer, he is like a man who looks intently at his natural face in a mirror. For he looks at himself and goes away and at once forgets what he was like. But the one who looks into the perfect law, the law of liberty, and perseveres, being no hearer who forgets but a doer who acts, he will be blessed in his doing." The passage from Titus says that if you profess to know God, but you deny Him by your way of life, then you are detestable, disobedient, and unfit for any good work. How can you want to be used by God when you know the truth and deny it by your habitual lifestyle of hypocrisy? It is better to be ignorant about the truth and not obey it than to know the truth and live contrary to it. Jesus warns against false prophets and gives us a way to examine ourselves to see if we are in the faith: "Every healthy tree bears good fruit, but the diseased tree bears bad fruit. A healthy tree cannot bear bad fruit, nor can a diseased tree bear good fruit" (Matthew 7:17-18). Today we must examine our works, fruit, and hypocrisy. Are we a hearer of the Word and a doer of it?

Day 240

For the LORD your God is a consuming fire, a jealous God.

Deuteronomy 4:24

Emphasis: For the LORD your God is a **consuming fire**, a **jealous God**.

Rewrite: The Lord is a devouring fire, and He is a jealous God.

Application: This attribute was what drove one famous woman to deny the true and the living God. She said, "God is all. God is omnipresent. And God is also jealous? God is jealous of me? And something about that didn't feel right in my spirit... and that is where the search for something more than doctrine started to stir within me." Her search for something more than doctrine led her to say, "One of the biggest mistakes humans make is to believe there is only one way. Actually, there are many diverse paths leading to what you call God." When people only believe what they like about God and deny the rest of what is true about God, they create an idol and no longer believe in the only true God. The Israelites were constantly lured away to worship idols instead of God. In this passage of Scripture, God is again teaching Israel that idolatry is forbidden. God warned them to not break the covenant He made with them by making a carved image in the form of anything (v. 23). The reason for this is because the Lord God is a consuming fire, a jealous God. God demands the full obedience of all His people. As a consuming fire, God consumes everything that is evil and purifies everything that is good. God wants our full devotion. "No one can serve two masters, for either he will hate the one and love the other, or he will be devoted to the one and despise the other" (Matthew 6:24). God has a zeal for His name, His righteousness, and His honor. God will never share His glory with any man (Isaiah 42:8) nor will allow the honor that is due to Him alone be given to another. God is not jealous of us as if He wants something from us that we have. God's jealousy is not like our sinful human jealousy. His jealousy is a holy jealousy. We belong to the jealous God. God loved us so much and was so perfectly jealous to have us as His possession that He killed His perfect Son, Jesus Christ, in our place. God's jealously should bring forth fear and delight to our souls.

Day 241

To speak evil of no one, to avoid quarreling, to be gentle, and to show perfect courtesy toward all people.

Titus 3:2

Emphasis: To **speak evil** of no one, to avoid **quarreling,** to be **gentle**, and to show perfect **courtesy** toward all people.

Rewrite: They should not slander or quarrel but be gentle and courteous to all people.

Application: You would think these instructions would be common sense, but Paul had to write this to Titus for a reason. All you have to do is look into any church and you will see that not everyone is obeying this verse. God has redeemed people for Himself through the blood of His precious Son, Jesus Christ, to give Him a possession of Christ-like people who are zealous for good works (Titus 2:14). The Christian should be submissive to rulers and authorities instead of always complaining about the government (v. 1). He must be obedient to the word of God and not justify being disobedient for any reason (v. 1). He must be zealous for and devoted to doing good works (vv. 1-8). He must not speak evil of anyone. This should be convicting. How often have we slandered other people to feed our pride and make ourselves feel better than others? The old saying, "If you don't have anything nice to say, then do not say anything" is something we have heard a lot growing up, but we probably have not seen it modeled. Speaking evil or slandering a person is an easy snare to fall into. We must fight against saying anything evil about anyone. The Christian must avoid quarreling. This is a common theme in all of Paul's epistles to the churches because all of the churches were quarreling. It seems that the churches in our age have followed suit, which proves the Bible's relevancy. The Christian must be gentle, not a strong-willed, aggressive person who everyone is afraid of upsetting. Finally, the Christian must show perfect courtesy toward all people. If we are courteous to our friends and family or to people in a high position over us, it is nothing; even the unbelievers of the world do this. We are called to be perfectly courteous to all people, even our enemies and the people who we think deserve worse.

Day 242

Tremble, O earth, at the presence of the Lord, at the presence of the God of Jacob.

Psalm 114:7

Emphasis: **Tremble**, O earth, at the **presence of the Lord,** at the presence of the God of Jacob.

Rewrite: Let all the earth tremble at the presence of the Lord.

Application: This Psalm reminds Israel of God's sovereign power recalling the parting of the Red Sea and the Jordan River. Why should the earth tremble at the presence of the Lord? Because God is sovereign over all His creation. In this Psalm, God assures and reminds believers that He can deliver them from their situation even when things are humanly impossible. God's creation is personified in this Psalm. The Red Sea and the Jordan River are said to have fled from the presence of the Lord (v. 3), and the mountains are said to have skipped like rams (v. 4). This paints the picture of why the earth should tremble at the presence of the Lord. We should not take God lightly but should have a healthy fear of Him. Fearing God should be the response to an all-powerful God who created and governs all things. If we could only grasp a little of the power of God, we would tremble before His mighty hand. All of creation responds to God in fear and obedience. God commands and it is done. It is amazing that man does not do what creation does. Everything obeys God but man. The unregenerate man has reason to fear God more than anything, but he has no fear. The unregenerate man is in more danger than all of God's creation, yet he lives as though God has no power over him. "The heavens declare the glory of God, and the sky above proclaims his handiwork" (Psalm 19:1), yet the unregenerate man seeks all the glory for himself. All the earth is called to tremble at the presence of the Lord, but the unregenerate man sets his face boldly against God. How bold and daring is man in his depraved state? He is very bold against God until he stands before His presence for one second, and then his bold rebellion will be crushed, and he will only be able to tremble. We must fear the living God and tremble in His presence.

Day 243

Not because of your righteousness or the uprightness of your heart are you going in to possess their land, but because of the wickedness of these nations.

Deuteronomy 9:5

Emphasis: **Not because of your righteousness** or the uprightness of your heart are you going in to possess their land, but **because of the wickedness of these nations.**

Rewrite: It is not because of your righteousness or your moral integrity that you will receive the land, but because of the wickedness of these nations that I am driving out.

Application: Many times we think we deserve something more than other people because we are better people. Israel was warned in verse four, by God, not to fall into the same trap: "Do not say in your heart, after the LORD your God has thrust them out before you, 'It is because of my righteousness that the LORD has brought me in to possess this land,' whereas it is because of the wickedness of these nations that the LORD is driving them out before you." Then in verse six, God emphasizes this truth; he says, "Know, therefore, that the LORD your God is not giving you this good land to possess because of your righteousness, for you are a stubborn people." The rest of the chapter is used to demonstrate the sinfulness and stubbornness of Israel so they would understand that they did not deserve the land. God gives Israel two reasons why He is allowing them to take the land. The first is because the nations were so wicked that God was going to annihilate them, and the second was that God wanted to confirm His covenant with Abraham, Isaac, and Jacob (v. 5). God does all things for His glory according to the purpose of His will. We must not fall into the same snare as Israel. Everything that we have comes through the blessing of Christ. In Christ and because of Christ we receive all blessings. God even gives us the power to get the wealth we have (Deuteronomy 8:17-18), and no matter how much we work, we would not have anything that God does not give. Today we must meditate on the fact that God gives us all things for His glory and purposes, not because of our goodness.

Day 244

For I have derived much joy and comfort from your love, my brother, because the hearts of the saints have been refreshed through you.

Philemon 7

Emphasis: For I have derived much joy and comfort from your **love**, my brother, because the hearts of the saints have been **refreshed** through you.

Rewrite: You love has comforted me, and it has given me great joy, my brother, because the saints have been refreshed through you.

Application: Paul is writing this letter to a man named Philemon in order to make an appeal to him for the life of Onesimus. Before Paul makes his appeal, he thanks Philemon for his love and faith in Christ toward other Christians (v. 5). Philemon was a man marked by showing love to the brothers, for his comforting, his faith, and his evangelism (vv. 4-7). Paul saw Philemon acting like a Christian and modeling Christ, and he derived much joy and comfort from knowing that Philemon was loving and refreshing the saints. Philemon, like Barnabas, was someone who encouraged and refreshed the hearts of people in a positive way. Philemon leaned on the side of grace instead of harshness. Paul was confident that Philemon would accept his plea and that he would even do more than Paul asked (v. 21). Philemon was a man of love, encouragement, and forgiveness. Now we must look at ourselves and ask if we are known as people who always encourage and refresh the saints in love and faith in Jesus Christ? Are we inserting the love of Christ into every conversation, or like the Pharisees, are we marked by being critical and always leaning on the side of harshness instead of mercy and grace? In the same way that God has demonstrated His love for us by mercifully sending His perfect Son to die for us, we must be men and women marked by mercy, love, and encouragement. God, the Father of mercy and God of all comfort, "comforts us in all our affliction, so that we may be able to comfort those who are in any affliction, with the comfort with which we ourselves are comforted by God" (2 Corinthians 1:3-4). As God comforts and encourages us in Christ, we must comfort and encourage others.

Day 245 – Your Meditation

...how shall we escape if we neglect such a great salvation?

Hebrews 2:3a

Read: Hebrews chapter 1 – 2:1-4

Emphasis:_____

_____

_____

Rewrite:_____

_____

_____

Application:_____

_____

_____

_____

_____

_____

_____

_____

_____

_____

_____

_____

_____

_____

_____

_____

_____

_____

_____

Day 246

But exhort one another every day, as long as it is called "today," that none of you may be hardened by the deceitfulness of sin.

Hebrews 3:13

Emphasis: But **exhort** one another every day, as long as it is called "today," that none of you may be **hardened** by the **deceitfulness of sin**.

Rewrite: Encourage each other every day so that you will not become hardened by the deception of sin.

Application: The author of Hebrews calls the people to consider Jesus, who was counted worthy of more glory than Moses (vv. 1-3), and warns the people to not harden their hearts as in the rebellion (v. 8). The Israelites who followed Moses were not allowed to enter the promised land because of their unbelief. The people are warned not to fall into the same snare of unbelief. Verse 12 says, "Take care, brothers, lest there be in any of you an evil, unbelieving heart, leading you to fall away from the living God." Unbelief is a grievous sin that God hates. The Israelites refused to believe God's promise to bring them into a land and give them rest, so they turned away from the living God. Unbelief can only lead you away from God. Continuing in unbelief will only harden your heart. Every time a person hears the gospel and chooses to disobey the gospel call to repent and believe, their heart is hardened by the deceitfulness of this grievous sin. A continual rejection of the gospel leads to a numbness to the things of God and eventually an open hatred for the gospel. The author urges the people to exhort one another every day so that none of them may be hardened by the deceitfulness of sin. The evidence that you are truly a Christian is that you will persevere to the end. Verse 14 says, "For we have come to share in Christ, if indeed we hold our original confidence firm to the end." If a person claims to believe in God but later rejects Him and hardens his heart, then the individual proves to be an unbeliever. We must seek a tender heart and fear God because good news came to us just as to Israel, but their unbelief kept them from God's rest. "Let us therefore strive to enter that rest, so that no one may fall by the same sort of disobedience" (Hebrews 4:11). "Today, if you hear his voice, do not harden your hearts as in the rebellion" (Hebrews 3:15).

Day 247

*And it shall be with him, and he shall read in it all the days of his life,
that he may learn to fear the LORD his God by keeping all the words of
this law and these statutes, and doing them.*

Deuteronomy 17:19

Emphasis: And it shall be with him, and he shall **read** in it **all the days** of his life, that he may **learn to fear** the LORD his God by **keeping** all the words of this law and these statutes, and **doing** them.

Rewrite: The Scriptures should be with him, and he should read them every day so that he will learn to fear the Lord by obeying His words.

Application: The future kings of Israel were instructed to write a copy of the law of God as approved by the Levitical priests (v. 18). They were required to always keep this copy with them and to read it all the days of their lives so they would learn to fear the Lord God. As they read it every day, they were to keep the words of the law and do them. They were not to be only readers, or hearers, of the word of God, but doers of the word of God. Everyone, even the highest authority, must put himself under the authority of the Scriptures because the word of God is the only authority, instruction, and source of truth about God. All men must give an account to how they have obeyed or disobeyed the Scriptures. "For the word of God is living and active, sharper than any two-edged sword, piercing to the division of soul and of spirit, of joints and of marrow, and discerning the thoughts and intentions of the heart. And no creature is hidden from his sight, but all are naked and exposed to the eyes of him to whom we must give account" (Hebrews 4:12–13). The more we read the Scriptures, the more we will know God. The more we know God, the more we will fear and obey Him. The more we know God, fear God, and obey God, the more we will die to our own desires in humility and live for Him. Our hearts will not be lifted up above others, and we will not turn aside from following God. However, if we stop reading the Scriptures on a daily basis, we forget about God and who He is. We stop fearing God and keeping His commandments, and we start justifying sin. A true Christian desires to feed on the Word of God. We must meditate on and conform to the Scriptures.

Day 248

But solid food is for the mature, for those who have the
discernment trained by constant practice to distinguish goo

Hebrews 5:14

Emphasis: But solid food is for the **mature**, for those who have t
powers of **discernment** trained by **constant practice** to **distinguis**
good from evil.

Rewrite: Solid food is for the mature in faith who, through constant
practice, have the skill of discerning good and evil.

Application: In verses 11 through 14 the author rebukes the Hebrews
for becoming dull in hearing and for their spiritual immaturity. The
Hebrews should have been teachers by this time, but they still needed to
understand the basic principles of the faith. They needed the milk of
basic Christianity instead of the solid food of the deep things of God.
The author calls the Hebrews children because they were still living on
milk and unskilled in the word of righteousness. This is a rebuke to
anyone who has been a Christian for years and still is unskilled in the
Bible. The person who has been a Christian for many years is expected
to have a thorough knowledge of the Bible and be skilled in discernment.
A Christian must be trained by the constant practice of knowing what the
Bible says and how it applies to his life. He must be able to discern
between what is good and evil, what is biblical and contrary to the Bible,
and what is the truth and what is a lie. The person who claims to have
been a Christian for the last 10 years but is still ignorant of the Bible and
immature in his character and practice should take this rebuke seriously
and change his ways immediately. Discernment is not a gift in the sense
of a special spiritual gift given to only some people and not others.
Discernment is a skill that is developed by knowing the Bible and
practicing what it teaches. Discernment is developed by being
enlightened by the Scripture and applying it to every situation in your
life. The more you read the Bible, the more you will know and fear God.
The more you know and fear God, the more you can rightly discern and
develop in maturity. For the Christian, sanctification is not an option.
We must strive to mature in the faith.

Day 249

This Book of the Law shall not depart from your mouth, but you shall meditate on it day and night, so that you may be careful to do according to all that is written in it.

Joshua 1:8a

Emphasis: This **Book of the Law** shall not depart from your mouth, but you shall **meditate** on it day and night, so that you may be careful to **do** according to all that is written in it.

Rewrite: Study the Bible and meditate on it day and night, so that you will be able to obey what is written in it.

Application: Joshua was just about to cross the Jordan and begin the conquest of the promised land of Canaan. In the first chapter, we see four times that the Lord exhorted Joshua to be strong and courageous. Joshua was to draw his strength and courage from the Book of the Law, which he was told to never abandon. Joshua was told to meditate on the Book of the Law, which is the first five books of the Bible. He was to meditate on it day and night so that he would be able to do everything that was written in it. God made promises in the first five books that Joshua was to know, meditate on, and obey, which would encourage him greatly and give him the courage he would need to fulfill the Lord's will. The Lord reminds Joshua of one of His promises; He says in verse three, "Every place that the sole of your foot will tread upon I have given to you, just as I promised to Moses." Another promise that strengthened Joshua was in verse five, the Lord says, "No man shall be able to stand before you all the days of your life. Just as I was with Moses, so I will be with you. I will not leave you or forsake you." Meditating on these promises from the Book of the Law gave Joshua strength and courage to obey the will of God even when the battle was the toughest. The second half of verse eight gives the results of obeying the first part of verse eight. It states: "For then you will make your way prosperous, and then you will have good success." This prosperity and success has nothing to do with material wealth. When we study the Bible, meditate on it day and night, and obey what we read, we will be prosperous and successful in doing the will of God and conforming ourselves to the Scriptures.

Day 250

Let us then with confidence draw near to the throne of grace, that we may receive mercy and find grace to help in time of need.

Hebrews 4:16

Emphasis: Let us then with **confidence** draw near to the **throne of grace**, that we may receive **mercy** and find **grace** to help in time of need.

Rewrite: Let us come boldly to God's throne of grace, so that we will receive mercy and grace in our time of need.

Application: We have access to God through Jesus Christ. He is the only intercessor that exists between man and God. Forgiveness of sins and reconciliation between man and God can only come through Jesus. Christ suffered for us and because of us. He voluntarily went through the sin and misery of this world, up to death itself, and suffered the full fury of the wrath of God due to us because of our sins, so that we could be saved from the punishment we deserve. Christ is our only high priest, so we no longer need an earthly priest. An earthly priest cannot intercede between us and God because he also is sinful. Christ is our perfect, sinless high priest who earned our salvation. Jesus can sympathize with our weaknesses because He was tempted in every respect that we are tempted, yet He did not sin (v. 15). Jesus suffered more in His life than any man has suffered since the foundation of the earth. Jesus "learned obedience through what he suffered" (Hebrews 5:8). Jesus felt what we feel when we suffer and are abused, and because He suffered and was tempted far more than us, we can boldly approach the throne of grace in search of mercy and grace in our times of need. Jesus is the fountain of all good, and He sustains and governs the universe by the word of His power. Jesus is our mediator and always intercedes for us. He atoned for our sin, He reveals the will of God to us, He rules and defends us, He prays for us, He comforts us, and He sustains our lives. What greater high priest should we go to? There is none but Jesus. Because He is our high priest who sympathizes with us in our weaknesses, we can go boldly to the throne of grace, as a child to a father, and expect to receive mercy and grace to persevere in our time of need.

Day 251

Consequently, he is able to save to the uttermost those who draw near to God through him, since he always lives to make intercession for them.

Hebrews 7:25

Emphasis: Consequently, He is able to **save** to the **uttermost** those who **draw near** to God through Him, since He always lives to make **intercession** for them.

Rewrite: Jesus is able to save completely for all time, those who come to God through Him, since He lives to continually intercede for them.

Application: In these verses, Jesus is proven to be the guarantee of the new covenant because of His eternality. Jesus is contrasted to the earthly priests of the old covenant who always died. "The former priests were many in number, because they were prevented by death from continuing in office, but he holds his priesthood permanently, because he continues forever" (vv. 23-24). Unlike the sinful, earthly priests who had to make offerings first for their own sins, Jesus is the perfect high priest, "holy, innocent, unstained, separated from sinners, and exalted above the heavens" (v. 26). "He has no need, like those high priests, to offer sacrifices daily, first for his own sins and then for those of the people, since he did this once for all when he offered up himself" (v. 27). Because Jesus offered Himself up, one time, to satisfy the divine justice of God and to reconcile His people to God, and because He lives continually to intercede for His people, He is able to save to the uttermost. Jesus is not dead but alive. He reigns at the right hand of the Father. He is able to save to the uttermost, that is to the greatest amount or degree possible. Jesus saves, keeps, and continually intercedes for those who trust in Him because of His great love for us. Jesus can save us from the uttermost depth of our sins, depression, sorrow, anguish, or temptation. "Who shall separate us from the love of Christ? Shall tribulation, or distress, or persecution, or famine, or nakedness, or danger, or sword? ...For I am sure that neither death nor life, nor angels nor rulers, nor things present nor things to come, nor powers, nor height nor depth, nor anything else in all creation, will be able to separate us from the love of God in Christ Jesus our Lord" (Romans 8:35,38–39).

Day 252 – Your Meditation

And let us consider how to stir up one another to love and good works, not neglecting to meet together, as is the habit of some, but encouraging one another, and all the more as you see the Day drawing near.

Hebrews 10:24-25

Read: Hebrews 10:1-25

Emphasis:_____
_____
_____

Rewrite:_____
_____
_____

Application:_____
_____
_____
_____
_____
_____
_____
_____
_____
_____
_____
_____
_____
_____
_____
_____
_____
_____
_____
_____

Day 253

They serve a copy and shadow of the heavenly things.

Hebrews 8:5a

Emphasis: They serve a **copy and shadow** of the **heavenly** things.

Rewrite: The priests were a copy and shadow of things in Heaven.

Application: Throughout the book of Hebrews the author is making the point that the system of worship in the old covenant was really pointing to Christ. It was only a copy and shadow of the reality of Christ in the new covenant. We see here that the imperfect priesthood was a shadow that pointed to reality. Hebrews 7:23-24 says "The former priests were many in number, because they were prevented by death from continuing in office, but he holds his priesthood permanently, because he continues forever." Jesus is our eternal high priest who continually intercedes for us. Christ is our high priest and "minister in the holy places, in the true tent that the Lord set up, not man" (Hebrews 8:2). The earthly tent, or tabernacle, was only a shadow of entering into the presence of God in Heaven, but the true tabernacle is in Heaven. We enter into the presence of God through Christ. The great Passover sacrifice was only a shadow of the reality that Christ is our Passover who has been sacrificed in our place (1 Corinthians 5:7). Christ was the spotless lamb that was slain. Circumcision was a shadow pointing to true circumcision of the heart through faith in Christ (Romans 2:29). In Christ we were "circumcised with a circumcision made without hands, by putting off the body of the flesh, by the circumcision of Christ" (Colossians 2:11). The feasts of the old covenant were a shadow of things to come, but the substance belongs to Christ (Colossians 2:16-17). God has ordained salvation through Christ from the foundation of the world and every book in the Bible points to this glorious truth. The Puritan Thomas Adams said, "Christ is the sum of the whole Bible, prophesied, typified, prefigured, exhibited, demonstrated, to be found in every leaf, almost every line, the Scriptures being but as it were the swaddling bands of the child Jesus."[28] We must meditate on the glorious Christ who is revealed in all of Scripture.

---

28 Thomas Adams, "Meditations upon Some Part of the Creed," in *The Works of Thomas Adams.* (1862; repr., Eureka, Calif.: Tanski, 1998), 3:224.

Day 254

But the word is very near you. It is in your mouth and in your heart, so that you can do it.

Deuteronomy 30:14

Emphasis: But the **word** is very **near** you. It is in your mouth and in your heart, so that you can **do it**.

Rewrite: The word is close to you. It is in your mouth and in your heart, so that you can obey it.

Application: In verse six we read that "The LORD your God will circumcise your heart and the heart of your offspring, so that you will love the LORD your God with all your heart and with all your soul, that you may live." From this verse we realize that a circumcised heart is necessary to love God with all one's heart and with all one's soul. Only by the regenerating work of the Holy Spirit can our hearts be circumcised or changed so that we will know God in a saving way. The result of a circumcised heart enables us to obey the gospel. Paul explains this verse in context of the new covenant. He says in Romans 10:8-10 that the word that is near to you is the word of faith that was proclaimed, that is, the gospel. He says that you know the word of faith is near to you because if you confess with your mouth that Jesus is Lord and believe in your heart that God raised Him from the dead, you will be saved. Christ brings the power to obey God from the heart. Paul again uses the words "mouth" and "heart" from Deuteronomy 30:14: "For with the heart one believes and is justified, and with the mouth one confesses and is saved" (Romans 10:10). God sets before us today life and good, death and evil, blessing and curse. These words of the gospel are very near to us so that we can obey them. The gospel call to repent and believe is not an option; we must obey them or face the consequences for disobedience. Moses desired that Israel fully submit themselves to God and to obey all that He commanded. In the new covenant, Paul urged the same commitment to God and obedience to His word. At the beginning of His ministry, Jesus demanded the same thing, stating, "The time is fulfilled, and the kingdom of God is at hand; repent and believe in the gospel" (Mark 1:15). These words are very near to us. We must obey them.

Day 255

He entered once for all into the holy places, not by means of the blood of goats and calves but by means of his own blood, thus securing an eternal redemption.

Hebrews 9:12

Emphasis: He entered **once** for all into the holy places, not by means of the blood of goats and calves but by means of **His own blood**, thus securing an eternal **redemption**.

Rewrite: He went into the holy places one time, not with the blood of animals but with His own blood, and secured an eternal redemption.

Application: Why did Jesus have to die by shedding His blood through severe torture? Why could Jesus not have secured redemption through a less bloody way? The answer is found in the Old Testament among the shadows of the sacrifices. In the sacrificial system, the spilling of blood was necessary to atone for the sin. However, these imperfect sacrifices were only a shadow that pointed to the reality of Christ's one time sacrifice. Hebrews 10:1 says, "For since the law has but a shadow of the good things to come instead of the true form of these realities, it can never, by the same sacrifices that are continually offered every year, make perfect those who draw near." Hebrews 10:4 says, "For it is impossible for the blood of bulls and goats to take away sins." These bloody sacrifices could never perfectly atone for sin, but they were a reminder that death was the result of sin. The law demands that someone must die for sin. Jesus had to shed His blood to pay the penalty for our sins. Under the law almost everything is purified with blood, and without the shedding of blood there is no forgiveness (v. 22). In verse 23, the author further explains the need for Christ to secure redemption by His blood: "Thus it was necessary for the copies of the heavenly things to be purified with these rites, but the heavenly things themselves with better sacrifices than these." Because Christ entered into Heaven by His own perfect blood, He has secured redemption for all who believe and He stands in the presence of God on our behalf (v. 24). "Christ, having been offered once to bear the sins of many, will appear a second time, not to deal with sin but to save those who are eagerly waiting for him" (v. 28).

Day 256

But we are not of those who shrink back and are destroyed, but of those who have faith and preserve their souls.

Hebrews 10:39

Emphasis: But we are not of those who **shrink back** and are **destroyed,** but of those who **have faith** and **preserve** their souls.

Rewrite: We are not like those who turn away from God and are destroyed, but of the faithful whose souls will be preserved.

Application: When we look at the people in the Bible we will find that not many of them finished well. This has always been a problem in the Church and is why perseverance to the end is true evidence of conversion. What happened to you at some point in time means nothing if you later shrink back and are destroyed. Perseverance is a guarantee for a true believer. Philippians 1:6 says, "And I am sure of this, that he who began a good work in you will bring it to completion at the day of Jesus Christ." In verse 38 of Hebrews 10 the author says that the righteous one shall live by faith, and if he shrinks back, God has no pleasure in him. Shrinking back is evidence that you were never really a Christian. 1 John 2:19 says, "They went out from us, but they were not of us; for if they had been of us, they would have continued with us. But they went out, that it might become plain that they all are not of us." Shrinking back results in destruction, not everlasting life. That is why the author says, "For you have need of endurance, so that when you have done the will of God you may receive what is promised" (v. 36). How do we get the endurance to press on to the end and finish the race? First we are to think back on those early days when we first learned about Christ (v. 32). We were full of zeal for Christ, and we remained faithful through many trials and suffering. Next we are to remember the reward that awaits us (v. 35). Our home is not on this earth but is in Heaven. We must live for eternity not earthly pleasure. We are not of those who shrink back and are destroyed, but of those who have faith and preserve their souls. God is always preserving and upholding every step of the true Christian, and no true Christian can fall from grace (John 10:28-29). We must press on and persevere to the end and never look back.

Day 257

And there has not arisen a prophet since in Israel like Moses, whom the LORD knew face to face.

Deuteronomy 34:10

Emphasis: And there has not arisen a **prophet** since in Israel like Moses, whom the LORD knew **face to face.**

Rewrite: There has never been a prophet in Israel like Moses, who the Lord knew face to face.

Application: Moses spoke to God face to face. This is an amazing thought worth dwelling on. Exodus 33:11 says, "Thus the LORD used to speak to Moses face to face, as a man speaks to his friend." Moses was a friend of God, and the relationship between God and Moses was like the friendship between the closest friends. This kind of relationship was rare because the text says that no other prophet like Moses had arisen after Moses. However, God promised Moses that He would raise up a prophet like him one day in the future. Deuteronomy 18:18 says, "I will raise up for them a prophet like you from among their brothers. And I will put my words in his mouth, and he shall speak to them all that I command him." Who is this prophet like Moses who arose from Israel and spoke the very words of God? None other than Jesus. In Acts 3:20-22, Peter quotes this text from Deuteronomy and says that Jesus is the prophet like Moses who spoke the words of God. Jesus fulfilled this prophecy. Jesus knew the Father face to face and had continual communion with Him. The Father put His words in the mouth of Jesus, and Jesus spoke all that the Father commanded Him. Jesus, by His Word and Spirit reveals God's will for our salvation. Moses was only a type of Christ, modeling the true relationship that Jesus has with the Father. Even though it was rare to have a relationship with God the way Moses did in the old covenant, through Jesus, we are fully reconciled with God, and we can speak to God face to face. We have full access to God through Christ. We are changed from an enemy to a friend. We are a friend of the sovereign God of the universe. What an incredible thought! We were once alienated from God and dead in our sins, but now we have communion with our loving, gracious, kind God.

Day 258

And without faith it is impossible to please him, for whoever would draw near to God must believe that he exists and that he rewards those who seek him.

Hebrews 11:6

Emphasis: And without **faith** it is impossible to **please** Him, for whoever would draw near to God must **believe** that He exists and that He rewards those who seek Him.

Rewrite: It is impossible to please God without faith. He who comes to God must believe that He exists and that He rewards those who seek Him.

Application: "Now faith is the assurance of things hoped for, the conviction of things not seen" (Hebrews 11:1). We can do many things for God without faith. God is not pleased with us when we read the Bible, when we pray, when we gather with the Church, or when we do countless duties in the ministry. God is pleased with us when we have faith. Faith is a firm confidence that God will fulfill all that He has promised in and through Christ. Without faith it is impossible to please God, who demands that we believe all that Scripture speaks about Him. The author of Hebrews speaks of a variety of people throughout the ages and all they did, but what they accomplished was not necessarily what pleased God. God was pleased with them all because of their faith. They believed God and then acted on it. They didn't just acknowledge that God would fulfill his promises. Their faith caused them to act. Their faith opened their eyes to reality. So often we say we believe something about God, but our belief is not a reality in our lives. Do you believe that God is in control of all things? How is this a reality in your life? How does it change the way that you handle trials or difficulties? Do you really believe that God hates sin? How is this a reality in your life? Do you take sin seriously or do you justify it? Do you really believe you can come with confidence and boldness to God through Christ in prayer? How is this a reality in your life? You can't believe this and only pray 15 minutes a day. If faith does not cause radical changes in your life, then you don't have faith and cannot please God.

Day 259 – Your Meditation

Looking to Jesus, the founder and perfecter of our faith, who for the joy that was set before him endured the cross, despising the shame, and is seated at the right hand of the throne of God.

Hebrews 12:2

Read: Hebrews 11:1-12:2

Emphasis:_____

_____

_____

Rewrite:_____

_____

_____

Application:_____

_____

_____

_____

_____

_____

_____

_____

_____

_____

_____

_____

_____

_____

_____

_____

_____

_____

_____

Day 260

But the people of Benjamin did not drive out the Jebusites who lived in Jerusalem.

Judges 1:21

Emphasis: But the people of Benjamin **did not drive out** the Jebusites who lived in Jerusalem.

Rewrite: The people of Benjamin failed at driving out the Jebusites who lived in Jerusalem.

Application: When Israel entered the land of Canaan they had strict instructions to devote all the inhabitants to complete destruction and to make no covenant with them and show no mercy to them (Deuteronomy 7:2). Judah did not drive out the inhabitants of the plains (Judges 1:19). Benjamin followed the example of Judah (v. 21). Israel continued to fail God's command to destroy the inhabitants of Canaan. Six other tribes, Manasseh, Ephraim, Zebulun, Asher, Naphtali, and Dan did not drive out the Canaanites from their territories (vv. 27-36). Failure to drive out the Canaanites in obedience to God caused the Israelites to turn away from God and worship Baal and the gods of the Canaanites. Israel saw the new land and became content and complacent in their obedience to God. They traded a comfortable life in a new land for their God who brought them into it, and they lost their zeal for God. We can fall into the same snare with sin. God commands us to kill the sin in our lives. He wants nothing less than complete destruction, and He requires that we never compromise with sin. Becoming comfortable in our spiritual growth leads to a tolerating of sin, disobedience to God, a loss of zeal for the things of God, and an eventual hardening of the heart and turning away from God. We must always be fighting and struggling against sin and never be satisfied with any hint of sin in our lives. We must "lay aside every weight, and sin which clings so closely, and we must run with endurance the race that is set before us" (Hebrews 12:1). We have not battled against sin to the point of shedding blood so we must take courage and not grow weary or fainthearted. We must never become comfortable and satisfied with earthly things or success at the cost of practical holiness, or we will have the same fate as Israel.

Day 261

Remember those who are in prison, as though in prison with them, and those who are mistreated, since you also are in the body.

Hebrews 13:3

Emphasis: Remember those who are in **prison**, as though in prison with them, and those who are **mistreated**, since you also are in the body.

Rewrite: Remember the Christians who are treated badly and in prison, as though you were in prison with them, since you are part of the same body.

Application: Christians have always suffered for their faith in Jesus Christ. Jesus said, "A servant is not greater than his master. If they persecuted me, they will also persecute you" (John 15:20a). The prophets of God were imprisoned and killed throughout history. Jesus suffered more than any man has ever suffered. The apostles were imprisoned and suffered greatly, and countless followers of Christ since have been mistreated, have suffered, have been imprisoned for their faith, and have been martyred. Hebrews 11:35-38 recounts the men and women of God who have suffered for their faith. "Some were tortured, refusing to accept release, so that they might rise again to a better life. Others suffered mocking and flogging, and even chains and imprisonment. They were stoned, they were sawn in two, they were killed with the sword. They went about in skins of sheep and goats, destitute, afflicted, mistreated—of whom the world was not worthy— wandering about in deserts and mountains, and in dens and caves of the earth." Even today countless Christians throughout the world are in prison and suffering for their faith in Jesus. When we remember those who are in prison as though in prison with them, Jesus says that as we do this to one of the least of the brothers, we do it to Him (Matthew 25:40). We must heed this exhortation and never forget the price that our brothers and sisters in Christ who suffer worldwide for their faith must pay for their faith. The Church has a responsibility to care for the persecuted in prison. We must physically help them when possible, and we must be in prayer for them, as if we were next to them in the prison cell. When we are comfortable, we must think of those who are not.

Day 262

Count it all joy, my brothers, when you meet trials of various kinds, for you know that the testing of your faith produces steadfastness.

James 1:2-3

Emphasis: Count it all **joy**, my brothers, when you meet **trials** of various kinds, for you know that the **testing** of your faith produces **steadfastness.**

Rewrite: Brothers, you should rejoice when you meet various trials because they test your faith and produce in you steadfastness.

Application: James writes to Jewish Christians who fell into a worldly life-style and stopped putting their faith into action because of the persecution and trials they were experiencing. The afflictions that they were enduring were causing them to lose faith. The devil in his schemes was using persecution to lead men into sin and worldliness. It was easier to hide their faith and live worldly than to steadfastly press on in the faith. James taught them to rejoice in their trials because God uses trials to conform them into the image of Christ. Like a refining fire purifies, trials test our faith to prove its genuineness. A continual testing of our faith through trials will produce steadfastness and resolve in us so that we can press on and finish the race. James teaches that if we endure trials, testing, and temptation, we will receive a reward. Verse twelve says, "God blesses those who patiently endure testing and temptation. Afterward they will receive the crown of life that God has promised to those who love him." We are not blessed just because we suffer. We are blessed if we patiently endure in suffering. We often fall into the snare of letting our circumstances steal our joy away. If we have a lot of money we rejoice, but when we lose money we become depressed. When things are good we rejoice, when trials of any kind come, we lose our joy. Our joy should always come because of and through Christ. If we are truly drawing our joy from Christ alone, then whatever happens in our earthly lives will never change our joy. Whether we are rich or poor, healthy or sick, resting easy or suffering, we should have the same joy. When we really understand sanctification we will have even more joy in trials because they are the means to build our faith and steadfastness.

Day 263

And she said, "I will surely go with you. Nevertheless, the road on which you are going will not lead to your glory, for the LORD will sell Sisera into the hand of a woman."

Judges 4:9

Emphasis: And she said, "I will surely go with you. Nevertheless, the road on which you are going **will not lead to your glory**, for the LORD will sell Sisera into the hand of a woman."

Rewrite: Deborah said, "I will go with you, but you will not get glory for yourself, for the Lord will kill Sisera by the hand of a woman."

Application: Deborah, a female judge of Israel, lived in a time when Israel did evil which resulted in God giving them over to their enemies. At this particular time, Israel did evil, and the Lord handed them over to Jabin king of Canaan (v. 2). The commander of Jabin's army was a wicked man named Sisera, who cruelly abused Israel for twenty years (v. 3). God raised up Deborah to lead Israel back to God and into victory over their enemies. She called on Barak to lead the army of Israel, but Barak was too afraid to go without Deborah. Barak agreed to lead the army only on the condition of Deborah going with him (v. 8). She agreed to go but prophesied that Barak would get no glory for the victory because the mighty enemy of Israel, Sisera, would be killed by a woman. The army of Sisera was lured into the Kishon Valley where God changed the brook of Kishon into a torrent which bogged down the 900 chariots of Sisera. Sisera fled by foot as his army was being slaughtered, and he came to the tent of a woman named Jael who killed him with a tent peg. Who was the hero? Deborah? Barak? Jael? No. God was the true hero (v. 23). The glory for every victory ultimately goes to God, not to men. God demonstrated this with Gideon when He reduced his army from 32,000 to 300 men and defeated over 130,000 men of Midian (Judges 8:10). God can conquer by few or many, and He demonstrated this most gloriously at the cross of Christ. One man, Jesus Christ, brought victory over death and sin for the glory of God. We must always hesitate when we think that we have done something in our own strength. Every victory comes from God for His glory, and the credit is due to Him.

Day 264

It is better to take refuge in the LORD than to trust in man.

Psalm 118:8

Emphasis: It is better to take **refuge** in the LORD than to **trust in man**.

Rewrite: It is better to take security in the Lord than to trust in man.

Application: This Psalm was written at a time when the nation of Israel was in great danger from their enemies. It seemed that they were in a situation without hope. They could trust in the Lord or trust in men. They chose to trust in the Lord, and the Lord delivered them from their enemies and their impossible situation. They learned it was far better to take refuge in God than to trust in man. Anyone who has faced an impossible situation that gave them the opportunity to choose God or man can relate to this verse. Everyone will be put in a desperate situation by the providence of God so that they can learn to trust in Him alone. It is infinitely better to put all our trust in God, who is worthy to be trusted and faithful in all things, than to put any trust in men. Men will always fail, but it is impossible for God to ever fail. God is immutable; He never changes. God must keep all of His promises because it is impossible for God to lie. This makes God dependable and gives us great hope in any situation. Hebrews 6:18 says, "...by two unchangeable things, in which it is impossible for God to lie, we who have fled for refuge might have strong encouragement to hold fast to the hope set before us." God has ultimately proven He can be trusted by delivering us from His own wrath through His Son, Jesus Christ. Men failed at gaining salvation, but God did not fail. It is vain to trust in anything other than Christ. Christ is our only refuge and hope. Every person in your life will fail you at some point. Your money, your mind, your security, your spouse, your children, your best friend, the people who you trust the most, your government, your health, and your beauty will fail you in the end. Everything in this world will fail you. However, we have hope in God, who will never fail. Christ is our only refuge and hope, and He is *the* only refuge and hope of all mankind. We really only have one option. Trust in God alone. Run to Him. He will never fail you.

Day 265

What good is it, my brothers, if someone says he has faith but does not have works? Can that faith save him?

James 2:14

Emphasis: What good is it, my brothers, if someone says he has faith but does not have works? Can that faith save him?

Rewrite: If someone says he has faith but does not demonstrate it by works, what good is it?

Application: James says that faith without works is dead (James 2:17), and Paul says "the one who does not work but believes in him who justifies the ungodly, his faith is counted as righteousness" (Romans 4:5). In Romans 3:28 he says, "For we hold that one is justified by faith apart from works of the law." There appears to be a conflict between Paul and James, but they are both really saying the same thing. They are both looking at faith but from different perspectives. The context of Paul's writings were to those who were trying to earn their way to Heaven by keeping the law. Paul said that it is impossible to be justified by works without faith. James writes to those who say they have faith but show no evidence by their works. James is saying that if you say you have faith but there is no evidence of your faith, then it is no good. He is saying that works are evidence of faith, and if you have no good works that come from faith, then it is proof that you really have no faith. Our theology will drive our practice. If you say you believe something but don't live your life as one who believes, then you prove you really don't believe. For example, many people today have deceived themselves into believing they are a Christian even when their lives do not bear good fruit. They have prayed a prayer at some point in their lives, or they have had a pastor tell them they were saved because they walked an aisle. They believe they are saved only because they did these things, but their lives bear only bad fruit. Jesus teaches that a person is known by their fruits, and a good tree cannot bear bad fruit (Matthew 7:15-20). We must always examine our faith to see if it is genuine or deceptive. A profession of faith without a changed life and continual conforming to Christ is of no saving value. In fact, it is damning.

Day 266 – Your Meditation

But be doers of the word, and not hearers only, deceiving yourselves.

James 1:22

Read: James 1:19-27

Emphasis:_____

_____

_____

Rewrite:_____

_____

_____

Application:_____

_____

_____

_____

_____

_____

_____

_____

_____

_____

_____

_____

_____

_____

_____

_____

_____

_____

_____

Day 267

...not one word has failed of all the good things that the LORD your God promised concerning you. All have come to pass for you; not one of them has failed.

Joshua 23:14

Emphasis: Not one **word** has **failed** of all the good things that the LORD your God **promised** concerning you. All have come to pass for you; not one of them has failed.

Rewrite: Everything that the Lord promised you has come to pass; not one promise of God has failed.

Application: God has always fulfilled His promises, and He always will fulfill His promises because He is faithful and immutable. God has not, cannot, and does not change. His promises do not and cannot change. What God has sworn to do in His Word, cannot fail. As the Israelites finished their conquest of the land of Canaan, Joshua gave a final charge to Israel's leaders before his death. He reminded them that it was not by their strength that they won the land, but it was the Lord who fought for them (v. 10). He also reminded the leaders that not one word had failed of all the good things the Lord had promised them. Joshua reminded them of God's faithfulness to fulfill all His promises: blessings and curses. Joshua warned them that if they strayed from the Lord then God would faithfully fulfill all He said. Joshua said, "But just as all the good things that the LORD your God promised concerning you have been fulfilled for you, so the LORD will bring upon you all the evil things, until he has destroyed you from off this good land that the LORD your God has given you" (Joshua 23:15). God gave us His Word to reveal His will for our lives. There are consequences for obeying or disobeying the will of God. God's will is that we believe in the Savior Jesus Christ and obey the gospel with grief and repentance for our sins. To do anything other than this will result in God's promise of punishment for those who have sinned. God promises eternal life to those who believe and eternal death for those who reject Him. God is faithful to fulfill all of His promises in the Bible. Even though everything and everyone on earth fail, God will never fail.

Day 268

But if you have bitter jealousy and selfish ambition in your hearts, do not boast and be false to the truth.

James 3:14

Emphasis: But if you have **bitter jealousy** and **selfish ambition** in your hearts, do not boast and be false to the truth.

Rewrite: If you have bitter jealousy and selfish ambition in your hearts, do not hide the truth behind bragging and lying.

Application: James contrasts bitter jealousy and selfish ambition with honor and humility in the previous verse. He says, "Who is wise and understanding among you? By his good conduct let him show his works in the meekness of wisdom" (James 3:13). Bitter jealousy and selfish ambition go hand in hand. When everything you do is to promote and advance yourself then you will be bitterly jealous when something impedes your advancement or rivals your promotion. A Christian must not have any trace of bitter jealousy or selfish ambition. We are to promote Christ and have zeal for God. Jesus Christ was the most selfless and humble man who has ever lived. Paul urges the Philippians to have the same mind as Christ and, "Do nothing from selfish ambition or conceit, but in humility count others more significant than yourselves" (Philippians 2:3). Selfishness and jealousy are part of our sin nature that we must destroy. It is challenging to put everyone's interests before our interests. It is difficult to make our ambition for the good of another while we suffer. It is arduous to pray for our co-workers to advance instead of ourselves. By our sinful nature we tend to tear down others so that we will look good. We find ourselves slandering another person so that we will win the favor of another and promote ourselves. We find deep bitterness in our souls when someone who we consider less worthy than us becomes successful or gets praise. How disgraceful is this sin and how opposite of our Lord Jesus are these attributes? We must never tolerate bitter jealousy and selfish ambition for any reason. We must mortify these vile sins and examine what we have deep in our beings and then fall on our faces in repentance. We should always live our lives in a way that our ambition and zeal is for God and His advancement.

Day 269

And if it is evil in your eyes to serve the LORD, choose this day whom you will serve, whether the gods your fathers served in the region beyond the River, or the gods of the Amorites in whose land you dwell. But as for me and my house, we will serve the LORD.

Joshua 24:15

Emphasis: And if it is **evil** in your eyes to serve the LORD, **choose** this day whom you will serve, whether the gods your fathers served in the region beyond the River, or the gods of the Amorites in whose land you dwell. But as for me and my house, **we will serve the LORD.**

Rewrite: If you think it is evil to serve the Lord, choose which of the other gods to serve. As for me and my house, we will serve the Lord.

Application: Joshua gives a bold ultimatum to Israel in his final exhortation. He tells them to fear the Lord and serve Him in sincerity and in faithfulness and put away the gods of their fathers (v. 14). If that seemed like an evil idea to Israel then Joshua gave them the second option. He said "choose this day whom you will serve, whether the gods your fathers served in the region beyond the River, or the gods of the Amorites in whose land you dwell." If Israel would not devote themselves fully and wholly to God alone then they should serve whatever gods they wanted and face condemnation. They could choose the gods of their fathers or the new gods of the Canaanites. Either way it would lead to their destruction. Joshua boldly said he and his house would serve the Lord. Joshua led the people in being fully dedicated to God alone. The Lord is a holy and jealous God, and He will not share His glory with anyone (vv. 19-20). God expects His people to be wholly devoted to Him. Jesus explained this in Matthew 6:24, "No one can serve two masters, for either he will hate the one and love the other, or he will be devoted to the one and despise the other." Ever since Christ ascended to Heaven, people have merged Christianity with other religions. They put Jesus on the shelf with their other gods, the world, superstitions, and man-made religions. This is worse than being an atheist and will only lead to condemnation. We must wholly serve God alone and put off everything else in our lives.

Day 270

For where you go I will go, and where you lodge I will lodge. Your people shall be my people, and your God my God.

Ruth 1:16b

Emphasis: For **where you go I will go**, and where you lodge I will lodge. Your people shall be my people, and **your God my God.**

Rewrite: Where you go I will go, and where you live I will live. I will make your people be my people, and your God my God.

Application: This bold statement from Ruth is a great example of salvation. Ruth forsook everything she knew to go with Naomi. She left her culture for the laws and customs of the people of God. She turned from her gods to the true and living God. She forsook her family for God's family, and she was resolved to go with Naomi, resolved to live in a new land with her, and resolved to worship her God. Ruth even says that she would remain where Naomi dies. She says, "Where you die I will die, and there will I be buried" (v. 17). Naomi was fully surrendered and resolved to persevere to the end. This foreshadows the importance of faith and the need to follow after Christ wherever He goes, wherever He is, to dwell with His people and to be fully surrendered and resolved to persevere in faith until death comes. This is truly how conversion should look. Often times we see the opposite. We see people say they will follow Christ, but they are still pursuing their own dreams instead of God's will. We see people say they will follow Christ where He leads, but they limit themselves to their home country and even their hometown. They will follow Christ as long as that doesn't mean uprooting themselves, like Ruth, and moving to a different country for the sake of the gospel. They say their new family is the people of God, but they look for an excuse to forsake the fellowship of the saints. They say they worship the true God, but their life does not look any different from the life of an atheist. They say they will faithfully serve Christ, but at the same time they pray for an easy, comfortable life and a peaceful death. We must be like Ruth and be resolved to forsake everything for the sake of following Christ. We must be willing to leave behind our comforts, culture, country, and relatives for Christ's glory.

Day 271

To an inheritance that is imperishable, undefiled, and unfading, kept in heaven for you.

1 Peter 1:4

Emphasis: To an **inheritance** that is **imperishable**, **undefiled**, and **unfading**, kept in **Heaven** for you.

Rewrite: We have an inheritance kept in Heaven, that will not decay, that is pure, and that will not change.

Application: Peter writes to a group that he calls "elect exiles." He uses this name to remind them that their inheritance is not in this earthly world but in the new world to come with Christ. He calls them to bless the God and Father of the Lord Jesus Christ for His great mercy. How did God show mercy? He "caused us to be born again to a living hope through the resurrection of Jesus Christ from the dead" (v. 3). Our sovereign God did all the work of salvation in us based on His motivation of love, mercy, and grace. The Christian has been born again, "not of perishable seed but of imperishable, through the living and abiding word of God" (v. 23). Because we have been born again spiritually which is imperishable and eternal, likewise, our inheritance is also imperishable. Our eternal home is in Heaven. It will never change or fade away. Our inheritance we received through Christ is waiting for us when we die and when we are united with Christ in Heaven. Meditating on the aspects of Heaven that we know from Scripture will encourage us to press on in this life with all that is in us. Our earthly inheritance will rot and perish, but our heavenly inheritance will remain perfect forever. Our earthly inheritance is defiled by sin and misery, but our heavenly inheritance is pure and perfect. Our earthly inheritance will be lost to another, but our heavenly inheritance is ours forever. When someone dies on earth there is always fighting over the inheritance, but the riches of our glorious inheritance are reserved for us in Heaven without question. Our unfathomable inheritance comes to us through Christ, and it is Christ. We have Christ which means we have everything and lack nothing. Thomas Goodwin said, "One saint in heaven has more glory and joy in his heart than all the joy that is on earth."

Day 272

But Samson said to his father, "Get her for me, for she is right in my eyes."

Judges 14:3b

Emphasis: But Samson said to his father, "Get her for me, for she is **right in my eyes**."

Rewrite: Samson said, "I want her because it is right to me."

Application: The last verse in the book of Judges summarizes the ideology of Israel, "In those days there was no king in Israel. Everyone did what was right in his own eyes" (Judges 21:25). We see an example of this ideology with Samson. In Deuteronomy 7:3, Israel is forbidden to intermarry with the Canaanite people. Samson knew this, but he chose to disobey God and obey his own lustful desires. Of course our sovereign God ordained this to bring deliverance to Israel from their enemies, but the choices of Samson to do what was right in his eyes eventually led to his demise. Like all of the judges, Samson was imperfect and could only lead his people for a short time before his fall. This points to the need for a perfect Savior King who would deliver His people once for all time. Doing what is right in our eyes will always lead to our downfall. The book of Proverbs speaks much about this. "There is a way that seems right to a man, but its end is the way to death" (Proverbs 14:12). We should never make decisions based on our feelings, and we should never trust our hearts. Jeremiah 17:9 makes this clear, "The heart is deceitful above all things, and desperately sick; who can understand it?" God gave us the Scriptures to teach us wisdom so that we will not depend on our fallible ideology. When we disobey what the Scriptures say is wise, and obey what we think is right, we put ourselves above Scripture. When we do this we prove to be foolish. "Do you see a man who is wise in his own eyes? There is more hope for a fool than for him" (Proverbs 26:12). God has given us the Holy Spirit, who speaks to us through the Scriptures, and godly brothers and sisters in Christ to help us in discernment. Before we make a decision based on what we think is right, we should seek the counsel of Scripture. "The way of a fool is right in his own eyes, but a wise man listens to advice" (Proverbs 12:15).

Day 273 – Your Meditation

Instead you ought to say, "If the Lord wills, we will live and do this or that."

James 4:15

Read: James 4:13-17

Emphasis:_____

_____

_____

Rewrite:_____

_____

_____

Application:_____

_____

_____

_____

_____

_____

_____

_____

_____

_____

_____

_____

_____

_____

_____

_____

_____

_____

_____

_____

_____

Day 274

But you are a chosen race, a royal priesthood, a holy nation, a people
for his own possession, that you may proclaim the excellencies of him
who called you out of darkness into his marvelous light.

1 Peter 2:9

Emphasis: But you are a chosen race, a royal priesthood, a holy nation, a people for His own possession, that you may proclaim the **excellencies** of Him who called you out of darkness into His marvelous light.

Rewrite: Because you are a chosen race, a royal priesthood, a holy nation, and God's own possession, you must proclaim the excellencies of Him who called you out of darkness into His marvelous light.

Application: Peter wrote primarily to Gentile Christians (1 Peter 1:1) and said, "But you are a chosen race, a royal priesthood, a holy nation, a people for his own possession." Peter applies special privileges and titles reserved for Old Testament Israel freely to the New Testament church. The Church is the one true people of God, made up of believing Jews and Gentiles. What does this mean, and how does it apply to us? This verse shows us our purpose of being God's own possession. We are to proclaim the excellencies of God. What are the excellencies? One of the many excellencies is God called us out of the darkness into His marvelous light. Once we lived in darkness without hope and without God. Once we were not a people, but now we are God's people; once we had not received mercy, but now we have received mercy (v. 10). If we could really grasp this fact then we would have no problems proclaiming the excellencies of Jesus Christ. It is odd that we can talk to strangers about the weather, sports, and just about any other thing, but when it comes to talking to someone about the excellencies of Christ, we freeze up and are ashamed. What a deplorable state we live in! What deadness we have in our souls! We don't proclaim the excellencies of Christ because we don't really know them and we don't really have communion with Him. What is the remedy? We must read the Scriptures and meditate on the excellencies of the person and work of Christ our Savior who brought us out of darkness into His marvelous light. The end of our meditation should drive us to act.

Day 275

And all who saw it said, "Such a thing has never happened or been seen from the day that the people of Israel came up out of the land of Egypt until this day.

Judges 19:30

Emphasis: And all who saw it said, "Such a thing **has never happened or been seen** from the day that the people of Israel came up out of the land of Egypt until this day.

Rewrite: They saw it and said that nothing so wicked has ever happened or been seen since Israel left Egypt.

Application: This is the gruesome story of a Levite and his concubine (Judges 19-20). The Levite was traveling from Bethlehem to Ephraim. It was getting late in the day so he sought refuge in a town called Gibeah. While they waited in the open square, an old man offered to take care of them. While at the old man's house, the worthless men in the city surround them and demanded that the old man turn over his guests so that they could molest them. The Levite seized his concubine and made her go out to them. The wicked men abused her all night, and she was found dead at the doorstep in the morning. The Levite took her home and cut her limb by limb into twelve pieces and sent her throughout all of Israel and demanded that this injustice be reckoned with. The people in Gibeah had become just like the people of Sodom and Gomorrah. They were given over to sin until they became numb to it. "God gave them up in the lusts of their hearts to impurity, to the dishonoring of their bodies among themselves" (Romans 1:24). The depths of sin always drive men to this point of madness. We often here about some new tragedy, another school shooting, another government attack against Christianity and we say with the Levite, "Such a thing has never happened or been seen since the foundation of our country." The further people dwell in the depths of sin, the more they harden their hearts and do worse things. God will eventually give them over to their sin and we will see unimaginable things. Every wicked tragedy that we see should remind us of the depth of sin and the need for salvation. It should cause us to proclaim the gospel, which is the only solution for sin and misery.

Day 276

You joyfully accepted the plundering of your property, since you knew that you yourselves had a better possession and an abiding one.

Hebrews 10:34

Emphasis: You joyfully accepted the plundering of your property, since you knew that you yourselves had a better possession and an abiding one.

Rewrite: When your property was robbed and plundered, you accepted it with joy, since you knew that a better and eternal possession awaited.

Application: When the gospel first went out from Jerusalem there was very intense persecution of Christians. The Hebrews in this letter faced a great deal of suffering. The author of Hebrews exhorts them to recall the former days right after their conversion and all of their suffering that they endured with joy. It can be easy for a person to forget his first zeal for the gospel when he becomes more comfortable with an easy life. In the former days these new believers joyfully accepted the plundering of their property. Because of their faith in Christ, their property was illegally seized, robbed, and pillaged. Christians were treated as the scum of the earth. Paul describes them like "men sentenced to death" and "men who have become a spectacle to the world, to angels, and to men." They became fools for Christ's sake (1 Corinthians 4:9–10). But in spite of all this, they counted it all joy to go through various trials, and they joyfully gave up all of their worldly wealth, possessions, and rights for the sake of Christ. They longed for Heaven where they would have a better life, better treasures, better liberty, better society, and better work. What a contrast from today where we see Christians defending their right to bear arms, their right to free speech, and their right to be wealthy. They spend more time building bunkers and resisting the government than they do proclaiming the glory of Christ. They have completely missed the battle. Sitting on a bucket of freeze dried potatoes in your bunker while holding your machine gun, threatening to murder anyone who takes your potatoes is an embarrassment to Christ and opposite of the Christians who joyfully accepted the plundering of their property for Christ's sake. Even if we lose everything, we have Christ, and He is enough.

Day 277

And I declare to him that I am about to punish his house forever, for the iniquity that he knew, because his sons were blaspheming God, and he did not restrain them.

1 Samuel 3:13

Emphasis: And I declare to him that I am about to punish his house forever, **for the iniquity that he knew,** because his sons were blaspheming God, and **he did not restrain them**.

Rewrite: I will punish his house forever because he allowed his sons to openly sin, and he did not restrain them.

Application: A priest named Eli had two worthless sons named Hophni and Phinehas who did not know the Lord (1 Samuel 2:12). Even though they did not know God, they became priests because their father was a priest. They abused the priesthood by treating the offering of the Lord with contempt, laying with the women of the temple, and dealing in an evil way with the people. Eli found this out and warned his sons, but he never removed them from the priesthood nor did he restrain them. God warned Eli that he would kill his wicked sons and raise up a faithful priest who would do according to what is in God's heart and mind (1 Samuel 2:35). Samuel would be this future priest, but ultimately this points to the need for a faithful high priest who would do the will of God forever. Jesus fulfills the role of our eternal priest. Regarding the wicked son's of Eli, we read in 1 Samuel 4:11 that God's promise comes to pass. The ark of God was captured, and the two sons of Eli died. When Eli heard the news of his sons and the that the ark of God was captured, he fell over dead. The wife of Phinehas went into labor early when she saw these events unfold. Before she died in childbirth she named her son Ichabod because the glory of the Lord had departed from Israel. This progression of destruction all stemmed from Eli tolerating the sin of his children under his roof. It is easy to fall into the same snare when you are more worried about your reputation than sin. Do we tolerate or ignore the sins of our children at home, but when we are in public we make them behave? If so, we are in sin and teaching our children to be hypocrites, both of which have deadly consequences.

Day 278

For Christ also suffered once for sins, the righteous for the unrighteous, that he might bring us to God, being put to death in the flesh but made alive in the spirit.

1 Peter 3:18

Emphasis: For Christ also suffered **once** for sins, the **righteous for the unrighteous**, that He might **bring us to God**, being put to death in the flesh but made alive in the spirit.

Rewrite: Christ suffered for our sins once. He, being righteous, died for us, who are unrighteous, so that He could bring us to God. He was put to death in His body but made alive in the spirit.

Application: This is one of the great proof texts of the doctrine of substitutionary atonement. We learn that Christ suffered for our sins once for all time. The Roman Catholic church teaches that Jesus must be sacrificed during each mass in order to forgive sins. However, Jesus did not have to offer Himself repeatedly, "as the high priest enters the holy places every year with blood not his own, for then he would have had to suffer repeatedly since the foundation of the world. But as it is, he has appeared once for all at the end of the ages to put away sin by the sacrifice of himself" (Hebrews 9:25–26). The reason Jesus suffered was for our sins. We are sinners, all of us, and we must reconcile our sins one day. We can pay the penalty for our sins in Hell for all eternity, or we can have a perfect Savior substitute Himself in our place and pay our penalty. Jesus did this. He who is perfect and sinless suffered for the sinful and unrighteous. The purpose of all of Christ's suffering was to bring us to God. We are born in sin and separated from God. We are naturally an enemy of God from birth, but through the substitutionary death of Jesus, we can be reconciled with God and brought home to Him. Jesus died in His flesh but was made alive in the spirit so that He could make us alive spiritually for the first time in our lives. Peter wrote this letter to remind the persecuted Christians who were suffering unjustly that Christ also suffered unjustly. Christ suffered far more unjustly and more than any man has ever suffered when He bore the wrath of God. As we suffer, we must meditate on Christ's suffering for us.

Day 279

"No! But there shall be a king over us, that we also may be like all the nations, and that our king may judge us and go out before us and fight our battles."

1 Samuel 8:19b-20

Emphasis: "No! But there shall be a king over us, **that we also may be like all the nations**, and that our king may judge us and go out before us and fight our battles."

Rewrite: No! We want a king so that we can be like the other nations, and that our king may judge and fight our battles.

Application: Israel traded the King of kings for a corrupt king of men. When Samuel heard this request he was grieved, but God told him to give the people what they wanted because they had rejected God from being king over them. Israel rejected God as their perfect, eternal king so that they could be like the other nations. This was the consistent pattern of Israel throughout their existence. Like all people, Israel wanted the world instead of God. Israel wanted praise from men rather than God. They wanted to be like the nations instead of the people who God wanted them to be. The people's rejection of God as their king is a picture of the rejection of Christ as the King of kings and Lord of lords. Peter shows that the heart of Israel had never changed throughout the ages. He says to Israel concerning their rejection of Jesus for Barabbas, "But you denied the Holy and Righteous One, and asked for a murderer to be granted to you, and you killed the Author of life, whom God raised from the dead" (Acts 3:14–15). Israel got what they wanted. God gave them over to their own wicked desires and gave them king Saul. Saul utterly failed Israel as their king, and God eventually killed him. We read of Saul's tragic end in 1 Chronicles 10:13-14; it says, "So Saul died for his breach of faith. He broke faith with the LORD in that he did not keep the command of the LORD, and also consulted a medium, seeking guidance. He did not seek guidance from the LORD. Therefore the LORD put him to death." We can't have God and the world. It is impossible to serve two masters. We must be fully surrendered to God and His will and mortify our sinful desires for the world.

Day 280 – Your Meditation

He himself bore our sins in his body on the tree, that we might die to sin and live to righteousness. By his wounds you have been healed.

1 Peter 2:24

Read: 1 Peter 2:13-25

Emphasis:_____

_____

_____

Rewrite:_____

_____

_____

Application:_____

_____

_____

_____

_____

_____

_____

_____

_____

_____

_____

_____

_____

_____

_____

_____

_____

_____

_____

_____

Day 281

And God gave Solomon wisdom and understanding beyond measure, and breadth of mind like the sand on the seashore.

1 Kings 4:29

Emphasis: And God gave Solomon wisdom and understanding **beyond measure,** and breadth of mind like the sand on the seashore.

Rewrite: God gave Solomon wisdom, knowledge, and understanding beyond measure.

Application: Solomon had more than any man has ever had. He had the "American Dream" beyond anyone else. He ruled a vast land, people always brought him tribute, he lived in peace and security, he had 40,000 stalls of horses, and all his days he lacked nothing (1 Kings 4:20-28). He had wealth, health, security, and wisdom beyond any man (v. 31). One would think Solomon would have been the happiest man on earth. However, this same man wrote the words, "Vanity of vanities, says the Preacher, vanity of vanities! All is vanity" (Ecclesiastes 1:2). Solomon found vanity in self indulgence, wisdom, toil, and wealth. He called life vanity and came to the conclusion that no matter what a person has or who a person is, death comes to all (Ecclesiastes 9:1-9). He coined the proverb: "in the place where the tree falls, there it will lie" (Ecclesiastes 11:3). Everyone must die and, whether a friend or enemy, one's relationship with God will be what remains when we die. At the end of Solomon's life he came to one conclusion: "Fear God and keep his commandments, for this is the whole duty of man. For God will bring every deed into judgment, with every secret thing, whether good or evil" (Ecclesiastes 12:13–14). We must stop and look at what we are living for. What are our motives? What are the goals we have in life? Most people spend their life pursuing the things Solomon had achieved. They think that achieving what Solomon did will bring them great joy and contentment. We must learn from Solomon and know that all of it is vanity. We must live for Christ or nothing. Everything we live for apart from Christ will only be kindling for the fires of Hell. We must put away the vain thoughts of satisfying our flesh on this earth and live for Christ.

Day 282

But in your hearts honor Christ the Lord as holy, always being prepared to make a defense to anyone who asks you for a reason for the hope that is in you; yet do it with gentleness and respect.

1 Peter 3:15

Emphasis: But in your hearts **honor Christ** the Lord as **holy**, always being **prepared** to make a defense to anyone who asks you for a reason for the **hope** that is in you; yet do it with **gentleness and respect.**

Rewrite: Honor Christ the Lord as holy and always be prepared to proclaim the hope that we have in Him to anyone who asks, but do it gently with respect.

Application: This is a well known verse that urges people on in evangelism. The context of this verse is Peter exhorting Christians who have been suffering for the gospel. He urges them to suffer for doing what is right because God will reward them for it. Peter exhorts them to not worry about or fear their persecutors, but to honor Christ in the manner in which they live. People are going to see them suffering and ask what possible reason of hope they could have amidst all their suffering. They were to be prepared at that moment to explain their glorious hope in the risen Christ. Just as Christ is holy, they also should live a holy life and explain their hope in holiness. They are not to spread the gospel by force or by mocking people who don't understand or be marked by anger. Paul exhorts Timothy to do the same thing. He says, "The Lord's servant must not be quarrelsome but kind to everyone, able to teach, patiently enduring evil, correcting his opponents with gentleness" (2 Timothy 2:24–25). There is a wrong way to explain something that is true. Always seeking controversy or seeking to boast in your own knowledge or always trying to win an argument are wrong ways to defend our hope in Christ. If we suffer, we should suffer for our faith in Christ, not because we are loudmouthed fools who offend everyone. Often people think they are being persecuted for their faith, but in reality they are suffering for their own stupidity. We must be like Christ and explain the truth of the gospel in a gentle, respectful, but bold manner and demonstrate a bold joy in proclaiming Christ.

Day 283

Sing to the LORD, all the earth! Tell of his salvation from day to day. Declare his glory among the nations, his marvelous works among all the peoples!

1 Chronicles 16:23-24

Emphasis: Sing to the LORD, all the earth! **Tell of His salvation** from day to day. **Declare His glory** among the nations, His marvelous works among **all the peoples!**

Rewrite: Let the earth sing to the Lord and every day proclaim His salvation. Declare His glory and amazing works to all the people and nations.

Application: This passage is a song of thanksgiving by David which is composed of three different Psalms (105, 96, 106). David wrote this after the ark was successfully brought back to Jerusalem. The philosophy of missions today can be taken from this song. We see that we are to rejoice in the Lord and tell of His salvation from day to day. When we have the cure for death, and don't share it, we are worse than a wicked doctor who finds the cure for cancer and refuses to share it. Also, we must declare the glory of God and His marvelous works to all the nations. The word *nations* does not mean the nation of Israel but a foreign nation. God has wondrous works which are worthy of proclaiming. David exhorts Israel to tell all the nations of God's wonderful works, His wonderful deeds, His wonderful salvation, and His wonderful glory, in that all things were worked out by God for His own glory and purpose. The same principle applies to missions by exhorting us to tell all the nations of God's wonderful works, His wonderful deeds, His wonderful salvation, which was accomplished by God sending His Son Jesus Christ to suffer and die in our place and satisfy divine justice by crushing Him instead of us. We must not stay home! We must go to all the nations because we have such good news and such hope for all the nations that we cannot hide it. Paul was willing to throw himself into Hell for the salvation of the nations (Romans 9:3). How much less should our burden be to declare the glory of Christ to every last person on this planet?

Day 284

They are surprised when you do not join them in the same flood of debauchery, and they malign you.

1 Peter 4:4

Emphasis: They are surprised when you do not **join them** in the same flood of **debauchery**, and they **malign** you.

Rewrite: They are surprised when you do not join them in wickedness like you once did, so they slander you.

Application: Peter calls Christians to stopping living to fulfill the passions of the flesh but to live for the will of God (v. 2). No longer is a Christian a slave to sin and debauchery. Verse three says, "For the time that is past suffices for doing what the Gentiles want to do, living in sensuality, passions, drunkenness, orgies, drinking parties, and lawless idolatry." When God converts the soul and brings it out of darkness into the marvelous light, all desires and motivations change. No longer will a Christian desire to live in these sins. A true Christian will begin to hate sin more and more and desire to do the will of God. This is the normal and expected result of true conversion. Every Christian has experienced this verse. Once changed by the Holy Spirit, your friends are shocked at your change and at the fact that you will not join them in debauchery anymore. Before Christ, you may have been the leader of your friends in drunkenness and debauchery, but now you refuse to join in any of these sins. Your old friends can't understand it, and at first they try to lure you back into these sins, but when they fail, they begin to malign you and slander you. Eventually they disconnect themselves from you because they hate the light that shines from you. "For everyone who does wicked things hates the light and does not come to the light, lest his works should be exposed" (John 3:20). Verse four tells us not to be surprised when this happens. It is the inevitable outcome of true conversion. However, when your old friends malign you for your faith in Christ and your changed life, they are only further condemning themselves. Verse five says, "But they will give account to him who is ready to judge the living and the dead." We must never give into sin and pressure from wicked friends, but strive for holiness, no matter what the cost.

Day 285

Behold, to obey is better than sacrifice...

1 Samuel 15:22b

Emphasis: Behold, to **obey** is better than **sacrifice.**

Rewrite: Obedience to God is better than sacrifice.

Application: This verse is from the story where the Lord rejects Saul as king. At this point Saul was already failing as king and moving away from God. Saul was instructed to strike the city of Amalek and devote everything to destruction, sparing no people or animals (v. 3). Saul attacked and defeated Amalek, but he did not obey God by destroying everything. Saul and the people spared king Agag and the best of the animals (v. 9). When Samuel arrived, Saul came to him in excitement about his defeat of Amalek, and he told Samuel that he performed all that the Lord had said. Samuel responded by saying, "What then is this bleating of the sheep in my ears and the lowing of the oxen that I hear?" (v. 14). Samuel then went on to tell Saul that God was removing him from being king because of his disobedience. Through Samuel, God said these hard words to Saul, "Has the LORD as great delight in burnt offerings and sacrifices, as in obeying the voice of the LORD? Behold, to obey is better than sacrifice, and to listen than the fat of rams. For rebellion is as the sin of divination, and presumption is as iniquity and idolatry. Because you have rejected the word of the LORD, he has also rejected you from being king" (vv. 22-23). Saul admitted that he disobeyed God because of the pressure of the people. Saul feared the people more than God. It is interesting that God equates the sin of disobedience to witchcraft and the sin of presumption to idolatry. This shows that when we choose to disobey God there is something deeper behind the simple act. Our sin lures us into witchcraft and idolatry when we disobey. We are serving the devil rather than God. When we disobey God it is because we fear men and devils far more than our sovereign God. Peter and the apostles understood this principle. When the high priest charged them not to teach in the name of Jesus, they responded with the bold words, "We must obey God rather than men" (Acts 5:29). If we could only live by this principle we would change the world.

Day 286

...casting all your anxieties on him, because he cares for you.

1 Peter 5:7

Emphasis: Casting all your **anxieties** on Him, because **He cares** for you.

Rewrite: Give all your worries to God because He cares for you.

Application: He cares for you. God really cares for you. He loves you. He is concerned for you. He wants to take your worries and troubles. Jesus says, "Come to me, all who labor and are heavy laden, and I will give you rest" (Matthew 11:28). Because of God's attributes, we can trust God with all our anxieties and troubles. God is merciful, patient, gracious, and loving. God is also sovereign over all and has all power. We should cast all our anxieties and cares upon God because He wants us to, and we can cast all of our anxieties on God because He is able to bear them. Again, Jesus says, "Take my yoke upon you, and learn from me, for I am gentle and lowly in heart, and you will find rest for your souls. For my yoke is easy, and my burden is light" (Matthew 11:29–30). Peter writes to suffering Christians and exhorts them to grow in humility in suffering and cast their anxieties on God instead of pridefully trying to take the battle into their own hands. 1 Peter 5:5 says, "Clothe yourselves, all of you, with humility toward one another, for 'God opposes the proud but gives grace to the humble.'" We must humbly submit to God, who is in control of all things, amidst our suffering. We must fully surrender to Him and His will because He ordained our suffering and is working it out for His glory and our good. One day our suffering will end so we must "humble yourselves under the mighty hand of God so that at the proper time he may exalt us" (v. 6). Knowing that one day our suffering will cease, and we will be exalted in Heaven, should give us great resolve to persevere through suffering as well as cause greater dependence on God. When we worry and are anxious, we are prideful. We think we can handle our troubles better than God, and we disbelieve that God can bear our burdens. "Therefore do not be anxious about tomorrow, for tomorrow will be anxious for itself. Sufficient for the day is its own trouble" (Matthew 6:34). Cast your cares upon Him. He cares.

Day 287 – Your Meditation

For the LORD sees not as man sees: man looks on the outward appearance, but the LORD looks on the heart.

1 Samuel 16:7b

Read: 1 Samuel 16:1-13

Emphasis:_____

_____

_____

Rewrite:_____

_____

_____

Application:_____

_____

_____

_____

_____

_____

_____

_____

_____

_____

_____

_____

_____

_____

_____

_____

_____

_____

Day 288

God did not spare angels when they sinned, but cast them into hell and committed them to chains of gloomy darkness to be kept until the judgment.

2 Peter 2:4

Emphasis: **God did not spare angels** when they sinned, **but cast them into Hell** and committed them to chains of gloomy darkness to be kept until the judgment.

Rewrite: God did not spare the rebellious angels but cast them into Hell to be kept until the judgment.

Application: Peter writes about the sure judgment of false prophets and the sure rescue of the his people. Peter uses "if" and "then" statements to make his point. He says, "For if God did not spare angels when they sinned, but cast them into hell and committed them to chains of gloomy darkness to be kept until the judgment; if he did not spare the ancient world, but preserved Noah, a herald of righteousness, with seven others, when he brought a flood upon the world of the ungodly; if by turning the cities of Sodom and Gomorrah to ashes he condemned them to extinction, making them an example of what is going to happen to the ungodly; and if he rescued righteous Lot, greatly distressed by the sensual conduct of the wicked (for as that righteous man lived among them day after day, he was tormenting his righteous soul over their lawless deeds that he saw and heard); then the Lord knows how to rescue the godly from trials, and to keep the unrighteous under punishment until the day of judgment" (2 Peter 2:4–9). If all of these statements are true then Peter makes it clear that it is impossible for an unrepentant sinner to be saved, and it is a guarantee that a repentant sinner who has faith in Jesus will be rescued from the punishment they deserve. No one can escape judgment. Because of God's great love, He ordained a divine rescue plan to save His people from the punishment they deserve. God punished His own Son on the cross instead of us. Jesus bore our punishment so that the divine justice of God would be satisfied and we would be rescued. It is amazing that God did not spare angels when they sinned once, but He crushed His Son for the vilest sinners on earth.

Day 289

And he said to him, "I also am a prophet as you are, and an angel spoke to me by the word of the LORD, saying, 'Bring him back with you into your house that he may eat bread and drink water.'" But he lied to him.

1 Kings 13:18

Emphasis: And he said to him, "**I also am a prophet** as you are, and an **angel spoke to me** by the word of the LORD, saying, 'Bring him back with you into your house that he may eat bread and drink water.'" But **he lied** to him.

Rewrite: He said to him, "I also am a prophet, and an angel of God told me to tell you to come back to my house so that you can eat and drink." But he lied to him.

Application: A man of God, a prophet, was sent by the word of the Lord to Bethel to confront Jeroboam for his wickedness. Jeroboam stretched out his hand to seize the man of God, but his hand was dried up by God so that he could not draw it back in. The man of God returned as God had commanded. When an old prophet, who lived in Bethel, had heard of all that the man of God did to the king, he ran after him with great excitement. The old prophet found the man of God resting under a tree and asked him to come back to his house to eat and drink. The man of God had clear instructions from God to neither eat bread nor drink water nor return by the way that he came (v. 9), so he refused to go with the old prophet. The old prophet then said, "I also am a prophet as you are, and an angel spoke to me by the word of the LORD, saying, 'Bring him back with you into your house that he may eat bread and drink water.'" But he lied to him. The man of God was deceived by his lie and faced the swift justice of God for his disobedience and was killed (v. 24). Often when we have clear instructions from God in the Scriptures, the devil sends a false prophet to tempt us to disobey God. Sometimes people will approach us and say, "God told me to tell you..." This should be a red flag to us. God has already told us all that we need in the Scriptures, and God works one-on-one with His children. We must be very cautious with these self-proclaimed prophets and avoid falling into the same snare as the man of God in Bethel.

Day 290

The Lord is not slow to fulfill his promise as some count slowness, but is patient toward you, not wishing that any should perish, but that all should reach repentance.

2 Peter 3:9

Emphasis: The Lord is not slow to **fulfill** His promise as some count slowness, but is **patient** toward you, not wishing that **any should perish,** but that **all should reach repentance.**

Rewrite: God is not slow in fulfilling His promise, but His delay is because of His patience toward you, not wishing that any should die, but that all would come to repentance.

Application: Peter calls his readers to remember the predictions of the holy prophets and the commandment of the Lord and Savior through the apostles. The concern here is the delayed return of Christ. We have all heard people say that Jesus has not returned in 2000 years so He is not going to return. When people say this, they are fulfilling prophesy. Verses three and four say, "scoffers will come in the last days with scoffing, following their own sinful desires. They will say, 'Where is the promise of his coming? For ever since the fathers fell asleep, all things are continuing as they were from the beginning of creation.'" Peter rebukes these scoffers by saying they deliberately overlook that God did create everything and that He destroyed everything in the flood (v. 6). In the same way, the heavens and the earth are being stored up for fire on the day of judgment when the ungodly will be destroyed (v. 7). Peter also reminds his readers that God is outside of time, so with the Lord, one day is as a thousand years, and a thousand years as one day (v. 8). The good news about the delay in Christ's second coming is God has ordained this time because of His patience toward His people. God reveals His love for all men when He says that He does not wish that any should perish but that all should reach repentance. God loves the world and wants all men to repent. God's delay in judgment, His patience toward us, and His kindness are all meant to lead us to repentance (Romans 2:4). We long for Christ's return, but we can rejoice in the delay because God is revealing His love and patience toward His people.

Day 291

She fell at his feet and said, "On me alone, my lord, be the guilt."

1 Samuel 25:24a

Emphasis: She fell at his feet and said, "**On me alone**, my lord, be the **guilt**."

Rewrite: She said, "Let all the guilt fall on me, my lord."

Application: After David spared Saul's life, Saul temporarily ended his pursuit of David. While in the wilderness David found a large herd of sheep and goats owned by a very rich, but foolish, man named Nabal. David could have been like other men and ran off the shepherds and had a feast on the sheep, but instead, he protected the massive flocks and their shepherds from roaming bandits. David heard that it was time to shear the sheep. Nabal would be in good spirits. It was his biggest pay day of the year. He would have had plenty of food on hand for the great feast that was held for all the shearers, shepherds, and buyers. David must have thought that any man, especially a rich man like Nabal, would have an open heart because of this great time of feasting. David sent ten men to greet Nabal with great humility and respect. They explained that they were sent by David, who protected Nabal's sheep and shepherds all this time, and then they asked Nabal for whatever food he had on hand. Nabal, living up to his name, responds in foolishness and pride. He began putting David down accusing David of being a worthless runaway slave. At the same time that David was arming his men, there was a providential scene unfolding in Nabal's camp. When Abigail heard about how her husband treated David, she immediately put a plan into action that would save many lives. When Abigail saw David, she hurried and got down from the donkey and fell before David on her face and bowed to the ground. She fell at his feet and said, "On me alone, my lord, be the guilt." Abigail's guilt-bearing intercession appeased the wrath of David and her family was saved. This act prefigures the gracious guilt-bearing of Christ. Because of the amazing love of God, He sent a great sin-bearer and intercessor to stand in our place condemned, pay our penalty, and appease the just wrath of God. We must meditate upon Jesus, get a glimpse of His beauty and the beauty of the atonement.

Day 292

And we are writing these things so that our joy may be complete.

1 John 1:4

Emphasis: And we are writing these things so that our **joy** may be **complete.**

Rewrite: We are writing these things so that we will have fullness of joy.

Application: John writes this letter so that his readers will have joy and so that their joy will be complete. The joy that he speaks of is the joy of eternal life through the gospel. Our salvation should bring us fullness of joy. We were once enemies of God and without hope, but Jesus came down from Heaven to seek and save us. He bore the punishment that was due to us for our sins, and He imputed His righteousness to us. He atoned for our sins because He loves us. He willingly and joyfully went to the cross and was condemned in our place. "Jesus, the founder and perfecter of our faith, who for the joy that was set before him endured the cross, despising the shame, and is seated at the right hand of the throne of God" (Hebrews 12:2). We were reconciled to God at the cross, and we now can have communion with Him. This should bring us the greatest possible joy in our lives. The gospel brings joy to people. Jesus spoke of this purpose in John 15:11, stating, "These things I have spoken to you, that my joy may be in you, and that your joy may be full." True joy comes only through Christ. Jesus speaks of bringing us joy again in John 16:24. He says, "Until now you have asked nothing in my name. Ask, and you will receive, that your joy may be full." The greatest joy we will ever have in this life or the life to come is in our relationship with God through the gospel of Christ. The happiest moment we have ever had on earth apart from Christ will seem like misery in comparison to the joy we have in knowing Christ. When we understand that all of our sins are forgiven, they are all gone, we can do nothing but be overwhelmed in our joy towards God. We spend so much time trying to get joy out of life and the world, but it all fails in the end. When we truly understand that fullness of joy comes by knowing Christ, we will seek Him more and the world less. We will proclaim the gospel of joy more and be afraid less.

Day 293

And Elijah came near to all the people and said, "How long will you go limping between two different opinions? If the LORD is God, follow him; but if Baal, then follow him."

1 Kings 18:21

Emphasis: And Elijah came near to all the people and said, "How long will you go limping between **two different opinions**? **If the LORD is God, follow Him**; but if Baal, then follow him."

Rewrite: Elijah drew near to the people and said, "How long will you be undecided? If the Lord is God, follow Him; but if Baal, then follow him."

Application: This is the famous account of Elijah and the prophets of Baal. Elijah gathered Ahab, the evil king of Israel, the 450 prophets of Baal, and the 400 prophets of Asherah on top of Mount Carmel to once and for all demonstrate who is the true God of Israel. Elijah boldly challenges all of Israel to stop wavering in their beliefs. Whoever proved to be the true and living God should be worshiped by Israel. Elijah and the prophets of the false gods each set up a burnt offering to be consumed by the true God. Whichever God consumed the burnt offering with fire was the true God. The prophets of Baal and Asherah began their ceremony, crying out to Baal and cutting themselves until blood gushed from them, but they heard no response. Elijah mocked them in confidence that he worshiped the true and living God. Elijah made a trench around his burnt offering and poured so much water over the bull and wood that it was filled with water. Elijah then began to pray to God for His glory to be manifested and that the people would know that He was the true God. The fire of the Lord instantly fell and consumed the burnt offering and the wood and the stones and the dust (v. 38). The people saw it, and they fell on their faces and said, "The Lord, he is God; the Lord, he is God" (v. 39). This is the question for every man. If the God of the Bible is truly the living God, then He is worthy to be worshiped and followed. He is worthy to give our lives entirely. We must stop wavering in our struggle between our desires to follow the world and God. If God is your Lord, you must be fully surrendered to Him.

Day 294 – Your Meditation

For all things come from you, and of your own have we given you.

1 Chronicles 29:14b

Read: 1 Chronicles 29:10-19

Emphasis:_____
_____
_____

Rewrite:_____
_____
_____

Application:_____
_____
_____
_____
_____
_____
_____
_____
_____
_____
_____
_____
_____
_____
_____
_____
_____
_____
_____
_____
_____
_____

Day 295

And by this we know that we have come to know him, if we keep his commandments.

1 John 2:3

Emphasis: And **by this** we know that we have come to **know Him**, **if** we keep His commandments.

Rewrite: The evidence that we know God is that we keep His commandments.

Application: The letter of first John is a great letter to discover if you are truly a Christian. In the letter we see clear evidence of one who follows Christ and one who does not. John says that we know we are a child of God if we keep His commandments. When we were lost and without God, we were not concerned with keeping God's commandments. We broke them willingly, and we justified them daily. When a person is converted through faith in Christ, through the regeneration of the Holy Spirit, everything changes. Our desires, thoughts, motivations, and tenderness to sin all change. After conversion we have a new relationship with sin. We once loved and justified sin, but now we hate and mortify sin. Evidence of a true child of God is that we desire to obey God and walk in His ways. John says, "Whoever says 'I know him' but does not keep his commandments is a liar, and the truth is not in him, but whoever keeps his word, in him truly the love of God is perfected. By this we may know that we are in him: whoever says he abides in him ought to walk in the same way in which he walked" (vv. 4–6). This does not mean that a Christian will be sinless. In verse one John says, "My little children, I am writing these things to you so that you may not sin. But if anyone does sin, we have an advocate with the Father, Jesus Christ the righteous." A Christian will sin and will be forgiven by our advocate Jesus Christ. The difference is in our relationship with sin. We don't make a practice of sin. When a Christian falls into sin he has grief and hatred of the sin and then repents. "Whoever makes a practice of sinning is of the devil, for the devil has been sinning from the beginning (1 John 3:8). Living a lifestyle of justifying sin proves you are not of God.

Day 296

Blessed are the poor in spirit, for theirs is the kingdom of heaven.

Matthew 5:3

Emphasis: **Blessed** are the **poor in spirit,** for theirs is the kingdom of Heaven.

Rewrite: Blessed are those who know that they need God, for the kingdom of Heaven is theirs.

Application: After Jesus returned from being tempted by the devil in the wilderness, He began His public ministry. His first major discourse in the book of Matthew is called "The Sermon on the Mount." The fame of Jesus was spreading throughout the land, and great crowds were following Jesus everywhere to hear His teaching, to be healed, and to see His miracles. When Jesus saw the crowds, He went up on a mountain overlooking the Sea of Galilee and sat down. His disciples came to Him (v. 1), and the crowds gathered around to hear Him teach (Matthew 7:28). Jesus opened His mouth and began to teach what are now called the Beatitudes. The first Beatitude is this verse, "Blessed are the poor in spirit, for theirs is the kingdom of heaven." The Beatitudes are what the life of a Christian should look like. A Christian should be conforming to the image of Christ that we see in the Beatitudes. Christ is the perfection of the Beatitudes. He lived the Beatitudes perfectly. When we examine this Beatitude and want an actual example of the character trait "poor in spirit," we only need to look to Jesus. To be poor in spirit is to recognize a total dependence on God. It means to not depend on yourself but to be fully surrendered and dependent on God. Jesus demonstrated this perfectly. He was in continual communion with His Father and fully surrendered His will (Luke 22:42). Many times God crushes us through providential events to teach us to be poor in spirit. As a Christian is sanctified, he increasingly dies to himself and his ability, and instead he lives more for God and becomes more dependent on Him. In fact, at the point of conversion we see more clearly our desperate depravity and need for a Savior who we can depend on. It is only those who recognize their sins and their need for God who will enter the kingdom of Heaven. We must examine our dependence on God and surrender fully to Him.

Day 297

Blessed are those who mourn, for they shall be comforted.

Matthew 5:4

Emphasis: **Blessed** are those who **mourn**, for they shall be **comforted.**

Rewrite: Blessed are those who grieve, for they will be comforted.

Application: This Beatitude is quite strange when we first read it. Blessed means happy, and to mourn means to be sad. This verse could be read, "Happy are those who are sad." The world would never equate mourning for happiness. There are several types of mourning but only one type is blessed. There is a sinful mourning which is when you mourn over your physical condition so that others will feel sorry for you. You use self-pity so that others will pity you. A gracious mourning is the type of mourning that is blessed. A mourning over our sins and a godly sorrow which leads to repentance is blessed. A mourning over the sin, misery and corruption in this world which causes us to act is a blessed mourning. A mourning over the justification of sin and those who call evil good and good evil, is blessed. A mourning over the afflictions of others because of sin is a blessed mourning. When we mourn over the holocaust of abortion, we are blessed. When we weep with those who weep, we are blessed. When we mourn over the name of Christ being blasphemed, we are blessed. When we mourn over the multitude who have never heard the name of Christ, we are blessed. When we mourn, or have a deep concern for holiness, we are blessed. How are we blessed by this gracious mourning? When we mourn with a godly sorrow we are lead to repentance of our sins which leads to a conformity to the character of Christ. We are blessed because we are becoming more like Christ who wept and was a man of sorrows. We are blessed when we mourn because we will be comforted. We will be encouraged and consoled by the Holy Spirit. Psalm 34:18 says, "The LORD is near to the brokenhearted and saves the crushed in spirit." We will ultimately be comforted in Heaven, where we will have fulness of joy and all our tears will be wiped away. Blessed are the dead who die in the Lord from now on." "Blessed indeed," says the Spirit, "that they may rest from their labors, for their deeds follow them!" (Revelation 14:13b).

Day 298

Blessed are the meek, for they shall inherit the earth.

Matthew 5:5

Emphasis: **Blessed** are the **meek**, for they shall **inherit** the earth.

Rewrite: Blessed are the humble and gentle, for they will inherit the earth.

Application: Jesus quotes this verse from Psalm 37:11, which says, "But the meek shall inherit the land and delight themselves in abundant peace." Moses was the most meek man of his day (Numbers 12:3), but Jesus was the meekest man of all time. Paul boasts of Christ's meekness and gentleness (2 Corinthians 10:1). Christ is the perfect example of a meek man. Peter describes Christ's meekness in 1 Peter 2:23: "When he was reviled, he did not revile in return; when he suffered, he did not threaten, but continued entrusting himself to him who judges justly." Jesus refers to His own meekness in Matthew 11:29; he says, "Take my yoke upon you, and learn from me, for I am gentle and lowly in heart, and you will find rest for your souls." The meek are those who humbly submit their lives to God and walk in submission to His will. The meek are not weak, as the world may think today. The meek are bold as a lion but harmless as a dove. The meek have a gentle spirit to them and are disciplined and controlled by the Spirit rather than the flesh. They are considerate and have no problem surrendering their will for the benefit of others. They have thick skin and are hard to provoke to anger. It is easy for the meek to forgive, and they would rather forgive people a multitude of times rather than take revenge once. They build people up and keep a humble spirit rather than slander others to exalt themselves. A good test to see if you are meek is to observe how children treat you. Are they scared of you or do they run to you and always want to be around you? The meek will inherit the earth. The meek have the promise of eternal life. Meekness is an attribute of Christ, and it is an attribute that every true believer will develop in his walk. At the end of one's life, he should be more humble and broken over his sin than at the point of his conversion. He should be more meek and less proud. He should see less of himself and more of Christ.

Day 299

Blessed are those who hunger and thirst for righteousness, for they shall be satisfied.

Matthew 5:6

Emphasis: **Blessed** are those who **hunger and thirst** for **righteousness**, for they shall be **satisfied**.

Rewrite: Blessed are those who desire and long for righteousness, for they will be satisfied.

Application: We always hunger and thirst after something; whether it is more money, a better job, a good marriage, good children, a dream home, a great vacation, or better health, there is always a longing for an object or a dream that we think will improve our lives. God's desire is that we hunger and thirst for righteousness. Blessed is the man who longs for the right object. All other things that we long for in this life will fail us and leave us disappointed, but when we pursue righteousness, we will be satisfied. The Christian is already accounted as perfectly righteous by the imputed righteousness of Christ. 2 Corinthians 5:21 says, "For our sake he made him to be sin who knew no sin, so that in him we might become the righteousness of God." However, as long as we live on this sin filled earth and in a sin filled body, we will never be righteous. A Christian must hunger and pursue after righteousness, practical holiness, and Christ-likeness. Becoming like Christ in character should be the desperate longing of every Christian. As the body hungers for food and thirsts for water, we are to have a hunger and a thirst for God and to become less like ourselves and more like Christ each day. When a wolf gets hungry, it longs for blood, and it will never be satisfied until it kills and tastes that which it thirsted for. When a Christian has a hunger and thirst for righteousness, nothing will satisfy him in this world until he tastes that which he has longed for. We must kill sin in our lives and strive for practical holiness. When we truly desire righteousness, and we seek after it with all our heart, God will satisfy our desire, and we will be conformed to the image of Christ. Psalm 42:1 expresses the hunger for God that we should have: "As a deer pants for flowing streams, so pants my soul for you, O God."

Day 300

Blessed are the merciful, for they shall receive mercy.

Matthew 5:7

Emphasis: Blessed are the **merciful**, for they shall receive **mercy**.

Rewrite: Blessed are those who show mercy, for they shall receive it.

Application: God is the Father of mercies and God of all comfort (2 Corinthians 1:3). God's greatest act of mercy was sending His perfect Son to die for the vilest of sinners and cause us to be born again to a living hope through Christ (1 Peter 1:3). Throughout the New Testament are scenes of people crying out to Jesus for mercy, and He grants it to them through healing, miracles, and ultimately by giving up His own life on the cross. Jesus is the perfect demonstration of what it means to be merciful. We are to live out this attribute of God in the way we treat others. Jesus says in Luke 6:36, "Be merciful, even as your Father is merciful." God desires mercy, and not sacrifice (Matthew 9:13). God would rather see us demonstrate mercy to others than do a multitude of good works. A merciful man not only bears his own burdens but the burdens of others. A merciful man has compassion on the souls of others and weeps with those who are suffering. A merciful man supplies the needs of others. A merciful man pities and defends the helpless. A merciful man gets great joy out of forgiving others. A merciful man is someone who people will take refuge in and run to in times of great affliction. We have been saved from an eternity in Hell and given eternal life by the mercy of God. How much more should we give mercy to others? When we show mercy to others in the same way that God shows mercy to us, we are blessed. James says, "For judgment is without mercy to one who has shown no mercy. Mercy triumphs over judgment" (James 2:13). When we are merciful, we will obtain mercy from men in this world and especially from God. Psalm 18:25a says, "With the merciful you show yourself merciful." Just as we cry out to God for mercy, we should show the same mercy to those who do not deserve it. We receive the mercy of God each morning when we wake up, and the mercy that God gave yesterday is not sufficient for today. Our merciful God pours out His new mercy faithfully so that we can meet today.

Day 301 – Your Meditation

Do not love the world or the things in the world. If anyone loves the world, the love of the Father is not in him.

1 John 2:15

Read: 1 John 2:1-17

Emphasis:_____

_____

_____

Rewrite:_____

_____

_____

Application:_____

_____

_____

_____

_____

_____

_____

_____

_____

_____

_____

_____

_____

_____

_____

_____

_____

_____

_____

_____

Day 302

Blessed are the pure in heart, for they shall see God.

Matthew 5:8

Emphasis: **Blessed** are the **pure** in heart, for they shall **see** God.

Rewrite: Blessed are the inwardly pure, for they will see God.

Application: To be pure in heart is to be undivided in our thoughts, words, and deeds. A pure heart will affect every area of our lives. Jesus says, "What comes out of the mouth proceeds from the heart, and this defiles a person" (Matthew 15:18). The heart must be pure, not divided. The Bible is full of dichotomies that show us this. You can't serve God and money (Matthew 6:24); we can only be on one road, a narrow road or a wide road (Matthew 7:13); we are a friend of the world or of God. We either hate sin or we love it. Jesus was perfect in purity, without sin, and without divided motives and desires. Jesus was fully dedicated to His Father, and He was fully surrendered to do His will. He had a pure hatred for sin and a complete love for God. Psalm 24 describes the King of glory, Jesus. It says, "Who shall ascend the hill of the LORD? And who shall stand in his holy place? He who has clean hands and a pure heart" (Psalm 24:3-4a). Only Jesus has a pure heart and can see God, but through faith in Him, we receive His imputed righteousness so that we too can see God. Even though we are accounted as righteous through Jesus, we are not pure in heart and must pursue purity. We must seek sin in our lives and kill it. We can't have mixed desires. In the spring, the normally pure water of a mountain stream is mixed with mud from the runoff, and the stream becomes filthy and unfit to drink. Whereas, when the stream is clear and pure, undefiled with mud, it is the best water. We must not be like a muddy stream in our devotion to God and our desires for sin and the things of this world. We must never tolerate sin but strive for practical holiness. When we find ourselves justifying sin, we are muddying our souls and are becoming more practically impure. The pure in heart will ultimately see God in Heaven. Revelation 22:4 says that the servants of God, "will see his face, and his name will be on their foreheads." To see God will bring us ultimate joy and satisfaction.

Day 303

Blessed are the peacemakers, for they shall be called sons of God.

Matthew 5:9

Emphasis: **Blessed** are the **peacemakers**, for they shall be called **sons of God.**

Rewrite: Blessed are those who promote peace, for they will be called sons of God.

Application: Jesus personifies peace because He is the Prince of peace (Isaiah 9:6). Paul says that Jesus Himself is our peace and that He makes peace between us and God through His death on the cross (Ephesians 2:14-16). A peacemaker reconciles two parties. Jesus reconciled us to God by taking our sins upon Himself and paying the penalty, thus satisfying divine justice. This brought peace between us and God through faith in Christ. Jesus preached this message of peace to all people near and far (Ephesians 2:17). When we are converted, we are given the Spirit of peace, and, therefore, we must be eager to maintain the unity of the Spirit and the bond of peace (Ephesians 4:3). To be a peacemaker is to promote peace between people instead of contention. A peacemaker is not someone who craves controversy but is a meek man who seeks peace between men. The peacemaker resolves conflicts instead of starts them. Peace is a fruit of the Spirit that all true Christians have and will develop as they are sanctified. Ultimately to be a peacemaker is to carry the gospel message of peace to all people so that they can have peace with God. 2 Corinthians 5:18 speaks of our mission of peace. It says, "God, who through Christ reconciled us to himself and gave us the ministry of reconciliation." Therefore we are ambassadors for Christ, calling men to be reconciled to God (2 Corinthians 5:20). The peacemakers will be called sons of God. Galatians 3:26 says "in Christ Jesus you are all sons of God, through faith." The true sons of God always promote peace, and they are blessed. The imposters always promote controversy and strife and are known for peace-breaking and causing division among brothers. These are not blessed but cursed. We must, "Strive for peace with everyone, and for the holiness without which no one will see the Lord" (Hebrews 12:14).

Day 304

Blessed are those who are persecuted for righteousness' sake, for theirs is the kingdom of heaven.

Matthew 5:10

Emphasis: **Blessed** are those who are **persecuted** for righteousness' sake, for theirs is the **kingdom of Heaven**.

Rewrite: Blessed are those who are treated badly for their faith in Christ and their desire to do what is right, for theirs is the kingdom of Heaven.

Application: This statement seems like the greatest contradiction ever. How can persecution make someone happy? God says, "Blessed are those who are persecuted," while the world says that the advantageous or those who are healthy, wealthy, and wise are blessed. The world views someone who fulfills all of his selfish desires as one who is happy. Jesus was persecuted for righteousness sake more than anyone. He, being without sins, was killed for our sins. Jesus was mocked, beaten, reviled, persecuted, and wicked men uttered all kinds of evil against him falsely because of His righteousness. The second part of this beatitude says the same thing. Jesus said in verses 11-12, "Blessed are you when others revile you and persecute you and utter all kinds of evil against you falsely on my account. Rejoice and be glad, for your reward is great in heaven, for so they persecuted the prophets who were before you." All Christians will face this treatment at some level. Paul said, "Indeed, all who desire to live a godly life in Christ Jesus will be persecuted" (2 Timothy 3:12). If we are not suffering for righteousness in some way then we are probably not striving to be righteous. Christians throughout history have been persecuted, hunted, pursued, run down, treated as animals, fined, imprisoned, banished, excluded, scourged, racked, tortured, slaughtered, and have had their property plundered on account of Jesus. These Christians were very blessed, happy, and ecstatic in their sufferings because they knew theirs was the kingdom of Heaven and their reward awaited. It is an honor to suffer because of the One who suffered so sacrificially for us. Paul says, "The sufferings of this present time are not worth comparing with the glory that is to be revealed to us" (Romans 8:18). We must rejoice over the honor of suffering for Christ.

Day 305

Help us, O LORD our God, for we rely on you, and in your name we have come against this multitude.

2 Chronicles 14:11b

Emphasis: **Help** us, O LORD our God, for we **rely** on you, and in your name we have come against this multitude.

Rewrite: Help us Lord God; we can rely on you alone against this multitude that we have come against in your name.

Application: King Asa found himself in a desperate situation when the Ethiopian king came out against him with a million man army. Asa knew he did not have a chance with only a small army. He could only do one thing in this situation: cry to the Lord for help. Asa pleads with God for His name to be glorified and Judah to be saved. He says, "O LORD, there is none like you to help, between the mighty and the weak. Help us, O LORD our God, for we rely on you, and in your name we have come against this multitude. O LORD, you are our God; let not man prevail against you" (v. 11). The Lord answered his prayers and defeated the mighty army of the Ethiopians (v. 12). Asa did right in depending on *El Shaddai*, God Almighty. Sadly, at the end of his reign, Asa forgot God and depended on men instead. Baasha, king of Israel, went up against Judah, and Asa ran to the king of Syria instead of to God. He paid him in gold to fight against Israel, which he successfully did. We read in 2 Chronicles 16:7-9 that God sent Hanani the seer to rebuke Asa for trusting in the king of Syria instead of God. Hanani reminds Asa, saying, "Were not the Ethiopians and the Libyans a huge army with very many chariots and horsemen? Yet because you relied on the LORD, he gave them into your hand." He then rebukes him, saying, "You have done foolishly in this, for from now on you will have wars." Asa did not repent after this but only hardened his heart (2 Chronicles 16:12). Are we not the same as Asa in our own lives? One day we trust completely in God and God delivers us, but the next day, when trials come, we forget all about it and trust in something else. In every circumstance we have the opportunity to trust in God or something else. Every time we trust in something else, we harden our hearts. We must trust in God alone.

Day 306

When he appears we shall be like him, because we shall see him as he is.

1 John 3:2

Emphasis: When He appears we shall be **like Him**, because we shall **see Him** as He is.

Rewrite: When Christ appears, we will see Him as He is, and we will be like Him.

Application: God loves us so much that He gave us to His Son Jesus so that we could be called sons of God. We are adopted sons of the living God and ambassadors of Christ. God is our Father, and He is not ashamed to call us His sons and daughters. At regeneration we were given a new heart and new desires. A Christian has the desire to conform to the image of Christ, and by the grace of God and the work of the Holy Spirit, he is "being transformed into the same image from one degree of glory to another" (2 Corinthians 3:18). We are children of God now, but what we will be has not yet appeared. Jesus told us that we would one day be with Him. He said in John 14:3, "And if I go and prepare a place for you, I will come again and will take you to myself, that where I am you may be also." When Christ appears we will be made perfect in holiness. Right now God has only begun a good work in us, but when Christ appears, He will bring it to completion (Philippians 1:6). We will be glorified in body and soul. Our glorified bodies will never grow old or become ill. We will be completely sinless in our thoughts, words, and deeds. Our desires and motivations will always be pure. We will never die, but live for all eternity in this perfect state. We will be like Christ in His character, but we will not be like Him in every way since Christ has divine attributes, like omnipotence and omniscience, that we will never obtain. We will see Jesus as He is. Only the pure in heart will see God (Matthew 5:8). When Christ appears, we will be perfectly pure in heart; therefore, we will see Christ, and it will be an unfathomable joy. "What no eye has seen, nor ear heard, nor the heart of man imagined, what God has prepared for those who love him" (1 Corinthians 2:9). Meditating on seeing Christ as He truly is and that we will be like Him is an incredible exercise that will encourage us on the worst day.

Day 307

I will make myself yet more contemptible than this, and I will be abased in your eyes.

2 Samuel 6:22a

Emphasis: I will make myself yet more **contemptible** than this, and I will be **abased in your eyes**.

Rewrite: I will make myself even more foolish than this, and I will be more humbled.

Application: David had tried to bring the ark of the Lord back to its place in Jerusalem, but the Lord struck Uzzah down because of his error (v. 7). David recognized his error, and on his second try he brought the ark of the Lord in with much rejoicing. David danced before the Lord with all his might (v. 14) as he brought in the ark of the Lord. All of Israel rejoiced and shouted and sounded horns in celebration. Michal, David's wife, did not share in this joy. Verse 16 says, "As the ark of the LORD came into the city of David, Michal the daughter of Saul looked out of the window and saw King David leaping and dancing before the LORD, and she despised him in her heart." Michal despised David because she thought that he made a fool of himself in wearing a linen ephod. She probably thought he should have entered with his kingly robes and with much dignity and pomp. David responds to her in verse 22 by saying, "I will make myself yet more contemptible than this, and I will be abased in your eyes." David was dressed simply before the Lord and rejoiced and praised God with all his might, not caring what the world might think. David made himself a fool in the sight of the world for the sake of God. In the same way, Christians are fools for Christ's sake. In 1 Corinthians 4:9-10, Paul shares how he and the other apostles were made fools for Christ. He says, "For I think that God has exhibited us apostles as last of all, like men sentenced to death, because we have become a spectacle to the world, to angels, and to men. We are fools for Christ's sake..." In the eyes of the world, the Christian life is foolish. However, we are not out to impress the world but to serve the living God with all of our being. God chose what is foolish in the world to shame the wise (1 Corinthians 1:27). We must serve God with boldness.

Day 308 – Your Meditation

In the time of his distress he became yet more faithless to the LORD...

2 Chronicles 28:22

Read: 2 Chronicles chapter 28

Emphasis:_____
_____
_____

Rewrite:_____
_____
_____

Application:_____
_____
_____
_____
_____
_____
_____
_____
_____
_____
_____
_____
_____
_____
_____
_____
_____
_____
_____
_____
_____

Day 309

But if anyone has the world's goods and sees his brother in need, yet closes his heart against him, how does God's love abide in him?

1 John 3:17

Emphasis: But if anyone has the **world's goods** and sees his brother in **need**, yet **closes his heart** against him, how does God's love **abide** in him?

Rewrite: If anyone has all that he needs and sees a fellow brother in need, yet he refuses to show compassion towards him, how does the love of God dwell in him?

Application: It has pleased God, according to His decree, to make some Christians poor and others rich. This providential act was to give the body of Christ the opportunity to function as the body was intended. Christ demonstrated His unconditional love for us by laying down His life for us and because of us. Verse 16 says, "By this we know love, that he laid down his life for us, and we ought to lay down our lives for the brothers." Because of Christ's example of love, we know how we must demonstrate our love to others. We must show our love, not by words, but by deeds. Verse 18 says: "let us not love in word or talk but in deed and in truth." If nobody had a need, there would be no opportunity to give sacrificially. The rich have the world's goods so that they can show their compassion and grace to others, just as Christ has shown it to them. If God has loved us and has demonstrated this love by sending His Son into the world for us, how much more should we model this by loving others. Demonstrating love is evidence that you belong to God. Those who see a brother in need, yet close their hearts, prove that the love of God does not abide in them. We have a great responsibility as Christians to use all of our time and resources to demonstrate love to the body of Christ and to advance the kingdom of Christ. We should not have our own plans and goals for our money any longer, but we should look for opportunities to use what God has given us for His will and glory. How different would things be in the Church if all the members got down on their knees with their money before them and asked God in prayer how they should specifically use it for His glory?

Day 310

And they demolished the pillar of Baal, and demolished the house of Baal, and made it a latrine to this day.

2 Kings 10:27

Emphasis: And they **demolished** the pillar of **Baal**, and demolished the house of Baal, and made it a latrine to this day.

Rewrite: They destroyed the pillar and house of Baal and made the area a public toilet to this day.

Application: Jehu had a zeal for the Lord. His zeal was manifested in his actions when he assassinated Joram and Ahaziah, the two evil kings of Israel and Judah. He went on to execute Jezebel, possibly the most vile woman in all of Scripture. His zeal for the Lord led him to kill all the descendants of Ahab, Israel's most wicked king. His zeal led him to gather all the prophets of Baal, all his worshipers and all his priests, and then strike them down. After the slaughter of the Baal worshipers, Jehu went into the house of Baal, brought out their sacred pillar and burned it and demolished the house of Baal. To further demonstrate his hatred for Baal, he turned the demolished temple into a public toilet. Some would say the zeal of Jehu was extreme, and maybe it was, but Christians today have a greater problem with a lack of zeal than with too much. A missionary to barbarians in the eighth century named saint Boniface had the same zeal of Jehu. The pagan and hostile German barbarians worshiped a giant oak tree. Boniface, in his zeal and courage, walked into the village with an axe, and began to chop down the giant oak. As he was chopping, the Lord sent a wind, and the tree fell over. He challenged the pagans to allow their god to kill him for what he did. Nothing happened. From the stump, Boniface spoke of the true and living God, which when the pagans heard, they fell in fear and worshiped God. These men had a hatred for sin and zeal for the Lord, which is lacking today. Killing abortion doctors or demolishing statues is not the way we fight the battle, but we should have zeal to fight the battle. We must zealously fight by the means of preaching the gospel and prayer. "For the weapons of our warfare are not of the flesh but have divine power to destroy strongholds" (2 Corinthians 10:4).

Day 311

For everyone who has been born of God overcomes the world. And this is the victory that has overcome the world—our faith.

1 John 5:4

Emphasis: For everyone who has been born of God **overcomes** the world. And this is the victory that has overcome the world—**our faith.**

Rewrite: Every Christian has continual victory over the world. And the victory that has conquered the world is our faith in Jesus.

Application: Jesus overcame the world at the cross (John 16:33). When a Christian puts his faith and trust in Jesus, nothing can separate him from the love of God in Christ, and he becomes more than a conqueror through Christ (Romans 8:37-39). When we overcome the world by faith in Jesus, we are guaranteed to never look away from Christ and return to slavery of sin in the world again. To leave Christ to return to the world is absolute proof of never being in Christ in the first place (1 John 2:19). A true Christian overcomes the world. He is not blinded by the god of this age any longer, nor a slave to sin. Because Christ defeated death on the cross, we no longer have to fear death. "But thanks be to God, who gives us the victory through our Lord Jesus Christ" (1 Corinthians 15:57). Our faith in Christ has brought us victory over the world. The Christian does not control the world or have power over the world as a world dictator would have. The Christian has a joyful confidence that Jesus has dominion and sovereignty over the world and that He reigns from Heaven. We faithfully trust that Christ is greater than the terrors of death and the temptations of the world. We have victory in Jesus, like the hymn writer says, "Victory in Jesus, my Savior, forever, He sought me and bo't me with his redeeming blood; he loved me ere I knew him, and all my love is due him, He plunged me to victory beneath the cleansing flood."[29] All the authority, honor, and glory is due to Jesus because He overcame the world at the cross. When we put our faith in Christ, we overcome the world by the blood of the Lamb and the word of our testimony. We have freedom and victory in Christ, which we should rejoice in greatly.

---

29 E.M. Bartlett, "Victory in Jesus," 1939

Day 312

For many deceivers have gone out into the world, those who do not confess the coming of Jesus Christ in the flesh. Such a one is the deceiver and the antichrist.

2 John 7

Emphasis: For many **deceivers** have gone out into the world, those who do not confess the **coming** of Jesus Christ in the **flesh**. Such a one is the deceiver and the **antichrist**.

Rewrite: There are many deceivers in the world who deny that Jesus came as fully human with a real body. These deceivers are the antichrist.

Application: In the first century there were many false prophets who were teaching that Jesus only appeared to be man but really was only a spirit. These people taught that all material things were sinful, therefore, Jesus could not have had a real body, nor have suffered on the cross. These deceivers were those who did not confess the coming of Jesus Christ in the flesh and therefore were labeled antichrist. This is the heresy called Docetism, and it still exists today among various sects. John is warning the believers to avoid these people and this false doctrine. He says in verse nine, "Everyone who goes on ahead and does not abide in the teaching of Christ, does not have God." Theology of Christ is very important. It is so important that if you have a wrong belief about the person and work of Christ, you can't be saved. In his first letter, John gave the same warning. He said, "Beloved, do not believe every spirit, but test the spirits to see whether they are from God, for many false prophets have gone out into the world. By this you know the Spirit of God: every spirit that confesses that Jesus Christ has come in the flesh is from God, and every spirit that does not confess Jesus is not from God. This is the spirit of the antichrist" (1 John 4:1–3). Jesus predicted the same thing and gave us something by which to test these false teachers. He said we would know them by their fruit (Matthew 7:15-20). Many people claim to be Christians but deny the teachings of Christ. Those who deny Christ's doctrine of Hell is a common example in this age. These are the antichrist and false teachers, and we must not only watch for them, but avoid them.

Day 313

You will do well to send them on their journey in a manner worthy of God.

3 John 6b

Emphasis: You will do well to **send** them on their journey in a **manner worthy** of God.

Rewrite: It will be good to send these missionaries out into the world in a manner worthy of God.

Application: The brothers who John spoke about were missionaries traveling from one place to the next, doing the work of the ministry. These missionaries had gone out for the sake of God's name, accepting nothing from the Gentiles (v. 7). Because they were working for God and in the name of God, as ambassadors of Christ, John encourages the brothers to support people like these, that they all could be fellow workers for the truth together (v. 8). A church has not validated its existence until it is involved, in some way, in going to all the world, making disciples and teaching them to observe all the things that Jesus taught (Matthew 28:19-20). Not everyone is called to go to all the world, and not everyone is called to stay home and hold the rope. However, everyone is called to obey the great commission by either going or sending. Hudson Taylor said, "The great commission is not an option to be considered, but a command to be obeyed." The brothers here were those who went into the world, and John's readers were those who were to send them on their journey in a worthy manner. The missionaries never took any physical or financial support from the Gentiles, and rightly so. It was the responsibility of the church to send out missionaries, not the world. Because the missionaries did not receive support from pagans, John says, "We ought to support people like these" (v. 8). We must now examine our involvement in the great commission. Are we going to all the world for the sake of Christ and His kingdom, or are we staying home and sending missionaries out in a manner worthy of God? We must ask ourselves what the great commission has cost us. If it has cost us nothing, we must radically rethink our lives and what we are living for. We must go, send, or disobey.

Day 314

And he read from it facing the square before the Water Gate from early morning until midday, in the presence of the men and the women and those who could understand. And the ears of all the people were attentive to the Book of the Law.

Nehemiah 8:3

Emphasis: And he **read** from it facing the square before the Water Gate from **early morning until midday**, in the **presence** of the men and the women and those who could **understand**. And the ears of all the people were **attentive** to the Book of the Law.

Rewrite: He read the Scriptures aloud from early morning until midday to all who could understand. The people intently listened to the Word of God.

Application: This event is a great model for the centrality of Scripture in the church, our homes, and our lives. All the people gathered in unity (v. 1). Ezra brought out the Book of the Law before the congregation, which was made up of everyone who could understand (v. 2). He stood above the people on a platform that he made to put the Word of God above the people (v. 4). All the people stood up in reverence to hear the Word of God (v. 5). He read the Scriptures for half the day (v. 3). The people were attentive and listened to every word (v. 3). Ezra blessed the Lord and exalted His name, and the congregation acknowledged that what he said was true with a hearty *Amen* and bowed their heads and worshiped the Lord (v. 6). The Word of God was read "clearly and they gave the sense, so that the people understood the reading" (v. 8). The Scripture was the main focus of every part of this meeting. Ezra simply stood up before the people, read the Word of God, expounded the Scripture so that the people were able to understand it, and all the congregation listened attentively. The whole "service" was based on a high, reverent view of the Scriptures. The congregation then responded to the word in obedience. They wept as they heard the Word of God because of their conviction of sin (v. 9). Ezra comforted them with the solution (v. 10). Finally the congregation went their way in great rejoicing because they understood the words that were declared (v. 12).

Day 315 – Your Meditation

His name shall be called Wonderful Counselor, Mighty God, Everlasting Father, Prince of Peace.

Isaiah 9:6

Read: Isaiah 8:11-9:7

Emphasis:_____
_____
_____

Rewrite:_____
_____
_____

Application:_____
_____
_____
_____
_____
_____
_____
_____
_____
_____
_____
_____
_____
_____
_____
_____
_____
_____
_____
_____
_____
_____

Day 316

Yet in like manner these people also, relying on their dreams, defile the flesh, reject authority, and blaspheme the glorious ones.

Jude 8

Emphasis: Yet in like manner these people also, **relying on their dreams**, defile the flesh, **reject authority**, and blaspheme the glorious ones.

Rewrite: These false teachers follow their dreams, which lead them into sin, cause them to reject authority, and blaspheme the glorious ones.

Application: The book of Jude is largely about the coming judgment on false teachers. Jude describes the judgment of sinful Israel, rebellious angels, and the people of Sodom and Gomorrah. In this verse, Jude describes the false teachers and their devices. He says they rely on their dreams, instead of the Scriptures, which lead them astray. These dreams lead them to reject the authority of the Scriptures and lead them to defile their flesh, which is sexual immorality. This has been so common among false teachers since the beginning until today. It is quite interesting that the Quaker movement started in the mid 1600s in the same way. The Quakers gave more authority to the "light of their consciences" than to the Scriptures. They rejected the authority of the Scriptures in favor of being "led by the spirit," or directed by other means, such as dreams. This led them to progressively reject any authority of the Word of God. They "quaked" in their services as the people were supposedly taken over by the spirit. Their reliance on dreams and the inner light led them into sin and to contradict the Scriptures. They rejected education and the use of books or commentaries. They rejected the Trinity and depended on hearing from God instead of obeying the Word of God. They allowed anyone to step up into the pulpit to express his or her thoughts and opinions and accepted it as authority from God. This led to bizarre behavior in the name of God, even as far as their female leader going half-naked to protest education. When we rely on anything other than the Scripture as our authority, this is the only behavior that will be manifested. We must beware of those who claim authority from their dreams and we must stand on Scripture alone.

Day 317

Behold, he is coming with the clouds, and every eye will see him, even those who pierced him, and all tribes of the earth will wail on account of him. Even so. Amen.

Revelation 1:7

Emphasis: Behold, **He is coming** with the clouds, and **every eye will see Him**, even those who pierced Him, and all tribes of the earth will **wail** on account of Him. Even so. Amen.

Rewrite: Look, Jesus is coming with the clouds, everyone will see Him, even those who killed Him, and every people group on earth will mourn over Him. It is true.

Application: In His revelation, Jesus, uses two Old Testament verses to speak of His second coming. In Daniel 7:13, Daniel has a vision of Jesus coming in the clouds to be given an everlasting dominion, glory, and a kingdom that will never be destroyed. The other verse referenced is Zechariah 12:10, in which, the Lord promises that He will pour out a spirit of grace on Israel so that when they see Jesus, the One whom they crucified, they will mourn and weep over their sin of rejecting the Messiah. Jesus speaks about His return in Matthew 24:30-31 when He says: "all the tribes of the earth will mourn, and they will see the Son of Man coming on the clouds of heaven with power and great glory. And he will send out his angels with a loud trumpet call, and they will gather his elect from the four winds, from one end of heaven to the other." Jesus is coming back at any time now. He is coming for judgment. Every eye will see Him. All of Israel that killed the Messiah and all those who have rejected the only hope of salvation through Christ will mourn when they see Jesus coming. On that day, every atheist will not be an atheist any longer. People will flee in terror of Christ and judgment, but it will be too late. We should meditate frequently on the second coming of Christ and long for His return. Doing this will keep our minds on eternal things instead of earthly things. We must ask ourselves what we would do or how we would live differently today if we knew that Jesus would return tomorrow. We must live in light of Christ's return. We must live for eternity and be busy about His work until He comes.

Day 318

To the one who conquers I will give some of the hidden manna, and I will give him a white stone, with a new name written on the stone that no one knows except the one who receives it.

Revelation 2:17b

Emphasis: To the one who **conquers** I will give some of the **hidden manna**, and I will give him a white stone, with a **new name** written on the stone that no one knows except the one who receives it.

Rewrite: Everyone who overcomes will receive hidden manna and a white stone with a new name written on it that no one knows but him.

Application: The one who conquers is the Christian (1 John 5:4). Because Jesus conquered the world (John 16:33), we are more than conquerors through Him (Romans 8:37). We are more than conquerors over tribulation, distress, persecution, danger, and the sword (Romans 8:35). In the book of Revelation, Jesus explains that there are many rewards for the one who conquers through Christ. The conqueror will eat of the tree of life (2:7), he will not be hurt by the second death (2:11), he will have authority over the nations (2:26), he will never be removed from the book of life (3:5), he will be made a pillar in the temple of God (3:12), and he will sit on the throne with Christ (3:21). In this verse we see that the one who conquers will receive some of the hidden manna and a white stone with a new name written on it. The hidden manna represents Christ, the Bread of life, who will spiritually nourish His people for all eternity. This spiritual nourishment is unknown and hidden from the world. Just as a white stone was given to those acquitted on trial and a black stone to those condemned, we receive a white stone since our sins have been pardoned. Our sins are gone! They are washed in the blood of Christ! When an adopted son becomes part of the family, he takes the name of his new family. We will also receive a new name as we are now part of the family of God. Our salvation is undeserved and a greater gift than we can imagine, but it doesn't stop there. The true believer will receive all of these promises through Christ. This should make us fall on our faces in worship of our merciful and gracious God, who loved us so much that He sent His Son to be crushed in our place.

Day 319

I know your works. You have the reputation of being alive, but you are dead.

Revelation 3:1b

Emphasis: I know your works. You have the **reputation** of being **alive,** but you are **dead.**

Rewrite: I know all that you do. People think that you are spiritually alive, but really you are dead.

Application: Even though the church at Sardis had the reputation of being alive, Jesus in His omniscience knew that they were dead spiritually. Because the church gave the impression they were alive but were in reality dead, they were charged with hypocrisy. They may have been flourishing in numbers and outwardly doing all the right things. They may have had sound doctrine, and their worship may have appeared true. Everything appeared to be going very well on the outside, but inside the church was dead. They had the appearance of godliness, but no power. They had a lot of people but not many Christians. They had the numbers, but the people were goats. However, there was a remnant of true believers who were worthy (v. 4). Jesus calls the sleeping church of Sardis to wake up and strengthen what remained before there was no hope of recovery. Jesus exhorts them to remember what they had received and had heard in the beginning, the gospel, which went forth in power and was a demonstration of the Spirit (1 Corinthians 2:4). If the church at Sardis did not wake up, Jesus threatened to come like a thief at an unknown hour. Jesus would come to remove their lampstand and write ichabod on the door, for the glory of God would depart. Jesus gave the same warning to the church of Ephesus. He said, "Remember therefore from where you have fallen; repent, and do the works you did at first. If not, I will come to you and remove your lampstand from its place, unless you repent" (Revelation 2:5). In today's age of number driven methods, we must take heed and not fall into the same snare as Sardis. God does remove lampstands. Worse yet, is when a flourishing, yet non-biblical, dead church is allowed to exist as a form of judgment on the people who want to have their ears tickled.

Day 320

Worthy are you, our Lord and God, to receive glory and honor and power, for you created all things, and by your will they existed and were created.

Revelation 4:11

Emphasis: **Worthy** are you, our Lord and God, **to receive** glory and honor and power, for **you created** all things, and by your will **they existed** and were created.

Rewrite: Lord God, you are worthy to receive all glory, honor, and power because you have created all things and you sustain them.

Application: Because it pleased God to create everything that exists and because God sustains all living things by the power of His word, all the credit, glory, honor and power is due to Him. No one can take any claim in creation or in sustaining anything. Only God can be worthy of glory. Oftentimes non-Christians get very angry about the truth that all the glory is due to God. They say that God is egocentric and self-absorbed. However, in reality, the glory must go to either God or man. Man is a finite, created being who is sustained by the living God. Man cannot live another day or take another breath without the sustaining grace of God. God, on the other hand, is the Creator, Sustainer, and cause of all things. He created man and upholds his life. Logic can only lead to God receiving all the glory and man none of it. Because of this fact, God created unfathomable creatures to remain around His throne and never cease to say day and night, "Holy, holy, holy, is the Lord God Almighty, who was and is and is to come" (v. 8)! Those who have received the reward of a crown willingly cast their crowns before the throne of God to demonstrate that only God deserves the glory, honor, and power (v. 10). They understood that they only received the crown based on the finished work of Christ and the gracious work of the Holy Spirit in their lives. A true Christian understands this and will never grudgingly give God the glory instead of himself. A Christian gets far greater joy out of giving God the glory than hoarding it for himself. A true Christian can only say, "Worthy is the Lamb who was slain, to receive power and wealth and wisdom and might and honor and glory and blessing!" (Revelation 5:12)

Day 321

They who wait for the LORD shall renew their strength; they shall mount up with wings like eagles; they shall run and not be weary; they shall walk and not faint.

Isaiah 40:31

Emphasis: They who **wait** for the LORD shall **renew** their strength; they shall mount up with wings like eagles; they shall run and **not be weary**; they shall walk and **not faint**.

Rewrite: They who wait for and trust in the Lord will gain strength; they will soar like eagles; they will not grow weary or faint.

Application: God rebukes Israel for their unbelief and lack of trust in Him (v. 27). They said, "My way is hidden from the LORD, and my right is disregarded by my God?" They said this as if God was unable to see their situation or that He had no interest in delivering them. The Lord sharply reminds them that He is the sovereign Creator who upholds everything that exists. He says, "The LORD is the everlasting God, the Creator of the ends of the earth. He does not faint or grow weary; his understanding is unsearchable. He gives power to the faint, and to him who has no might he increases strength" (vv. 28-29). When we know who God is by looking at His unchanging character, it is far easier to trust in Him. God is the Creator of all things, eternal, and all-powerful. He does not get tired or need to sleep like we do. God can do anything that He pleases, and He is pleased to help His people. He gives power to the weak and strengthens those who are worn out. God gives the promise here in this verse that those who wait for Him, trust in Him, and depend on Him, will be renewed in strength by Him. They will be renewed to persevere until the end. They will be renewed to press on and finish the race. God ordains circumstances in our lives to show us our weakness. He allows us to run ourselves into the ground to show us we can't do anything without Him. At these times of weakness and despair, we turn to God, and He strengthens us. When we finally realize that we can do nothing, we will then depend on and trust in God alone to deliver us. When we simply wait on and trust in the Lord instead of ourselves, we will find He will never fail.

Day 322 – Your Meditation

You have made them a kingdom and priests to our God, and they shall reign on the earth.

Revelation 5:10

Read: Revelation chapter 5

Emphasis:_____
_____
_____

Rewrite:_____
_____
_____

Application:_____
_____
_____
_____
_____
_____
_____
_____
_____
_____
_____
_____
_____
_____
_____
_____
_____
_____
_____
_____
_____

Day 323

After this I looked, and behold, a great multitude that no one could number, from every nation, from all tribes and peoples and languages, standing before the throne and before the Lamb, clothed in white robes, with palm branches in their hands.

Revelation 7:9

Emphasis: After this I looked, and behold, a **great multitude** that no one could number, from every **nation**, from all **tribes** and **peoples** and **languages**, standing before the throne and **before the Lamb**, clothed in white robes, with palm branches in their hands.

Rewrite: Then I saw a vast multitude of people who could not be counted, from every nation, tribe, people group, and language, standing before the throne of God and Jesus, wearing white robes and holding palm branches.

Application: Jesus, the worthy one, was slain on the cross for the sins of His people. By His blood He ransomed people for God from every tribe and language and people and nation. This great multitude standing before the Lamb is the one, true people of God. These are those who suffered in their earthly lives but persevered and finished the race. These are those who were tortured, refusing to accept release, so that they might rise again to a better life. Those who suffered mocking and flogging, and even chains and imprisonment. Those who were stoned, sawn in two, and killed with the sword. Those who went about in skins of sheep and goats, destitute, afflicted, mistreated, of whom the world was not worthy (Hebrews 11:35–38). These people were ransomed from every nation on earth, every tribe in the deepest jungle, every people group, and every known language. These people, the Church, stand before the almighty throne of God, and they can only cry out with a loud voice, "Salvation belongs to our God who sits on the throne, and to the Lamb" (v. 7)! What a glorious picture this is, and the greatest thing about it is we will be part of this great event in the future if we are in Christ. We will stand with the multitude and cry out these very words. We will worship God in the most pure, perfect worship that is imaginable. Even though this life is misery, this is our future!

Day 324

There is in my heart as it were a burning fire shut up in my bones, and I am weary with holding it in, and I cannot.

Jeremiah 20:9

Emphasis: There is in my heart as it were a **burning fire** shut up in my bones, and I am **weary** with **holding it in**, and I cannot.

Rewrite: There is a burning fire within me, and I cannot hold it in any longer.

Application: Jeremiah was appointed a prophet to the nations and charged with the difficult task of proclaiming the Lord's words of judgment and destruction. Jeremiah went wherever God sent him, and he spoke all the commands of God for 40 years of ministry. The people did not respond in repentance but rejected his words and persecuted him. Because of constant ridicule, mocking, and rejection, Jeremiah went through bouts of depression and temptation to stop preaching the word of God. In his weakness, he cries out in anguish, "I have become a laughingstock all the day; everyone mocks me. For whenever I speak, I cry out, I shout, 'Violence and destruction!' For the word of the LORD has become for me a reproach and derision all day long" (vv. 7-8). He is tempted to give up because he expected different results than God had planned. However, something deep in his soul prevented him from giving up. He says, "If I say, 'I will not mention him, or speak any more in his name,' there is in my heart as it were a burning fire shut up in my bones, and I am weary with holding it in, and I cannot." He wants to quit, but there is a fire in his bones, and he cannot hold the truth in. He must preach it or die. The apostle Paul had this same fire. He said, "Woe to me if I do not preach the gospel" (1 Corinthians 9:16)! Do we have this fire in our bones that makes it impossible to hold in the truth? When we see the vileness of the world and its rejection, mocking, and ridicule of Christ, do we quietly hide in a corner in a quiet desperation, or is a fire kindled inside of us to preach the gospel to the heathen world around us no matter what the cost? Are we willing to stand alone for truth, even when it seems every other Christian has compromised? We must have this fire burning inside of us, and we must not hold it in.

Day 325

The rest of mankind, who were not killed by these plagues, did not repent of the works of their hands nor give up worshiping demons and idols of gold and silver and bronze and stone and wood.

Revelation 9:20

Emphasis: The rest of **mankind**, who were not killed by these plagues, **did not repent** of the works of their hands nor give up worshiping demons and idols of gold and silver and bronze and stone and wood.

Rewrite: All those not killed by these plagues refused to repent and turn to God; instead they chose to continue worshiping demons and idols.

Application: This large group of people demonstrate the only attitude that sin can produce. Even after they went through devastation and judgment that was sent by God, they hardened their hearts and refused to repent. They loved sin so much and hated God with such a passion that they chose to worship their father the devil instead of God. Every time Christ called them to repent, they refused and hardened themselves. When they were scorched by the fierce heat of the sun, they cursed the name of God and did not repent and give Him glory (Revelation 16:9). When darkness overcame them in another plague from God, they gnawed their tongues in anguish and cursed the God of Heaven for their pain and sores. They did not repent of their deeds (v. 11). This is the state of the unregenerate man. He would rather be in Hell for all eternity than submit to God in any way. They worshiped every idol that their depraved mind could invent. These were religious people, not atheists. They willingly worshiped demons. They knew God existed, and they hated Him for it. This is where sin leads. It is so dangerous to think that we could not be like this. People don't become this hardened in an instant but over years of hardening their hearts. When we sin and don't repent, we slowly fade into wickedness, deeper sin, and further harden our hearts, enabling us to do things even more heinous without conscience. When we let sin take root in us, we will soon be in this situation, proving that we are not a child of God. "If we confess our sins, he is faithful and just to forgive us our sins and to cleanse us from all unrighteousness" (1 John 1:9).

Day 326

And the great dragon was thrown down, that ancient serpent, who is called the devil and Satan, the deceiver of the whole world.

Revelation 12:9

Emphasis: And the great **dragon** was **thrown down**, that ancient **serpent**, who is called the **devil** and **Satan**, the **deceiver** of the whole world.

Rewrite: The great dragon, who is called the ancient serpent, the devil or Satan, has been cast down.

Application: This text speaks of a great war in Heaven between Michael and the other angels of Heaven fighting against the dragon, or Satan (v. 7). Satan and his angels were defeated and thrown down from Heaven. From this passage we can learn a few things about Satan, the great enemy of our souls. We learn that Satan is a defeated foe. The victory has already been won. Satan knows he is defeated but now dwells on earth to vent his anger and great wrath on its inhabitants. Satan is called the dragon, ancient serpent, and the devil. He is the deceiver of the whole world. He is the god of this world who has "blinded the minds of the unbelievers, to keep them from seeing the light of the gospel of the glory of Christ, who is the image of God" (2 Corinthians 4:4). He is our enemy, but he has been conquered at the cross. Verses 10-12 of Revelation 12 say, "Now the salvation and the power and the kingdom of our God and the authority of his Christ have come, for the accuser of our brothers has been thrown down, who accuses them day and night before our God. And they have conquered him by the blood of the Lamb and by the word of their testimony, for they loved not their lives even unto death." Through Christ, the devil no longer has power over the believer. Through His death on the cross, Jesus conquered the one who has the power of death, that is, the devil (Hebrews 2:14). What is the application? Everyone under Heaven should rejoice. We have victory in Jesus our Savior forever. Peter gives us a final exhortation, "Be sober-minded; be watchful. Your adversary the devil prowls around like a roaring lion, seeking someone to devour. Resist him, firm in your faith" (1 Peter 5:8–9).

Day 327

...all who dwell on earth will worship it, everyone whose name has not been written before the foundation of the world in the book of life of the Lamb who was slain.

Revelation 13:8

Emphasis: All who dwell on earth will worship it, everyone whose **name** has not been written **before the foundation of the world** in the **book of life** of the **Lamb** who was slain.

Rewrite: All the people on the earth will worship the beast, everyone whose name has not been written in the Lamb's book of life before the foundation of the world.

Application: We learn that a book exists, which contains the names of all of the children of God since the beginning of time. The name of the book is the book of life. The owner of the book is the Lamb who had been slaughtered, which is Jesus Christ. The book was written before the world existed, and it holds the names of all those who would be given eternal life through the person and work of Jesus Christ on the cross, which they would receive by faith. Before creation, by His grace and His mere good pleasure, God chose which individuals would be redeemed by the Lamb who was slain. Ephesians 1:4-5 is one of many places that confirms this fact; it says, "He chose us in him before the foundation of the world, that we should be holy and blameless before him. In love he predestined us for adoption as sons through Jesus Christ, according to the purpose of his will." How can we take any credit for our salvation when it was already ordained before we existed? God can only receive all the glory and praise for His electing purposes. A true believer will discover this truth and rejoice with weeping because of the unfathomable mercy and grace of God. A worldly person will discover this fact and hate it with a passion and then use it as an excuse to reject Christ and refuse to repent. Those whose names are not written in the book of life will hate God by their nature and gladly worship the beast. They will go down into the depths of the lake of fire with the devil and reap what they have sown. If we are united with Christ, we will rejoice at our election and meditate on the goodness and mercy of God.

Day 328

He also will drink the wine of God's wrath, poured full strength into the cup of his anger, and he will be tormented with fire and sulfur in the presence of the holy angels and in the presence of the Lamb.

Revelation 14:10

Emphasis: He also will drink the wine of **God's wrath**, poured full strength into the cup of **his anger**, and he will be **tormented** with fire and sulfur in the presence of the holy angels and in the **presence of the Lamb.**

Rewrite: He will drink the wine of God's wrath, poured into the cup of His anger. He will be tormented in the presence of holy angels and Jesus.

Application: An angel proclaims that if anyone worships the beast, he also will drink the wine of God's wrath, poured full strength into the cup of his anger, and he will be tormented with fire and sulfur in the presence of the holy angels and in the presence of the Lamb (vv. 9-10). This is the fate of all who refuse to repent and who reject the only way of escape through Jesus. Torment and painful suffering for all eternity is the due penalty for sin against a holy God. God has been storing up His wrath and anger for this judgment. It is interesting that many people say that Hell is an eternity separated from God. Is God not in Hell? Is God not omnipresent? Who is the one pouring out punishment for sin? Notice here that all of these people in Hell will be tormented in the presence of Jesus and the holy angels. Jesus will be in Hell. This is very important to understand in the context of justification. If God is just, He must punish all sin. God satisfied His divine justice by pouring out the full cup of His wrath upon the head of Christ on the cross. In this way all who repent and believe in Jesus can have their sins pardoned. Because we are united with Christ, we receive His righteousness, and He receives our sins. Someone has to pay the penalty of sin for justice to be satisfied. Jesus stood condemned in our place and bore it all. If God is not in Hell punishing sinners, then He can't be just or omnipresent. God is not in Hell for a short time but for all eternity. Verse 11 says, "And the smoke of their torment goes up forever and ever." Meditating on God's eternal punishment will better help us to understand justification.

Day 329 – Your Meditation

Great and amazing are your deeds, O Lord God the Almighty! Just and true are your ways, O King of the nations! Who will not fear, O Lord, and glorify your name? For you alone are holy. All nations will come and worship you, for your righteous acts have been revealed.

Revelation 15:3-4

Read: Revelation chapter 15

Emphasis:_____

_____

_____

Rewrite:_____

_____

_____

Application:_____

_____

_____

_____

_____

_____

_____

_____

_____

_____

_____

_____

_____

_____

_____

_____

_____

_____

_____

Day 330

For you bless the righteous, O LORD; you cover him with favor as with a shield.

Psalm 5:12

Emphasis: For you bless the **righteous**, O LORD; you cover him with **favor** as with a shield.

Rewrite: Lord, you bless the godly and like a shield, you cover them with your favor.

Application: David, the author of this Psalm, had a very high view of God, which resulted in him being used greatly by God. When we get even a small glimpse of God, we can only have a high view of Him. A high view of God leads to a holy fear of Him. This fear leads to a hatred of sin and a willingness to read the Scripture and obey what it says. A desperate longing for practical holiness and conforming to Christ in His character is the result of this longing. This kind of person is the one who is used by God. Paul writes to Timothy, "[I]f anyone cleanses himself from what is dishonorable, he will be a vessel for honorable use, set apart as holy, useful to the master of the house, ready for every good work" (2 Timothy 2:21). Practical holiness, which is the process of cleansing sin and pursing righteousness, will make a Christian useful to the Lord. God blesses the righteous and covers him with His favor. All Christians have God's favor and are blessed because of the righteousness of Jesus that is imputed to us. However, to be useful to the Lord, we must pursue a life of practical holiness, developing the character of Christ. David begs God to lead him on this path, stating, "Lead me, O LORD, in your righteousness because of my enemies; make your way straight before me" (Psalm 5:8). The Scriptures illuminate our path to becoming useful vessels. The Scriptures lead us in the path of Christ-likeness and holiness. John Wesley said, "Give me one hundred men who fear nothing but sin and desire nothing but God, and I care not whether they be clergymen or laymen, they alone will shake the gates of hell." If we want to be used by God we must be fully devoted to Him and His plan to conform us to the image of His Son. Being a good preacher without holiness means nothing. We must seek to be like Christ.

Day 331

They will make war on the Lamb, and the Lamb will conquer them, for he is Lord of lords and King of kings...

Revelation 17:14

Emphasis: They will make war on the Lamb, and the Lamb will conquer them, for he is Lord of lords and King of kings.

Rewrite: They will wage war against the Lamb, and the Lamb will destroy them because He is the Lord of lords and King of kings.

Application: The ten kings who worship the beast will receive kingly authority from it, but they shall willingly hand over their power and authority to be of one mind, forming a strong coalition with a single purpose. They are to wage war against the Lamb. After these kings of the earth saw the power of the beast whom they worshiped, they confidently said, "Who is like the beast, and who can fight against it" (Revelation 13:4). All worldly power is gathered and allied in a common hatred against the Lord of lords. They approach the battle line with great confidence. They have every human and spiritually evil strength and ability on their side. Foolishly, they believe that the victory is at hand. What they don't realize is that they are waging war against the Creator and Sustainer of all life. The reason they are breathing at the moment is because of the grace of God. The reason they will have strength to draw near to the front line is because God gives them the strength. They have no more chance of raising a finger against the Lamb than an ant has of destroying the sun. They are simply deplorable kings of the earth, starting a war with the King of kings. Their question from 13:4 is about to be answered. The battle would start and end with a word. We get a more detailed look at the short battle in Revelation 19:19-21, "And I saw the beast and the kings of the earth with their armies gathered to make war against him who was sitting on the horse and against his army. And the beast was captured, and with it the false prophet." "These two were thrown alive into the lake of fire and the rest were slain by the sword that came from the mouth of him who was sitting on the horse, and all the birds were gorged with their flesh." Who can stand against our mighty Lord? No one! The Lamb already won the victory at the cross.

Day 332

Do not think that I have come to abolish the Law or the Prophets; I have not come to abolish them but to fulfill them.

Matthew 5:17

Emphasis: Do not think that I have come to **abolish** the Law or the Prophets; I have not come to abolish them but to **fulfill** them.

Rewrite: Don't misunderstand. I have not come to destroy the Law or the Prophets. I have come to fulfill them.

Application: Today in the Church, there is a common misunderstanding about the Christian's relationship with the Law of God. There is a false belief that says the Law of God has been abolished by Jesus. In this belief called antinomianism, the Law is irrelevant. The people who hold to this view abuse the doctrine of grace in order to live a sinful, carnal, or worldly life. They use grace to justify the satisfaction of their flesh and worldly desires. However Paul says: "What then? Are we to sin because we are not under Law but under grace? By no means!" Before, we were slaves to sin, but now, under grace, we are set free from the bondage of sin and free to pursue righteousness. The other extreme in understanding the Christian's relationship to the Law is to say that the Christian is still under the Law. In this view, its adherents believe they must still keep dietary and ceremonial laws. However, Jesus completely fulfilled all of these laws that pointed to Him. What is the Christian's relationship with the Law? In one sense, the grace of God enables us to fulfill the Law. When we were not Christians, we hated the Law and had no desire to keep it. After God saved us and the Spirit of God came to dwell in us, our desires changed. Now, by the grace of God, the Law is not a burden, and we have joy in keeping it. Jesus came to enable us to keep the Law, not abolish it. A Christian does not look for ways to break the Law, but to fulfill it. If you are reading the Bible to justify satisfying your carnal desires, it is evident that you have not received the grace which you claim you are under. Grace enables us to love God and His Law. Psalm 1:2 says for the Christian, "...his delight is in the law of the LORD, and on his law he meditates day and night." The Law is not abolished, but now we have the grace to love the Law.

Day 333

Let us rejoice and exult and give him the glory, for the marriage of the Lamb has come, and his Bride has made herself ready.

Revelation 19:7

Emphasis: Let us **rejoice** and exult and give Him the glory, for the **marriage** of the **Lamb** has come, and His **Bride** has made herself ready.

Rewrite: Rejoice and be glad and give Him all the glory, for the marriage of the Lamb and His Bride has come.

Application: The judgment of the great prostitute caused the great multitude in Heaven from every nation, tribe, people, and language to cry out, "Hallelujah!" The great multitude cries out again, like the roar of many waters, because the Lord Almighty reigns and because the great marriage supper of the Lamb has come. The Lamb, Jesus Christ, was the One who was slain, and by His blood He ransomed people for God from every tribe and language and people and nation, which is His Bride (Revelation 5:9). The Bride of the Lamb is the Church, the one true people of God from all ages. She adorns herself with righteous deeds. The Bride is clothed in salvation and righteousness that comes through Christ (Isaiah 61:10). The Bride, being betrothed to Christ before the foundation of the world (Ephesians 1:4), is now perfectly united with Christ in this great marriage ceremony. She is made holy and shares in the joy and glory of her Bridegroom. The great multitude is called to rejoice and exult and give God glory for this great event. What a day of rejoicing it will be when we are finally united to our Bridegroom Jesus. What an unfathomable celebration will it be with all of Heaven present and watching in anticipation as the Bridegroom takes the hand of the Bride in perfect union, never to be separated. Marriage in this world is only a shadow of this true marriage in Heaven. When a husband is away from his wife for a time, he longs intensely to be with her. Soon all of his thoughts are only on his wife, and he can do nothing else but wait for this hopeful reunion. When he finally is united with her, unspeakable joy bursts from him and her. This is only a taste of what awaits us in this great heavenly ceremony that we long for now. Our desire for Christ should consume our thoughts and motivate us to be like Him.

Day 334

Behold, all souls are mine; the soul of the father as well as the soul of the son is mine: the soul who sins shall die.

Ezekiel 18:4

Emphasis: Behold, **all souls** are **mine**; the soul of the father as well as the soul of the son is mine: the soul who **sins shall die**.

Rewrite: All souls, both of the father and the son, are mine. Whoever sins is the one who will die.

Application: At the beginning of this chapter, the Lord rebukes Israel for using an evil and untrue proverb that said, "The fathers have eaten sour grapes, and the children's teeth are set on edge" (v. 2). They believed that if the father had eaten sour grapes, the children would suffer the consequences of bad teeth, because of their father's behavior. They used the proverb to say that they were suffering punishment because of the sins of their ancestors, not their own transgressions. They were condemning God because of their suffering and asserting their innocence. The Lord said that this proverb would not be used by them any longer (v. 3). The Lord then makes a very clear statement, "Behold, all souls are mine; the soul of the father as well as the soul of the son is mine: the soul who sins shall die." All souls belong to God alone. He is the maker and sustainer of every living thing. God has more right to the soul than the soul has to itself. God can do what He desires with both fathers and sons because He is the sovereign Creator. God is just, and He confirms this by saying, "the soul who sins shall die." God is not punishing Israel for the sins of their ancestors but for their own unrighteousness. We cannot blame God, our parents, or anyone else for our behavior. We cannot say that we only sin because others have influenced us. We alone are responsible for every sin we commit. We must ask ourselves if we have blamed others for our sins. Have we thought that we would be less sinful if it were not for others in our lives? God called Israel to stop making excuses and repent of their sins so that they would live. God does not take pleasure in the death of the wicked. He says, "For I have no pleasure in the death of anyone, declares the Lord GOD; so turn, and live" (v. 32). God also calls us to turn and live.

Day 335

Then I saw a new heaven and a new earth, for the first heaven and the first earth had passed away, and the sea was no more.

Revelation 21:1

Emphasis: Then I saw a **new heaven** and a **new earth**, for the first heaven and the first earth had **passed** away, and the sea was no more.

Rewrite: I saw new heavens and a new earth, for the former ones have faded away, and the sea was gone.

Application: There are many unclear details about what will happen after Jesus returns, but we do get a glimpse of the future state in this chapter. Isaiah prophesied about a new heaven and a new earth that God would create in the future (Isaiah 65:17). This passage in the book of Revelation is the fulfillment of it. The heavens and earth will not be obliterated and then a completely new heavens and earth created, but they will be renewed or restored to a perfect state. The stars, planets, and countless galaxies will be restored to perfection, and the earth will once again be perfect, as it was before the fall of Adam. The dwelling place of God will be with man on the earth and He will be their God and they will be His people (Revelation 21:3). God will wipe away every tear and all mourning, crying, and pain will cease to exist. The wages of sin is death, but death will be no more since Christ defeated death on the cross. The holy city, the new Jerusalem, prepared as a bride adorned for her husband, will be on the earth (v. 2). All those who hunger and thirst for righteousness will be satisfied. All the thirsty will drink from the spring of the water of life without payment (v. 6). There will be no temple in the city because God is the temple (v. 22). Darkness will be no more, and there will be no need for the sun or moon to give light because the glory of God and Jesus, the light of the world, will shine brightly (v. 23). Everyone will be guided by this perfect light (v. 26). There will be no more sin in us or on earth, which is something that we cannot begin to contemplate while we live on a cursed earth with indwelling sin (v. 27). What an amazing future is in store for those who trust in the Lamb who was slain to make propitiation for our sins. How grateful should we be to Jesus? How joyfully should we serve Him?

Day 336 – Your Meditation

Behold, I am coming soon, bringing my recompense with me, to repay each one for what he has done.

Revelation 22:12

Read: Revelation 22:6-21

Emphasis:_____

_____

_____

Rewrite:_____

_____

_____

Application:_____

_____

_____

_____

_____

_____

_____

_____

_____

_____

_____

_____

_____

_____

_____

_____

_____

_____

Day 337

The wicked flee when no one pursues, but the righteous are bold as a lion.

Proverbs 28:1

Emphasis: The **wicked flee** when no one pursues, but the **righteous are bold** as a lion.

Rewrite: The wicked run away when no one is chasing them, but the followers of Christ are bold as a lion.

Application: People who have many skeletons in their closet generally have secret fears. They have a guilty conscience, but they refuse to obey it. Their many secrets create in them a constant fear of being exposed. They begin to develop conspiracy theories about all those in their lives. The first hint at their secrets being exposed, they run from their potential problems and hide deeper. No one is pursuing them, but because of their hidden sins, they flee. These people are a slave to fear. On the other hand, the righteous have confessed their sins, and God is faithful to forgive them through the propitiatory work of Christ on the cross. They have nothing to hide because their skeletons were exposed and destroyed. The Christian has nothing to fear in this world. "God gave us a spirit not of fear but of power and love and self-control" (2 Timothy 1:7). The Christian should be the least fearful and most bold person on the planet. Guillaume Farel, an evangelist in France in the 1500s, was an example of a bold lion for the gospel. He had no fear of anything. He constantly preached against the Pope and the idolatrous mass. Various priests tried to assassinate him, but he did not fear the bullets. Like Jeremiah, he had a fire burning in his bones to preach the gospel. He was eventually banned from preaching in France, so he fled the country and preached boldly in the open air to anyone who would listen. The people responded with mocking and attempts on his life. He did not give up, but eventually established a church and trained a young minister named John Calvin to take his place. Why do we live in fear of anything? We must ask ourselves if we are as bold as a lion or as cowardly as a mouse. If we lack courage, we must look deep within us to find out why. The Christian must be marked by boldness and resolve.

Day 338

For everyone who asks receives, and the one who seeks finds, and to the one who knocks it will be opened.

Luke 11:10

Emphasis: For everyone who asks **receives**, and the one who seeks **finds**, and to the one who knocks it will **be opened**.

Rewrite: Everyone who asks will receive, seeks will find, and knocks will find the door opened.

Application: The Puritan Richard Baxter said about seeking God in prayer, "It was among the Parthians the custom that none was to give their children any meat in the morning before they saw the sweat on their faces, and you shall find this to be God's usual course not to give His children the taste of His delights till they begin to sweat in seeking after them." Prayer seems to be our greatest struggle. Most Christians still pray before they eat and when they are with the Church, but how many people spend much time asking, seeking, and knocking in their prayer closets today? Jesus plainly says here that everyone who asks will receive, seeks will find, and knocks will find the door opened. So why do we have a hard time doing what Jesus tells us? The men who God has used most greatly throughout the ages had one thing in common, they were men devoted to prayer. Most of these men of old spent three hours in prayer each morning and some spent up to eight hours a day in prayer. When we hear stories of this dedication to prayer, we can't even contemplate it because most of the time we kneel down to pray, we spend the first half hour thinking a variety of scattered thoughts about anything from the weather to what we will eat for dinner. We don't have because we don't ask, and our prayers are not answered because of our hidden sins, lack of faith and trust, and our sheer laziness of going to God. When was the last time we sought God in so much agony that we broke out into a sweat? Most people are completely unaware of the power in prayer. If we truly understood prayer, we would pass many more hours praying than doing things. We must go to God in prayer as a humble child with a reverent boldness, knowing that when we pray in faith with a pure purpose, God will answer our petitions for His glory and our good.

Day 339

Obey my voice, and I will be your God, and you shall be my people. And walk in all the way that I command you, that it may be well with you.

Jeremiah 7:23

Emphasis: **Obey** my voice, and I will be **your God**, and you shall be my people. And walk in all the way that I **command** you, that it may be well with you.

Rewrite: If you perfectly obey my voice and do all that I command, then I will be your God, and it will be well with you.

Application: The Puritans loved to meditate on the promises of God because Jesus Christ is the fountain of all promises. We have every right and claim to the promises of God because Christ bought them all with His blood. This promise is a good example of taking hold of a conditional promise that is based on perfect righteousness because Jesus fulfilled the whole law of God and applied it to His people's account. In this promise, God gives the condition: If you obey my voice and walk in all the way that I command you, then I will be your God, and it will be well with you. For Israel this was a conditional promise based upon obedience. This promise assumes that if you disobey God's voice once, or if you don't walk in every way that God has commanded in His law, then He is not your God. If we don't love God with all our heart, soul, mind, and strength for even one moment, then this promise cannot be applied to us. If we gossip, slander, or tell one little lie, this promise can't be applied to us. This promise is impossible to attain for anyone outside of Christ. For those in Christ this is a promise that underpins our position because of Christ's perfect obedience in our place. Christ fulfilled the law for us. We uphold the law by faith in Him (Romans 3:31). God enabled us to receive this promise in faith by sending His perfect Son to be condemned for our failures, "in order that the righteous requirement of the law might be fulfilled in us, who walk not according to the flesh but according to the Spirit" (Romans 8:4). When we look at this promise we can boldly take hold of it because of what Christ did in our stead. When we meditate on the fact that the Lord is our God, our meditation will lead us to none other than Jesus Christ.

Day 340

Truly, truly, I say to you, whoever hears my word and believes him who sent me has eternal life. He does not come into judgment, but has passed from death to life.

John 5:24

Emphasis: Truly, truly, I say to you, whoever **hears** my word and **believes** Him who sent me has **eternal life**. He does not come into **judgment**, but has passed from **death to life.**

Rewrite: Whoever hears me and believes in Him who sent me has eternal life. He will not be judged for his sins, but will pass from death to life.

Application: This is a gospel promise that ensures that all who hear the shepherd's voice and believe in Him, will be saved from death and judgment, and given eternal life. This promise, together with the command to repent for the forgiveness of sins (Acts 3:19), offers salvation. "Whoever believes in him should not perish but have eternal life" (John 3:16). Whoever will hear the words of Scripture and believe in the Christ of Scripture will be led to repentance and given eternal life. This is a promise that brings great comfort to everyone. It doesn't say that whoever fulfills the law and does all his religious duties perfectly will be saved. It doesn't say that whoever is a good person will be saved. It doesn't say that whoever gives a large sum of money to the poor will be saved. It says that whoever hears and believes will be saved from judgment and given eternal life. This promise is for everyone. However, the reason the majority of the people in this world are not saved is because they refuse to repent and believe. They willing choose not to listen, not to believe, and not to repent. "Whoever believes in him is not condemned, but whoever does not believe is condemned already, because he has not believed in the name of the only Son of God" (John 3:18). Even though they refuse to repent and believe, they can still attain this promise by repenting and believing. Everyone who has breath has the opportunity to be saved. We must proclaim the gospel of faith in Christ and repentance of sins to everyone who is still breathing so they can take hold of this promise, repent of their sins, and be saved.

Day 341

For the LORD God is a sun and shield; the LORD bestows favor and honor. No good thing does he withhold from those who walk uprightly.

Psalm 84:11

Emphasis: For the LORD God is a sun and shield; the LORD bestows **favor and honor**. No good thing does He withhold from those who **walk uprightly**.

Rewrite: The Lord God is our sun and shield; He gives grace and glory to those who walk uprightly. No good thing will be withheld from them.

Application: This is one of the sweetest Psalms in the Psalter, and it has brought so much comfort in times of trials to countless saints throughout the ages. When Queen Mary sent thousands of saints to be burned at the stake because of their faith, many sang this Psalm as they were being burned alive. The Lord is our sun and shield. He guides our path with the light of His word, and He protects us. We have nothing to fear in this life because we know that God works all things for the good of those who love Him. Because of this great promise and other promises like it, we can trust in the character of God and have great hope in the times of great distress. We can say with David, "Even though I walk through the valley of the shadow of death, I will fear no evil, for you are with me; your rod and your staff, they comfort me" (Psalm 23:4). God gives us favor and honor through Jesus Christ. We receive everything good because we are Christ's and Christ is God's (1 Corinthians 3:23). God does not withhold any good thing from those who walk uprightly. By God's everlasting love, He gave us His own Son. "He who did not spare his own Son but gave him up for us all, how will he not also with him graciously give us all things?" (Romans 8:32) God did not withhold the greatest of all good things, Jesus Christ. When the Christian walks uprightly, he conforms to the image and character of Christ by dying to sin and becoming more practically holy. God gives us countless, undeserved blessings in this life, but ultimately He gives an inheritance as a reward to all those united in Christ. This is a great promise to memorize and meditate on during difficult times and good times because it will always bring sweet encouragement and refreshment.

Day 342

The LORD, the LORD, a God merciful and gracious, slow to anger, and abounding in steadfast love and faithfulness, keeping steadfast love for thousands, forgiving iniquity and transgression and sin, but who will by no means clear the guilty.

Exodus 34:6-7

Emphasis: The LORD, the LORD, a God **merciful** and **gracious**, **slow to anger**, and abounding in **steadfast love** and **faithfulness**, keeping steadfast love for thousands, **forgiving** iniquity and transgression and sin, but who will by no means clear the guilty.

Rewrite: The Lord God is merciful, gracious, slow to anger, filled with unfailing love and faithfulness, keeping loving-kindness for thousands, forgiving sin but who will never clear the guilty.

Application: This is another glorious promise that we can trust in concerning the character of God. The devil will always try to attack the character of God, making Him dissimilar to these attributes. The devil will say that God cannot love a sinner like you, or when a person is in the midst of deep trials, say that God is not faithful in caring for you and is punishing you for sin. To tempt you into a grievous sin, the devil will also say that God will clear you, the guilty, in order to tempt you into a grievous sin. Knowing the character of God in this verse is a promise we can depend on in any situation. At times when we are under great stress and depression due to sin we are fighting but can't seem to conquer, we can open up this promise and pray it. We can beg God for mercy, grace, patience, help, steadfast love, faithfulness to us, and forgiveness. We can plead this promise of God's character and put all our hope in His Word. God will give us comfort, and He will display these attributes to us because this is His character. He is Mercy, Grace, Patience, Love, and Faithfulness. He will never leave or forsake His children. His steadfast love will endure forever. In God alone our strength is found, and we have our hope bound up in Him. All of these character promises are found in and given to us in Christ and only through Jesus will God clear the guilty because He bore our guilt. In our deepest despair, we can cry out to God and beg Him for these things.

Day 343 – Your Meditation

In return for my love they accuse me,
but I give myself to prayer.

Psalm 109:4

Read: Psalm 109

Emphasis:_____
_____
_____

Rewrite:_____
_____
_____

Application:_____
_____
_____
_____
_____
_____
_____
_____
_____
_____
_____
_____
_____
_____
_____
_____
_____
_____
_____
_____

Day 344

He has granted to us his precious and very great promises, so that through them you may become partakers of the divine nature, having escaped from the corruption that is in the world because of sinful desire.

2 Peter 1:4

Emphasis: He has granted to us His precious and very great **promises**, so that through them you may become **partakers** of the divine nature, having **escaped** from the **corruption** that is in the world because of sinful desire.

Rewrite: God gave us His exceedingly precious promises, by which we become partakers of His divine nature and escape the sinful temptations of the corrupt world.

Application: We see from this verse the importance and role of the promises of God that we find in Scripture. Peter calls them "His precious and very great promises." Through the divine power of Christ, from which we draw our strength, we are given all things that pertain to life and godliness (v. 2). The Christian will persevere to the end because of the divine power of Christ that sustains him. He has been given all that is needed to live a godly life and conform to the image of Christ. The Christian is given the ability and called to supplement "faith with virtue, and virtue with knowledge, and knowledge with self-control, and self-control with steadfastness, and steadfastness with godliness, and godliness with brotherly affection, and brotherly affection with love" (vv. 5-7). Christ has granted His great promises so that we may become partakers of the divine nature. We participate in the divine nature of Christ by becoming like Him by the power of the Holy Spirit who dwells in us. We are partakers in the divine nature of Christ by being united with Him. "For if we have been united with him in a death like his, we shall certainly be united with him in a resurrection like his" (Romans 6:5). By believing the promises of God, we escape the corruption of the world and sinful desires and are able to live for Him. We are enabled to die to ourselves daily and live to do His will. We draw great strength and encouragement to mortify sin and become like Christ through His divine power given in His precious and great promises.

Day 345

When you pass through the waters, I will be with you; and through the rivers, they shall not overwhelm you; when you walk through fire you shall not be burned, and the flame shall not consume you.

Isaiah 43:2

Emphasis: When you pass through the waters, **I will be with you**; and through the rivers, they shall not overwhelm you; when you walk through fire you shall not be burned, and the flame shall not consume you.

Rewrite: When you pass through extreme danger and difficult times of trials, I will be with you.

Application: This proverbial phrase of passing through the waters was meant to remind Israel of God's deliverance from Egypt as they crossed the Red Sea on dry ground. Walking through fire symbolizes going through great trials. Psalm 66:12 says, "we went through fire and through water; yet you have brought us out to a place of abundance." The principle we can learn from this is that God will be with His people. No matter how bad our trials and temptations are, God will give us a way of escape (1 Corinthians 10:13). We will not be overwhelmed or consumed in our struggles. God is with us and will never leave us. We must hold on to this promise and pray that God would uphold and deliver us. Regarding the Lord's prayer, the *Westminster Shorter Catechism* explains how we should petition God concerning trials and temptations. Question 106 says, "In the sixth petition, which is, And lead us not into temptation, but deliver us from evil, we pray that God would either keep us from being tempted to sin, or support and deliver us when we are tempted." All of God's people will, at some point, go through fiery trials. When we go through trials in our own strength and ignore this promise that God will be with us, we will always fail miserably and fall into great despair. These trials should cause God's people to depend on Him to either deliver us from our situation or give us the strength to persevere through hard times, depending on Him alone. This is an exceedingly great promise that we must cling to and trust in. When we do, God will deliver us or strengthen us through any struggle.

Day 346

For still the vision awaits its appointed time; it hastens to the end—it will not lie. If it seems slow, wait for it; it will surely come; it will not delay.

Habakkuk 2:3

Emphasis: For still the vision awaits its **appointed time**; it hastens to the end—it **will not lie**. If it seems slow, **wait for it**; it will surely come; it will not delay.

Rewrite: The vision is for an appointed time, even though it may seem slow in being fulfilled, it will surely come to pass at the perfect time.

Application: Habakkuk, grieving over the Babylonians unjust treatment of God's people, was in a position where he could only pray and wait patiently for God to intervene. He says in verse one, "I will stand on my guard post and station myself on the rampart; and I will keep watch to see what He will speak to me." Habakkuk wanted God to punish the Chaldeans for their wickedness against His people, and he was resolved to stay where he was and wait for God's answer. God answered him starting in verse two, "Then the LORD answered me and said, 'Record the vision and inscribe it on tablets, that the one who reads it may run. For the vision is yet for the appointed time; it hastens toward the goal and it will not fail. Though it tarries, wait for it; for it will certainly come, it will not delay.'" God tells Habakkuk that He will punish Babylon and the nation will fall but in His appointed time, not when Habakkuk wanted to see it happen. God tells him to wait for it because it will surely come without delay. The vision about this event was eventually fulfilled when Babylon fell to the Medo-Persian kingdom. Habakkuk learned to trust in the promises of God and to not lose hope while waiting patiently for the Lord to accomplish everything in His time. We must learn the same thing. We often pray for years without receiving an answer. We often wait on God for a long time to bring His promises to pass. In these times it is easy to become impatient and discouraged, but we must repent of this since we are trying to accomplish our will instead of God's. We must learn to wait patiently on God and be resolved to persevere in prayer until God accomplishes His will.

Day 347

As far as the east is from the west,
so far does he remove our transgressions from us.

Psalm 103:12

Emphasis: As far as the east is from the west, so **far** does He **remove** our **transgressions** from us.

Rewrite: He has removed our sins from us as far as the east is from the west.

Application: After being delivered from great distress by the means of prayer in Psalm 102, David now breaks forth in thanksgiving because of his answered prayer in this Psalm. David exhorts his own soul to bless the Lord and never forget all His benefits (vv. 1-2). What are the benefits for which the Lord should be blessed? David says that God forgives, heals, redeems, shows steadfast love, mercy and goodness, gives justice for all who are oppressed, makes His ways known, is merciful, gracious and slow to anger, shows compassion for us, and He does not deal with us according to our sins, but as far as the east is from the west, so far does he remove our transgressions from us (vv. 3-13). What amazing benefits that are worthy to praise God! We have so many reasons to give thanks to God, but ultimately our redemption through our Savior and Substitute, Jesus Christ, is the greatest reason. God does not treat us as our sins deserve because He sent His perfect son to stand in our place, and He treated Him as our sins deserve. He satisfied divine justice on the cross so that our transgressions could be paid for, removed, and obliterated. When we believe in Christ and trust in Him as the only Savior, our sins are wiped away. We are made whiter than snow, we are redeemed by the Savior's blood, and we are granted eternal life. God's amazing, steadfast love is so infinite that He removes our transgressions from Himself an immeasurable distance. Our sins are gone! We must meditate on our redemption by the blood of Christ. W. G. Ovens penned a hymn that will help us meditate. He writes, "Wounded for me, wounded for me, there on the cross He was wounded for me; gone my transgressions, and now I am free, all because Jesus was wounded for me." How costly was our salvation?

Day 348

They have washed their robes and made them white in the blood of the Lamb.

Revelation 7:14

Emphasis: They have washed their robes and made them white in the blood of the Lamb.

Rewrite: They have washed their robes in the blood of the Lamb, and they became perfectly clean.

Application: The Kingdom of Christ is always advanced through the suffering of His servants for their faith. The road to Heaven is a progression through many trials and tribulations. The martyrs that this verse speaks of were faithful unto death and will receive the crown of life because of their faithfulness (Revelation 2:10). Because of the cross of Jesus Christ, the Christian should no longer fear death, but embrace it. At the cross, Jesus destroyed the one who had the power of death, the devil, and now delivers all those who were slaves to the fear of death (Hebrews 2:14-15). When a man does not fear death, he is the most bold and dangerous man in the world. In the nineteenth century, a man named James Chalmers demonstrated to the world what it means to have no fear of death. After hearing a letter read from a missionary in Fiji, Chalmers, in his zeal, dedicated his life to bring the gospel to the cannibals. He prepared himself in his studies and was sent out by a Presbyterian church. Chalmers was bold, courageous, and fearless in everything because he knew his position in Christ. He landed in New Guinea and had a very successful ministry. In 1901 Chalmers and his friend explored a new island of cannibals but upon touching the shore they were clubbed to death, chopped to pieces, cooked, and eaten. Chalmers entered Heaven as a martyr and washed his robe in the blood of the Lamb and was made clean. The martyrs for Jesus Christ are ordinary men who simply believe God and His word. They have no fear of death, and they have a special place in Heaven reserved for them before the throne of God, and they serve him day and night in His temple, being sheltered by His presence (v. 15). We must renew our zeal and fire inside of us to serve Christ with our whole being, even to the point of death.

Day 349

You are the salt of the earth, but if salt has lost its taste, how shall its saltiness be restored? It is no longer good for anything except to be thrown out and trampled under people's feet.

Matthew 5:13

Emphasis: You are the **salt** of the **earth,** but if salt has lost its taste, how shall its saltiness be restored? It is no longer good for anything except to be thrown out and trampled under people's feet.

Rewrite: You are the salt of the earth, but what good is salt that has lost its preserving effectiveness? It is no longer any good but should be thrown out.

Application: In today's corrupt, sin-filled, world we see unrighteous people engrossed in evil, covetousness, and malice. They are envious, murderers, and filled with strife, deceit, and maliciousness. They are gossips, slanderers, haters of God, insolent, haughty, boastful, inventors of evil, disobedient to parents, foolish, faithless, heartless, ruthless (Romans 1:29–31). When Jesus says that Christians are the salt of the earth, He implies that the earth is rotting away. The function of salt is to preserve and to prevent rotting. When you rub salt into meat that is going bad, the salt kills the bacteria that causes the meat to rot. Christians have the potential to delay the moral and spiritual decay of the earth when they live out the character of Christ in their daily lives. Jesus says that we are the salt of the world, but there is a possibility that we will lose our saltiness. If Christianity in the world conforms more to the world than to the character of Christ, the salt of Christianity loses its preserving effectiveness. If a Christian looks and acts more like the world than Christ, he has lost his effectiveness to be an influence in the world. A Christian must be salt by living his life like Christ, inside and outside the church, at his job, at the market, and everywhere public and private. People should notice that there is something completely different about you than the rest of the world. Like Jesus, you must be the opposite of the world in every way. We must live in such a way that we make others thirsty to know Christ. We must continue to conform to Christ; otherwise we are indistinguishable from pagans and useless.

Day 350 – Your Meditation

And Jesus said, "Father, forgive them, for they know not what they do."

Luke 23:34

Read: Luke 23:26-43

Emphasis:_____
_____
_____

Rewrite:_____
_____
_____

Application:_____
_____
_____
_____
_____
_____
_____
_____
_____
_____
_____
_____
_____
_____
_____
_____
_____
_____
_____
_____
_____
_____
_____

Day 351

By this my Father is glorified, that you bear much fruit and so prove to be my disciples.

John 15:8

Emphasis: By this my Father is **glorified**, that you bear much **fruit** and so **prove** to be my disciples.

Rewrite: When you bear much fruit, you prove to by my disciples, which glorifies my Father greatly.

Application: The Father gets glory from us when we bear fruit, which proves that we are His true children. All true Christians will bear fruit, which is developing the character of Christ. All true Christians will become more like Christ in His character and less like their old selves. We don't necessarily give God glory, since we have no glory to give, but we reflect God's glory when we are like Him in our character, doctrine, and practice. It is impossible to bear true, biblical fruit apart from being a Christian. Our union with Christ enables us to bear fruit. In verse 5, Jesus says, "I am the vine; you are the branches. Whoever abides in me and I in him, he it is that bears much fruit, for apart from me you can do nothing." Because we can't bear fruit apart from Christ, bearing fruit is evidence that we are united with Christ by faith. All those who are not united with Christ in faith, non-Christians, will not bear fruit, proving they are not abiding in Christ, and will not enter Heaven. Jesus says in verse 6, "If anyone does not abide in me he is thrown away like a branch and withers; and the branches are gathered, thrown into the fire, and burned." We now see the contrast between those who bear fruit and those who don't. Through our union with Christ, we abide in Him and His words abide in us. Verse 7 says, "If you abide in me, and my words abide in you, ask whatever you wish, and it will be done for you." When we are in Christ, we will joyfully obey the words of Christ, which will guide us to pray rightly and will give power to our prayers. When we pray rightly, God will give us whatever we wish, which will result in bearing much more fruit. We must meditate on abiding in Christ and His words, and then act by obeying His words, conforming to His image, and bearing much fruit, which will prove our salvation and glorify God.

Day 352

And now, Lord, look upon their threats and grant to your servants to continue to speak your word with all boldness.

Acts 4:29

Emphasis: And now, Lord, look upon their threats and grant to your servants to continue to **speak** your word with all **boldness**.

Rewrite: Lord, hear their threats and give your servants boldness to speak Your words.

Application: After Pentecost, God did amazing signs and wonders through the apostles and many people were saved. The Church was growing rapidly, but it was also facing resistance. The greatest resistance came from the religious leaders, the Sadducees, and the priests. When Peter and John went before the council, Peter demonstrated his boldness in proclaiming the gospel with a zealous fire within him. He boldly claimed that the healing of the crippled man was through the name of the resurrected Jesus Christ, the very one whom they crucified. When he finished speaking, the council was astonished. Acts 4:13 says, "Now when they saw the boldness of Peter and John, and perceived that they were uneducated, common men, they were astonished. And they recognized that they had been with Jesus." The bold claims of Peter and John caused anger in the chief priests and elders, but they could do nothing but lecture and finally release them. When they were released, they immediately began to pray to the Sovereign Lord for more boldness to preach the gospel, despite the threats that they received. God answered them. "And when they had prayed, the place in which they were gathered together was shaken, and they were all filled with the Holy Spirit and continued to speak the word of God with boldness" (Acts 4:31). The Kingdom of Christ will not be advanced by cowards. We are so weak in our flesh that we must pray for boldness everyday. We must pray for the power and unction of the Holy Spirit to control our lives and give us the boldness and resolve to press on, despite opposition to the gospel. Our lack of boldness is a result of our lack of prayer and misunderstanding of the reality in which we live. How often do we pray for boldness to speak the words of God to a lost and dying world?

Day 353

So we have come to know and to believe the love that God has for us.
God is love, and whoever abides in love abides in God, and God abides
in him.

1 John 4:16

Emphasis: So we have come to know and to believe the **love that God has for us**. **God is love**, and whoever abides in love abides in God, and God abides in him.

Rewrite: We know that God loves us. God is love, and whoever continues in love, continues to be in God, and God in him.

Application: The love of God is one of the most misunderstood divine attributes because of the world's definition of love without justice and because we cannot grasp even a little of the depth of God's love. Paul prays that the Ephesians would understand the love of God in Ephesians 3:18-19. He begs God that they would "have strength to comprehend with all the saints what is the breadth and length and height and depth, and to know the love of Christ that surpasses knowledge." We come to know and believe the love God has for us when we first look at a bloody Savior hanging on a cross. God demonstrates His love to us through the life, death, and resurrection of Jesus, however, this unconditional love of God is foreign to us. Why would the Creator of all things send His only Son to be murdered instead of us? In our finite minds, it makes no sense. We only deserved justice for our sins. John Bunyan wrote of the unfathomable love that God has for us, "To see a prince entreat a beggar to receive an alms would be a strange sight; to see a king entreat a traitor to accept of mercy would be a stranger sight than that; but to see God entreat a sinner, to hear Christ say, 'I stand at the door and knock,' with a heart full and a heaven full of grace to bestow upon him that opens, this is such a sight as dazzles the eyes of angels."[30] When we meditate on the love of God, we will always be left in wonder and amazement. We must strive to model this love in our lives in some measure and continue to abide in it, thereby demonstrating that God abides in us.

---

30 John Bunyan, "Saved by Grace," in *The Works of John Bunyan*, ed. George Offor. (1854; repr., Edinburgh: Banner of Truth Trust, 1991), 1:350.

Day 354

But I say to you that everyone who is angry with his brother will be liable to judgment; whoever insults his brother will be liable to the council; and whoever says, 'You fool!' will be liable to the hell of fire.

Matthew 5:22

Emphasis: But I say to you that everyone who is **angry** with his brother will be liable to **judgment**; whoever **insults** his brother will be liable to the council; and whoever says, 'You fool!' will be liable to the **Hell** of fire.

Rewrite: Everyone who is angry with his brother will be guilty; whoever slanders his brother will be guilty before the court; and whoever curses his brother will be guilty and in danger of Hell.

Application: Jesus explains the true meaning behind the law by first quoting the law from Exodus, "You shall not murder," and then uncovering a deeper layer. All sin starts in the heart. Before one murders, he is angry, bitter, slanderous, and filled with hate, which are all inward sins of the heart. If someone has these sinful motives, given opportunity, he will eventually murder. The consequences of our inward sins will be judgment. Holding a grudge against someone is a grievous sin, as well as slandering, insulting, and hating anyone. Having a continual hatred for someone will eventually be evidence that you are not a true Christian. John says, "Everyone who hates his brother is a murderer, and you know that no murderer has eternal life abiding in him" (1 John 3:15). These inward sins of the heart, which can be hidden from others, have dire consequences that must be dealt with immediately. Therefore, Jesus applies this teaching, "So if you are offering your gift at the altar and there remember that your brother has something against you, leave your gift there before the altar and go. First be reconciled to your brother, and then come and offer your gift" (Matthew 5:23–24). If we have something against someone, we must immediately address the issue before it creates a seed of bitterness that will develop into anger, slander, and hatred. Everyone struggles with these inward sins. Because of this, we see our desperate need for a perfect Savior to represent us and the work of a precious Spirit to help us kill every sin in our heart.

Day 355

You are the light of the world. A city set on a hill cannot be hidden.

Matthew 5:14

Emphasis: You are the **light** of the **world**. A city set on a hill cannot be **hidden.**

Rewrite: You are the light of the world, like a city set on a hill that cannot be hidden.

Application: Jesus said in John 8:12, "I am the light of the world. Whoever follows me will not walk in darkness, but will have the light of life." Jesus is the light, and in Him there is no darkness. We are only the light of the world because Jesus is the light of the world. We do not necessarily give light to the world, but we reflect the light of Christ. We must be light because the world is in darkness. The wisdom of the world has put a man on the moon, and it has advanced technology far beyond any point in history. Knowledge has increased tremendously, but all of the world's knowledge and technology have not changed the nature of man. Man is still wicked. The world is in darkness, and knowledge won't bring change. Jesus is the only true light, and His followers must be the same. When a lamp is lit in a dark room, the darkness flees from the light and cannot be in the presence of light. People who live in the darkness of sin will hate being around the light of a true Christian. When we are the salt of the earth and walking in the character of Christ, people know that there is something different about us. Being different is not unusual. However, this is when we must shine as light. We must expose the darkness of sin and show the light of the truth. We must walk as children of light and live like Christ. Next, Jesus said that a city set on a hill cannot be hidden. As Christians, we must be this city set on a hill. We must be a beacon of light to the nations. The nations must look at us and see their sins and their need for Christ. The greatest problem in Christianity today is that men have the light of Christ, they have sound doctrine, they proclaim the gospel, but the way they live shows the world that they are hypocrites and that their words are disqualified. We must meditate on how we are demonstrating we are the light of the world, what dims our light, and how we can shine brighter.

Day 356

For the kingdom of God does not consist in talk but in power.

1 Corinthians 4:20

Emphasis: For the **Kingdom of God** does not consist in talk but in **power**.

Rewrite: The Kingdom of God is not mere words, but power.

Application: Christians are part of the Kingdom of God through faith in Christ. Their inclusion is not guaranteed, based on a mere confession of faith, but is demonstrated by the power of a changed life, bearing the fruit of conforming to the image of Christ. Some of the Corinthians were arrogant, which demonstrated that they were not living as if they were part of the Kingdom of God. They boasted in great words but had no power in their lives. Paul demonstrated his inclusion in the Kingdom of God, both in words and power. He says in 1 Corinthians 2:3-5: "And I was with you in weakness and in fear and much trembling, and my speech and my message were not in plausible words of wisdom, but in demonstration of the Spirit and of power, so that your faith might not rest in the wisdom of men but in the power of God." True spirituality is not demonstrated in words, but in the Spirit indwelled power of a holy life. Our words mean nothing if our lives do not reflect our testimony. God demonstrates His power in us by making a spiritually dead, God-hating sinner into a new creation. God turns the vilest of sinners into Christ exalting men and women of God. God turns drug addicts into preachers of righteousness, blasphemers into orators of the words of life, slanderers into evangelists, racists into missionaries, murderers into good Samaritans, homosexuals into fathers and husbands, and atheists into apologists. When God changes the prideful to the humble, the lovers of sin into mourners, the arrogant to the meek, the lustful to the righteous, the vile heart into a pure heart, the haters into peacemakers, and persecutors into the persecuted for righteousness sake, the Kingdom of God is demonstrated in great power. A confession of faith only condemns if a changed life does not follow. Do our lives demonstrate power or only empty words? Do our lives reflect the character of Christ and holiness, or do we look just like the world?

Day 357 – Your Meditation

For as in Adam all die, so also in Christ shall all be made alive.

1 Corinthians 15:22

Read: 1 Corinthians 15:1-34

Emphasis:_____

_____

_____

Rewrite:_____

_____

_____

Application:_____

_____

_____

_____

_____

_____

_____

_____

_____

_____

_____

_____

_____

_____

_____

_____

_____

_____

_____

_____

_____

_____

_____

_____

_____

Day 358

Since we have these promises, beloved, let us cleanse ourselves from every defilement of body and spirit, bringing holiness to completion in the fear of God.

2 Corinthians 7:1

Emphasis: Since we have these **promises**, beloved, let us **cleanse** ourselves from every **defilement** of body and spirit, bringing **holiness** to **completion** in the fear of God.

Rewrite: Since we can depend on the promises of God, let us be motivated to mortify every sin that defiles the body and spirit, advancing in practical holiness in the fear of God.

Application: In the previous chapter, Paul emphasized the promises of God in which the Corinthians could put their hope and which could motivate them to holy living. God promised His people that He would be their God, and they would be His people. He calls His people to separate themselves from sin, and He gives them the promise that He will welcome them, and be their Father (2 Corinthians 6:17-18). Because of these great promises and call to separate from sin, Paul exhorts the Corinthians to pursue practical holiness by mortifying sin and conforming to the character of Christ. The motivation for living a life of holiness is the fear of God and His great promises. God not only calls us to make war against the sin in our lives and strive for holiness, He gives us great promises to motivate us to be like Christ. Many Christians use their misunderstanding of Christian liberty to justify satisfying the carnal desires of their flesh. Why would we do this when we could use our freedom in Christ to strive to conform to His image? Everyone has baggage that they drag with them. The Corinthians had the baggage of boastful attitudes and sinful practices which they learned from the false teachers in the midst of them. They were called to examine their baggage and kill every defilement of body and spirit so they could become practically more like Christ. This is our sanctification. We cannot develop the character of Christ in a positive sense without also killing sin in our lives. We have the motivation of the great promises of God to do this, and we have the great example of Christ to pursue.

Day 359

...so as to walk in a manner worthy of the Lord, fully pleasing to him, bearing fruit in every good work and increasing in the knowledge of God.

Colossians 1:10

Emphasis: ...so as to **walk** in a manner **worthy** of the Lord, fully **pleasing** to Him, **bearing fruit** in every good work and increasing in the **knowledge** of God.

Rewrite: So that you will walk in a manner worthy of the Lord, which is pleasing to Him, and be able to bear good fruit from your works and increase in the knowledge of God.

Application: In the previous verse Paul exhorts the Colossians to "be filled with the knowledge of his will in all spiritual wisdom and understanding" (Colossians 1:9). The purpose of gaining this knowledge of God is so that they will be able to walk in a manner worthy of the Lord. Paul calls Christians to this manner of living in other letters as well. In Ephesians 4:1, Paul said: "I therefore, a prisoner for the Lord, urge you to walk in a manner worthy of the calling to which you have been called." Again in his letter to the Philippians, he said: "Only let your manner of life be worthy of the gospel of Christ..." (Philippians 1:27a). Now that we have been made a new creature through the new birth, we must not walk in the ways of our old man. We must live our lives in a way that reflects Jesus Christ and His character. We must continue to repent and have faith in Him, which is what pleases Him. We must do the works of God, bearing good fruit. How are we to walk in a manner worthy of the Lord? We must be filled with the knowledge of God's will, which can only be found in the Scriptures. We can never know the will of God apart from His written Word. When we increase in the knowledge of God, we will understand how to live our lives in a manner worthy of the Lord, worthy of our calling, and worthy of the gospel of Christ. Paul urges us to walk in this way because he knows it will be a struggle. Paul struggled with this himself. The struggle between our old man, which is our flesh, and the Spirit of God living in us, will always be there until we die. We must fight to live in the Spirit.

Day 360

See to it that no one fails to obtain the grace of God; that no "root of bitterness" springs up and causes trouble, and by it many become defiled

Hebrews 12:15

Emphasis: See to it that no one fails to obtain the grace of God; that no **"root of bitterness"** springs up and **causes trouble**, and by it many become defiled

Rewrite: Watch after each other so that no one fails to receive the grace of God; that bitterness does not poison the mind and cause trouble, defiling many.

Application: The author of this book is urging the Christians to press on in their struggle with sin and to keep fighting it. Unlike the apostate who will continue in sin without discipline from God, the author tells the true Christian that God will discipline him to keep him on the narrow path that leads to life. Being disciplined by God is a sign that you are His true children. Because many people in a congregation have deceived themselves into thinking they are Christians, the author urges the people to watch after each other so that none fail to receive the grace of God. If a person fails to receive the grace of God, he does not belong to God. A root of bitterness is something that everyone must watch for because it is so common. It is so easy for us to be bitter and then justify this sinful behavior. Some proclaiming Christians live a life-style of bitterness for years, never forgiving and always holding grudges. The author warns that we must watch for this root of bitterness and kill it before it causes trouble amongst the whole congregation and many become defiled. A bitter person in the Church can spread the poison of bitterness among the congregation faster than the common cold is spread in the family home. Bitterness is contagious and must be sterilized. In the next verse, the author goes on to give a horrific example of the bitterness and apostasy of Esau. He urges the congregation not to be like Esau, "who sold his birthright for a single meal. For you know that afterward, when he desired to inherit the blessing, he was rejected, for he found no chance to repent, though he sought it with tears" (Hebrews 12:16–17). Bitterness leads to apostasy and to no further chance to repent. It must be killed.

Day 361

*For it is not an enemy who taunts me— then I could bear it; it is not an
adversary who deals insolently with me— then I could hide from him.
But it is you, a man, my equal, my companion, my familiar friend.*

Psalm 55:12-13

Emphasis: For it is not an enemy who **taunts** me— then I could bear it;
it is not an adversary who **deals insolently** with me— then I could hide
from him. But it is you, a man, my equal, **my companion**, my familiar
friend.

Rewrite: I could bear the reproach of an enemy and the exalted insults
of a foe, but they come from you, my companion and close friend.

Application: One of the most difficult times we will face is the betrayal
and deception of a close Christian friend. David wrote this Psalm about
being betrayed by a close friend who worshiped the Lord with him.
When a friend whom you have trusted turns against you and proves to
have been a false friend, the wound runs deeper than anything. You
expect to be taunted and attacked by an enemy, but when a friend stabs
you in the back, the pain is unbearable. When a friend turns against you
and lies, slanders, reviles, and utters all kind of evil against you falsely,
your first sinful reaction is to complain, defend yourself, hate the
accuser, and seek vengeance. Jesus was hated without cause and "when
he was reviled, he did not revile in return; when he suffered, he did not
threaten, but continued entrusting himself to him who judges justly" (1
Peter 2:23). No one is able to avoid slander and deception from a false
friend. At some point in your life you will be betrayed. It is at these
times when we must shine like Christ in our response and character. We
must fight the urge to vindicate ourselves and let God vindicate the
righteousness. We must avoid retaliation because vengeance is the
Lord's. Like Christ, we must not revile in return but entrust ourselves to
the Lord who judges justly. When we put our complete trust in the Lord,
He will save us. When we cast our burdens on the Lord, He will sustain
us. We must submit to the will of God and accept the trials that He
allows in our lives. One day, He will expose the evil that is done in
secret and make all things right. We must entrust ourselves to God
alone.

Day 362

...The harvest is plentiful, but the laborers are few. Therefore pray earnestly to the Lord of the harvest to send out laborers into his harvest.

Luke 10:2

Emphasis: ...The **harvest** is plentiful, but the **laborers** are few. Therefore pray earnestly to the **Lord of the harvest** to send out laborers into His harvest.

Rewrite: The harvest is great, but there are not enough laborers to harvest. Therefore beg the Lord, who owns the harvest, to send laborers into the fields.

Application: It is important to understand that the harvest is not ours. We do not own the harvest, God does. God is the Lord of the harvest, and He will reap all that belongs to Him. God is sovereign over the harvest because He made the seeds grow. We have the immense privilege of being a laborer in the harvest. We get to plant and water, but only God can make the seed grow. Paul explains our role in God's eternal plan: "I planted, Apollos watered, but God gave the growth. So neither he who plants nor he who waters is anything, but only God who gives the growth. He who plants and he who waters are one, and each will receive his wages according to his labor. For we are God's fellow workers. You are God's field, God's building" (1 Corinthians 3:6-9). The particular job that we hold in the harvest is not important. We may plant, water, gather, or do all three, but each is equally important and is a great privilege. The problem we see here is a lack of laborers for the harvest. There is a great harvest that is waiting to be reaped, but there are not sufficient harvesters. We are fellow workers with God in the harvest. God does not need us, but He gives us the tremendous privilege to work as laborers in the harvest. What greater joy and privilege do we have but to work in fields that are white for the harvest? We have received our commission to go into all the world and make disciples. All Christians have been called to work, so why is the work neglected? We must pray to the Lord of the harvest to send out laborers. God uses the means of prayer to raise up new laborers and to bring in the great harvest of souls. We must look at how we are laboring and praying for laborers.

Day 363

Answer not a fool according to his folly, lest you be like him yourself.
Answer a fool according to his folly, lest he be wise in his own eyes.

Proverbs 26:4-5

Emphasis: Answer not a **fool** according to his **folly**, lest you be like him yourself. Answer a fool according to his folly, lest he be wise in his own eyes.

Rewrite: Do not answer the foolish arguments of a fool in the same way he does, or you will become just as foolish as him. Answer the fool correctly, so that he does not become wise in his own eyes.

Application: These two verses have been used by atheists and skeptics to say there are contradictions in the Bible. This, however, is not the case. These verses teach two appropriate ways to answer the arguments of the foolish. We are told not to answer a fool according to his folly, which means we are not to stoop to his level and mimic his foolishness. If the fool exalts himself, we should not respond by boasting about ourselves. If the fool slanders, lies, mocks, and utters all kinds of evil against us falsely, we should not resort to the same tactics. If the fool reacts instantly in his emotions, we must patiently pray about our response. On the other hand, we must avoid the temptation to ignore the fool, lest he be wise in his own eyes. Sometimes if we remain silent and don't answer the fool, he becomes justified in his folly and his foolishness only increases. It takes great discernment to know which position should be held in each situation. When we think the point of an argument is to win at all costs, we fall into the same folly as the fool. We can be completely right about a matter, but handle the discussion in such a poor, sinful way that we have already lost because we fell into the trap of folly and have become a fool. A good principle to follow when discerning how you should answer a fool in his folly is to not respond immediately but to wait and pray for three days. Often times your potential response will radically change after three days when your emotions subside. After seeking God in prayer, studying how Christ responded to fools in their folly, and letting time pass, you will have far greater discernment of how to answer the fool, and therefore glorify God.

Day 364 – Your Meditation

Though he slay me, I will hope in him.

Job 13:15a

Read: Job chapter 13

Emphasis:_____
_____
_____

Rewrite:_____
_____
_____

Application:_____
_____
_____
_____
_____
_____
_____
_____
_____
_____
_____
_____
_____
_____
_____
_____
_____
_____
_____
_____
_____
_____
_____

Day 365

...for that which has not been told them they see, and that which they have not heard they understand.

Isaiah 52:15b

Emphasis: ...for that which has **not been told** them they **see**, and that which they have **not heard** they **understand.**

Rewrite: ...for they will see what they have not been told, and they will understand what they have not heard.

Application: This prophecy in Isaiah is about the predicted Messiah, Jesus Christ, who will astonish many nations and shut the mouths of kings (Isaiah 52:15a). When Jesus came, He was the light in great darkness, and He told the people of the redemption through Him alone. This was never before told so clearly. The nations would be told about reconciliation with God through Jesus Christ. Paul quotes this verse in Isaiah in his letter to the Romans to validate his ministry to the Gentiles. He says: "...I make it my ambition to preach the gospel, not where Christ has already been named, lest I build on someone else's foundation" (Romans 15:20). We know that Christians will go and proclaim the gospel, and that people will hear the gospel, resulting in the salvation of God's people from every tribe and language and people and nation (Revelation 5:9). We also know that today there are a great number of people who do not know the name of Jesus. Who will go and tell them? Charles Spurgeon urged the people of God when he said, "Millions have never heard the name of Jesus. Hundreds of millions have seen a missionary only once in their lives, and know nothing of our King. Shall we let them perish? Can we go to our beds and sleep, while China, India, Japan, and other nations are being damned? We ought to put it on this footing, - not, 'Can I prove that I ought to go?' but, 'Can I prove that I ought not to go?'"[31] God will accomplish His ordained plan, but the question is whether you will be part of it. I will finish this book with an exhortation from Spurgeon. "Brethren, do something; do something; DO SOMETHING."

---

31 C.H. Spurgeon, *An All-round Ministry: Addresses to Ministers and Students* (London: Passmore and Alabaster, 1900).

Recommendation

Now that you have meditated on the Scriptures for one year, you are already disciplined in meditation, you have read many examples of how to meditate on Scripture, and you have written out your own meditations 52 times. Now that the book is finished, don't quit. The point of this book is to not only learn how to meditate on the Scriptures but to continue to practice the spiritual discipline of meditating on the Word of God. As you continue to do your own meditating each day, I think it is important to read your Bible in its entirety in one year. This way your meditation will cover the whole will of God and be in proportion to the Scripture itself. There are 39 books in the Old Testament and 27 books in the New Testament. If we divide the Bible by books alone, we see that the Old Testament makes up roughly 59% of the Bible. Therefore, your meditation should be made up of roughly 59% of Old Testament verses. This is a good balance. The Old Testament, sadly, is often neglected, so meditating in this way should keep you balanced. To read the Bible in a year, it is necessary to read 3 chapters a day and then extra in the Psalms. For example, you could read two Old Testament chapters and 1 New Testament chapter. There are countless reading plans to read the Bible in a year, and the point is not to choose a certain plan but to be balanced in reading and meditating on the Scriptures.

Scott Doherty is a missionary in Cusco, Peru. He serves as one of the elders at Iglesia Cristiana de la Gracia. Scott and his wife, Kimberly, have four children. To find out more about their work in Peru, please visit their website: **2alltheworldperu.blogspot.com**